Study Guide for
Crooks & Baur's
Our Sexuality

EIGHTH EDITION

JUDY ZIMMERMAN

Portland Community College

WADSWORTH

THOMSON LEARNING

Australia • Canada • Mexico • Singapore • Spain • United Kingdom • United States

WADSWORTH

THOMSON LEARNING

Assistant Editors: *Jennifer Wilkinson, Kristin Parks*
Editorial Assistant: *Stacy Green*
Production Coordinator: *Dorothy Bell*
Cover Design: *Roy R. Neuhaus*

Cover Photo: *Robert Farber*
Print Buyer: *Christopher Burnham*
Printing and Binding: *Patterson Printing*

For more information about this or any other Wadsworth product, contact:
WADSWORTH
511 Forest Lodge Road
Pacific Grove, CA 93950 USA
www.wadsworth.com
1-800-423-0563 (Thomson Learning Academic Resource Center)

Printed in the United States of America

10 9 8 7 6 5 4 3 2 1

ISBN 0-534-57979-5

To The Student

Welcome to the study of Human Sexuality. An exciting journey of learning and personal discovery awaits you. I hope the eighth edition of *Our Sexuality* and this study guide will be helpful companions during your exploration.

Successful study of Human Sexuality requires that you develop a mastery of both scientific, factual information as well as apply that information to current social and political issues, and the world of your personal experience. A sound study strategy may help bring this about.

Prior to reading the text of each chapter, review the introduction in this study guide and the learning objectives. Develop a framework for the chapter's text by studying the Concept Map. The Concept Map identifies relationships among the chapter's elements, as well as pertinent "facts". You are building a memory structure in the same way a home is built from a frame and foundation.

Add layers to the memory structures you are creating by reading the text with a specific goal in mind. This is where the Learning Objectives are useful. Choose an objective and structure your reading and note-taking in order to master the objective. Be sure you know all bold-face and italicized terms in the text. A list of these Key Terms is provided in each study guide chapter. Proceed to the next objective when you have fully understood an objective and can answer the objective, using only your memory. This helps achieve *overlearning*, that is studying beyond what you really think you need. Mastering learning objectives step-by-step may seem like a long process, yet it helps build strong memory structures that are more resistant to forgetting and the hazards of a busy life, such as stress and lack of sleep.

When you have mastered the objectives that pertain to a section of the text, complete the Concept Checks in the corresponding study guide chapter. Review the text and your notes for items that you missed. Continue your study process by doing the Matching and Crossword Puzzle, and reviewing where necessary. Allowing sufficient time for this review process is a critical part of ensuring solid learning and retention. As a final step, complete the Multiple Choice and check your responses, reviewing your notes and the text where needed.

Congratulations on taking a Human Sexuality course. You have chosen to make an important investment -- in yourself and the world in which you live. Your comments and feedback regarding this study guide are most welcome. Email can be directed to: jzimmerm@pcc.edu.

Best wishes for your studies,

Judy Zimmerman

Contents

Introduction

The text's psychosocial orientation is introduced. The author's disagreement with Western culture's emphasis on sex-for-reproduction and rigid gender roles is discussed. The myriad ways that mass media and the Internet shape human sexuality are described. The origins of the sex-for-reproduction and gender role legacies are traced to Judeo-Christian religious traditions, slavery, and the Victorian era. The diversity of sexual expression is examined across three societies and within the United States. Key events of the past century that have moved human sexuality away from the public domain and closer to the realm of personal choice are explored as the chapter draws to a close.

Learning Objectives. *In order to derive maximum benefit from these objectives, use these as soon as you begin reading the chapter. After you have completed reading and studying this chapter, you should be able to do the things listed below with ease, using only your memory.*

1. Define the term "psychosocial" as it applies to the orientation of the text, and explain why the authors choose to emphasize this perspective.

2. Describe how the media influences and reflects sexuality today.

3. Discuss how the sex-for-reproduction legacy has evolved historically, and explain how this theme affects sexual attitudes and behaviors today.

4. Discuss how the gender-role legacy has evolved historically, and explain how this theme affects sexual attitudes and behaviors today.

5. Describe the difficulty in determining what constitutes "normal" sexual behavior, citing specific cross-cultural examples to support your explanation.

6. Discuss the sexual attitudes and behaviors of the people in China, the Islamic Middle East and Sweden.

7. Understand sexual diversity as it exists in various subcultures within the United States.

8. Give examples of specific psychological, scientific and social advances within the last century that have affected sexual values and behavior in today's society.

Concept Map

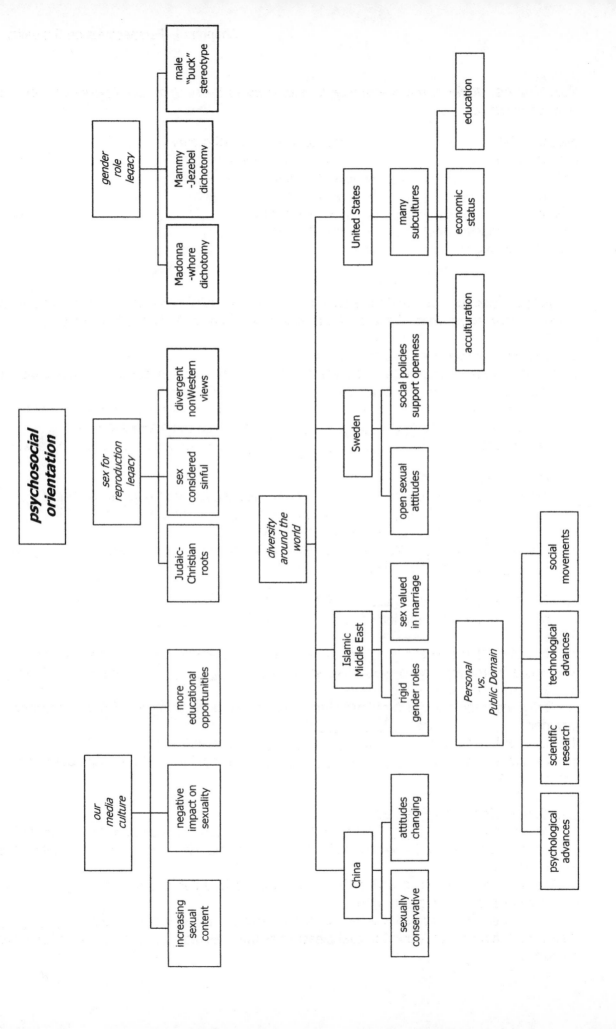

psychosocial orientation

our media culture
- increasing sexual content
- negative impact on sexuality
- more educational opportunities

sex for reproduction legacy
- Judaic-Christian roots
- sex considered sinful
- divergent nonWestern views

gender role legacy
- Madonna-whore dichotomy
- Mammy-Jezebel dichotomy
- male "buck" stereotype

diversity around the world
- China
  - sexually conservative
  - attitudes changing
- Islamic Middle East
  - rigid gender roles
  - sex valued in marriage
- Sweden
  - open sexual attitudes
  - social policies support openness
- United States
  - many subcultures
    - acculturation
    - economic status
    - education

Personal vs. Public Domain
- psychological advances
- scientific research
- technological advances
- social movements

Key Terms. *Refer to the glossary or subject index in the back of your textbook for definitions and information.*

psychosocial
homosexuality
coitus
socialization
celibacy
sex for reproduction legacy
gender role legacy

madonna-whore dichotomy
Mammy-Jezebel dichotomy
courtly love
polygyny
two spirit people
acculturation

Concept-Checks. *Complete this section by filling in each blank after you have studied the corresponding pages from the text. Answers are provided at the back of this chapter.*

The Author's Perspectives, pp. 2-4
1. A psychosocial orientation reflects the authors' view that human sexuality is influenced more by psychological and social factors than _____ factors.
2. Using the term foreplay implies that _____ is the only real type of sexual activity. This belief is an example of the _____ view, which the authors' oppose.
3. The authors' believe that _____ are limiting and can adversely affect our sexuality.

Our Media Culture, pp. 4-8
1. Recent studies point to an _____ in the sexual content of popular media.
2. Viewing stereotyped images of gender and sexuality in music videos may lead to _____ and _____ beliefs about the nature of intimate relationships.
3. Television has shown signs of its potential to educate by including more _____ and _____ characters and story lines in the 90's.

The Sex for Reproduction Legacy, pp. 8-11
1. The sex for reproduction legacy is important to the _____ and _____ religious faiths.
2. The notion that sexual organs were intended for procreation and using them in any other way was a "crime against nature" was discussed by _____ in *Summa Theologica,* one of many works associating sex with sin.
3. Religious traditions which did not share Western views equating sex with reproduction included _____ and _____.
4. Classical Islamic faith allows both _____ and concubinage.
5. The availability of _____ and _____ has enabled sex to be separated from reproduction.

The Gender Role Legacy, pp. 11-14
1. The practice of _____ is exemplified in the devotion of young knights to married women of nobility, even though such affection had no possibility of being consummated due to her marriage.
2. The witch-hunts which began in the 15th century stand as an example of _____ , one of two contradictory images of women.
3. In the book *The Vindication of the Rights of Women,* 18th century progressive _____ maintained that women valued sexual pleasure as much as men and that premarital sex was not sinful.

4. Gender roles during the Victorian era were _____, with men's and women's spheres remaining separated.

5. Even though Victorian men were admonished to follow the strict customs of the day,_____ thrived.

6. In contrast to popular notions of female sexuality in the Victorian era, research by Dr. Celia Mosher found that the majority of women experienced _____.

7. The institution of slavery was legitimized due to the presence of _____ of Black women and men.

8. The most common image of Black femininity during slavery was the _____, a seductress with incredible sexual desire.

9. Under slavery the black male was stereotyped as the _____ , a sexually violent predator.

A Cross Cultural Perspective: Social Norms and Sexual Diversity, pp. 14-17
1. Even though inadequate knowledge is viewed as the cause of sexual problems by Chinese doctors, no _____ is provided in Chinese schools.

2. One sign that Chinese attitudes toward sexuality are changing is that rates of _____ are increasing.

3. According to Islamic teachings, _____ is a serious offense which can be punished by death.

4. The prophet Mohammed encouraged _____ to be slow and delaying during sexual activity.

5. In Sweden _____ became mandatory in 1954, the same time in which American husbands and wives were shown sleeping in separate beds in TV and movies.

6. One reason ethnic groups and subcultures are not homogenous groups is because of _____, whereby customs and beliefs of the dominant culture begin to replace traditional values and practices.

7. In many Native American tribal groups, _____ and _____ were not associated with sin.

8. Among many Native American tribal groups, children were viewed as belonging to the entire tribe, thereby making _____ unnecessary.

Sexuality: Personal or Public Domain?, pp. 17-19
1. Among the key events of the 20th century which shaped public attitudes toward sexuality were the publication of research studies by _____, and *Human Sexual Response* by _____ and _____.

2. Taboos against _____ began to lessen somewhat in 1974 when this alleged mental disorder was removed from the American Psychiatric Association's manual of diagnostic categories.

3. The Clinton-Lewinsky scandal was instrumental in stimulating public discussion over what sorts of activities might be defined as _____.

Crossword

Across

1. Native American gender benders
4. Mary is to _____ as Eve is to whore
5. Paul of Tarsus' path to spiritual growth
9. one man to many wives
10. considered "real" sex by some
12. person who considered masturbation healthy
14. "Aunt Jemima" is an example of this racist and sexist stereotype

Down

2. authors' perspective on sexuality
3. these persons are negatively portrayed in music videos
5. Protestant reformer who valued sex in marriage
6. given secondary status as a sexual activity
7. this nation sought to eliminate decadent Western sexual behaviors
8. award given to TV programs promoting sexual health

Practice Test

This test will work best to guide your learning if you take it as part of a final review session before an exam.

1. A psychosocial orientation reflects a concern with _____ factors in the study of human sexuality.
   a. biological and anthropological
   b. sociological and medical
   c. psychological and social
   d. psychiatric and sociobiological

2. The sex for reproduction legacy is most clearly shown in which of the following statements?
   a. Jorge believes that foreplay is an essential part of a sexual encounter.
   b. Midori thinks she is still a virgin because she has done everything except penile-vaginal intercourse
   c. Sheila likes to initiate sexual activity with her partner.
   d. Mike enjoys masturbating and does not feel guilty about it.

3. Jamal believes that a "real" man always makes the first sexual advance in a relationship. Jamal's thinking best reflects
   a. the gender role legacy
   b. principles of courtly love
   c. a lesser degree of acculturation
   d. homophobia

4. Studies of television programming have demonstrated that prime-time shows
   a. have substantially decreased the sexual content in recent years
   b. are complying with government issued restrictions on the use of sexual language
   c. have reduced the number of commercials with sexual imagery
   d. have more sexual content than previous years

5. The increase of gay and lesbian characters and story lines on incest and condom use illustrates that television
   a. may help reduce taboos on the discussion of sensitive topics
   b. has failed to use realistic information about sexuality
   c. will soon include a rating system to alert viewers to homosexual content
   d. has completely failed to portray sexuality in a positive, healthy manner

6. Research on the effects of music videos has shown that
   a. watching videos promotes acceptance of dating violence
   b. filming techniques depersonalize women
   c. viewing encourages acceptance of exploitive beliefs about relationships
   d. all of the above

7. Who is associated with the belief that celibacy is superior to marriage?
   a. Paul of Tarsus
   b. Solomon
   c. Freud
   d. Lao Tsu

8. Which of the following persons is NOT associated with the view that sex is sinful?
   a. Thomas Aquinas
   b. Augustine
   c. Havelock Ellis
   d. Paul of Tarsus

9. What view did early Taoism and Hinduism have in common?
   a. masturbation was encouraged
   b. sex was primarily for procreation
   c. celibacy was prohibited
   d. sexual activity could help achieve spiritual growth and fulfillment

10. The opposing images of women as the virgin Madonna and evil temptress Eve originated during
    a. the Victorian era
    b. the Middle Ages
    c. the Roman Empire
    d. the Renaissance

11. Which statement best reflects gender roles during the Victorian era?
    a. Men's and women's worlds were deeply intertwined
    b. Men's and women's worlds were clearly separated
    c. Men were expected to adhere to strict mores, even in business affairs
    d. Men were expected fulfill their families' need for moral and spiritual guidance

12. Which of the following statements is inconsistent with the Jezebel stereotype of black women's sexuality under slavery?
    a. Black women were perceived as having an insatiable sexual appetite.
    b. Black women were thought to prefer short and scanty clothing.
    c. Black women were thought to lack self-respect.
    d. Black women were considered ladylike.

13. Which of the following statements is consistent with prevailing stereotypes about black male sexuality during slavery?
    a. Black men were considered asexual.
    b. Black men were wanton seducers of white women.
    c. Black men were peaceful and meek.
    d. Black men were alleged to have smaller penises than white men.

14. What basic generalization about world cultures and sexuality can be made, despite the fact that there is great diversity in human sexual expression?
    a. Every society regulates sexuality in some way.
    b. The world's cultures tend to universally view breasts as erotic.
    c. Sex is considered shameful in some way by all societies.
    d. Some form of kissing is considered arousing in each culture.

15. Most married Chinese women believe that sex is
    a. the preferred path to spiritual enlightenment
    b. for procreation only
    c. permissible for adolescents
    d. something that should be taught in college

16. Islamic customs such a wearing a veil and segregating the sexes until marriage are regarded as necessary because
    a. Islamic texts believe that men are rife with sexual desire
    b. Urbanization has made it more difficult to follow Islamic teachings
    c. Women have more sexual desire than men
    d. Sex outside of marriage is increasing

17. Attitudes toward sexuality in Sweden are exemplified by
    a. the availability of free contraception
    b. the acceptance of cohabitation
    c. parental leave for fathers
    d. all of the above

18. Diversity within a subculture or ethnic group is influenced by
    a. acculturation
    b. education
    c. socioeconomic status
    d. all of the above

20. Whose pioneering studies after World War II helped lead to a greater acceptance of a variety of sexual behaviors?
    a. Kinsey
    b. Klein
    c. Van de Velde
    d. Gagnon

21. Key events which helped change conceptions of gender roles during the latter part of the 20th century included all of the following except
    a. the availability of "the Pill"
    b. the reinstatement of Comstock laws
    c. the Roe vs. Wade decision
    d. the feminist movement

22. What key event of the 80's brought gay men and lesbians into the public limelight?
    a. the Stonewall riots
    b. publication of Evelyn Hooker's study
    c. the first AIDS diagnosis
    d. the murder of Matthew Shepherd

Answer Key - Chapter 1

<u>Concept Checks</u>

The Authors' Perspectives
1. biological
2. coitus; sex for reproduction
3. rigid gender roles

Our Media Culture
1. increase
2. adversarial; exploitative
3. gay; lesbian

The Sex for Reproduction Legacy
1. Christian; Judaic
2. Aquinas
3. Taoism; Hinduism; (or Islam)
4. polygyny
5. contraceptives; abortion

The Gender Role Legacy
1. courtly love
2. Eve
3. Mary Wollstonecraft
4. highly defined
5. prostitution
6. sexual desire
7. sexual stereotypes
8. Jezebel
9. buck

A Cross-Cultural Perspective: Social Norms and Sexual Diversity
1. sex education
2. sexually transmitted diseases
3. sex outside marriage
4. men
5. sex education
6. acculturation
7. nudity; sexual intercourse
8. monogamy

Sexuality: Personal or Public Domain?
1. Kinsey; Masters; Johnson
2. homosexuality
3. sex

Crossword Puzzle

Across
 1. two-spirit
 4. Madonna
 5. celibacy
 9. polygyny
11. education
12. Stone
13. Ellis
14. Mammy

Down
 2. psychosocial
 3. women
 5. Calvin
 6. foreplay
 7. China
 8. SHINE

Practice Test

1. c.   2. a   3. a.   4. d   5. a   6. d   7.a   8. c   9. d   10. b.
11. b   12. d   13. b   14. a   15. b   16. c   17. d   18. d   19. c   20. d
21. a   22. b.   23. a

Introduction

Three broad goals of the science of sexology are achieved using two classes of research methods, nonexperimental and experimental methods. Advantages and disadvantages of these methods are described, as well as technologies and ethical guidelines used in sex research. Discussion of the limits of sex research and the potential benefits of feminist theory follows. The quality of sex research presented in popular media is analyzed and guidelines for evaluating such research are offered. The chapter concludes with a look at what sexology in the 21st century might hold.

Learning Objectives*. In order to derive maximum benefit from these objectives, use these as soon as you begin reading the chapter. After you have completed reading and studying this chapter, you should be able to do the things listed below with ease, using only your memory.*

1. Define sexology and describe three of its goals, providing examples of each goal.

2. Describe when and how the discipline of sexology originated.

3. Describe each of the following research methods, including advantages and disadvantages of each method, and provide an example of each type of research: case study, survey, direct observation, experimental

4. Define each of the following and distinguish among them: survey sample, target population, representative sample, and random sample.

5. Discuss two types of survey methods, and the strengths and limitations of each.

6. Explain how nonresponse, self-selection, demographic bias and inaccuracy present problems in sex survey research.

7. Summarize the available research on "volunteer bias."

8. Describe the research studies of Alfred Kinsey and his associates, including research methods used, subject populations studied, and strengths and limitations of this work.

9. Describe the National Health and Social Life Survey, including research methods used, subject populations studied, and strengths and limitations of this work.

10. Describe the results of surveys on violent pornography and alcohol use.

11. Describe Masters and Johnson's research, including the research method used, subject populations studied, and the strengths and limitations of this work.

12. Describe new technologies in sex research.

13. Distinguish between independent and dependent variables, providing examples of each.

14. Describe how the experimental method has been used to study the effects of alcoholism on sexual arousal.

15. Describe the experimental method that has been used to study the relationship between sexually violent media and rape attitudes and behavior.

16. Describe how feminist theory has influenced research in sexology.

17. Discuss the reliability of sex research published in popular magazines.

18. Identify some criteria that would be helpful in evaluating various kinds of research.

19. Summarize some of the research findings on ethnicity and sexual behavior.

20. Discuss some ethical considerations in conducting sex research.

21. Summarize some of the results of a national sex survey in China.

22. Summarize some of the results of the NHSLS research on American ethnicity and sexuality.

Concept Map

sexology

- uses science
- goals
  - understanding
  - predicting
  - controlling

experimental method
- independent variable
- dependent variable
- causal relationships

nonexperimental research
- direct observation
  - Masters & Johnson
- case study
- survey
  - questionnaire
  - interview
    - socially desirable responses
  - target population
  - Survey sample
    - representative
    - random
    - nonresponse
    - demographic bias
- examples
  - Kinsey
  - NHSLS
  - violent pornography
  - alcohol use

technologies in research
- penile strain gauge
- vaginal photoplethysmograph
- computer assisted self interview
- cyberspace

feminist theory
- research ignored women
- male heterosexuality as the standard

ethical guidelines
- informed consent
- right of refusal
- careful use of deception
- confidentiality & anonymity

Key Terms. *Refer to the glossary or subject index in the back of your textbook for definitions and information.*

sexology	self-selection	penile strain gauge
case study	volunteer bias	vaginal photoplethysmograph
survey	demographic bias	computer assisted self interview
survey sample	socially desirable responses	informed consent
target population	direct observation	deception
representative sample	experimental research	confidentiality
random sample	independent variable	feminism
nonresponse	dependent variable	sexual science

Concept-Checks. *Complete this section by filling in each blank after you have studied the corresponding pages from the text. Answers are provided at the back of this chapter.*

The Goals of Sexology, pp. 23-25
1. The study of sexuality is called _____, which uses scientific methods rather than value judgements to gather new information about human sexual behavior.
2. Sexology includes the goals of understanding, _____, and _____ behavior.
3. Sexual behavior in other countries has been conducted by _____, anthropologists who specialize in studying the cultures of other societies.
4. A recent sex survey in China found that a majority of people approved of _____ sex.

Nonexperimental Research Methods, pp. 25-34

Case Study
1. A single person or _____ is studied using the case study method.
2. The case study allows the researcher great _____ in data collection and as a result _____ information can be obtained.
3. Foremost among the drawbacks of the case study method is an inability to _____ the findings to a larger group of people.

Survey
1. A survey uses a small group called a _____ that is a subset of a much larger group known as the _____. This allows the researchers to draw conclusions about this larger group.
2. A survey may be conducted using face-to-face or telephone _____ and _____ to gather information about sexual behavior.
3. Survey researchers prefer to use a _____ sample, which is a microcosm of the target population.
4. Sometimes researchers must randomly select a subset of a population in order to construct a _____ sample.
5. Questionnaires tend to be cheaper and quicker to administer than _____ and provide a greater amount of _____ .

6. Interviews have a format that is more _____, which enables a researcher to clarify questions a subject does not understand. Good interviewers may also build a sense of _____ , encouraging subjects to provide more truthful responses.

7. Obtaining representative samples is difficult because of _____, as people refuse to participate.

8. Volunteers for sex research are different than nonvolunteers so the problem of _____ remains a key issue for sexologists.

9. Caucasians, the middle class and college educated persons make up a disproportionate number of sex research volunteers so _____ may effect sex research results.

10. Sex research continues to deal with problems concerning the fallability of human memory and _____ responses, the tendency of people to give answers that enhance social image.

11. In the National Health and Social Life Survey, _____ reported substantially lower rates of masturbation and oral sex than White Americans.

12. Even though the sample excluded _____, some findings from Kinsey's landmark studies of human sexuality remain valid. For example, sexual orientation is not considered an either-or matter and _____ still influences sexual behavior.

13. An exceptionally high response rate of _____ was obtained in the National Health and Social Life Survey, which is widely considered the best sex survey to date.

14. The survey sample in the National Health and Social Life study was representative of White Americans, _____ Americans and _____ Americans aged 18-59.

15. Findings from the National Health and Social Life Survey showed that Americans are more_____ than was widely believed.

Direct Observation

1. The work of _____ and _____ has been widely acclaimed for its use of direct observation to record human physiological sexual response.

2. Direct observation is advantageous because the possibility of _____ is eliminated.

3. A subject's behavior may be influenced by the presence of _____ , a major disadvantage of direct observation.

The Experimental Method, pp. 34-35

1. Experimental research provides a _____ environment where subjects' behavior can be measured.

2. The researcher controls or manipulates the _____ variable in an experiment.

3.   The outcome or resulting behavior that is merely observed and recorded is called the _____ in an experiment.

4. In the study on alcohol consumption and sexual responsiveness, the amount of alcohol consumed was the _____ variable whereas sexual arousal, as measured by a penile strain gauge, was the _____ variable.

5. Experiments are the only research method that allow researchers to draw conclusions about _____ relationships.

6. The _____ of laboratory settings may bias a subject's responses in an undesirable way.

Technologies in Sex Research, pp. 35-37

1. Prior to the development of current technologies, early researchers had to rely upon_____ reports of sexual responses.
2. The _____ is a thin rubber tube filled with a strand of mercury, and measures changes in _____.
3. Another device used to directly observe male sexual arousal is the _____, a metal band gauge.
4. In order to measure changes in vaginal blood volume, researchers use a _____.
5. Devices used to measure arousal are typically inserted in _____ by the research participant.
6. Computer-assisted self interviews reduce problems associated with _____ and the adverse impact of _____ interviews.
7. One of two types of computer assisted self interviews (CASI) is _____ CASI, where respondents view questions on a _____ and press labeled keys on a computer keyboard.
8. When audio-CASI is used, respondents listen to questions using _____. This method does not require that subjects be _____.
9. The collection and management of _____ in Web-based surveys is more efficient, and the perception of _____ may encourage respondents to be more honest.
10. Even though Web-based surveys have many advantages, a great deal of _____ bias exists. Web users tend to be male, younger, more _____ and _____ .
11. A major ethical issue associated with Web-based surveys is the use of _____ to recruit research participants.
12. Providing _____ is also challenging for Web-based research.

Ethical Guidelines for Human Sex Research, p. 37

1. Guidelines established by professional associations demand that no _____ be exerted upon subjects in order to guarantee their participation and that researchers refrain from practices that might cause _____ to subjects.
2. Researchers are also required to obtain _____ consent from participants before the study begins.
3. The use of _____ in research continues to be disputed. If this is used, subjects must receive a debriefing and may request that their data be _____ from the study.
4. Before any data collection begins, a(n) _____ committee must examine the proposed study in order to assure that participants' welfare is protected.

Feminist Theory and Sex Research, pp. 38-40

1. Many feminist sexologists believe that research has been dominated by a model of _____ sexuality that presents _____ as the norm.
2. Feminist researchers also believe that research has stressed _____ data collection, and should be broadened to include qualitative data such as interviews with open ended questions.

Popular Media and Sex Research, pp. 40-41

1. Magazine surveys illustrate that large sample sizes are not necessarily better, as the sample represents only the readership of that magazine, and is not representative of a larger _____.

2. The recent "Sex on Campus" survey results may be cautiously interpreted, as data from this study are _____ to the findings of surveys using more representative sampling techniques.

3. Magazine surveys do not utilize _____ methodology, yet are useful if we keep in mind that study results represent the ways that certain select samples experience their sexuality.

Sexology in the New Millenium: A Look at the Future, p. 42

1. Sexologist John Bancroft has argued that sexologists adopt a more _____ to their science, taking into account biological, cultural, and psychological influences on sexuality.

2. Several sexologists have recommended that a new, separate discipline of _____ be founded which would include specialists in sex education, psychology, sexual medicine, and anthropology, among others.

Matching

Match the sex research method with the characteristic that best fits. Responses may be used more than once.

a. case study   b. survey   c. direct observation   d. experimental method

1. _____ Provides a controlled environment in which all possible factors that might influence participants' responses are ruled out

2. _____ Inexpensive and quick method for gathering data from large samples

3. _____ Difficult to generalize data to other populations

4. _____ Offers flexible data gathering methods

5. _____ Subjects' behavior may be affected by the presence of observers

6. _____ Examines the behavior of individuals or small groups in great depth

7. _____ Uses independent and dependent variables

8. _____ Demographic bias and nonresponse may affect results

9. _____ Possibility of data falsification is greatly reduced

10. _____ Permits exploration of causal relationships between variables

Crossword

<u>Across</u>

3. a researcher manipulates this variable
5. _____ and Johnson
8. the ideal sample
9. "I won't participate"
10. a case study lacks this quality
11. a survey sample is drawn from this population
12. a field of study and social movement

<u>Down</u>

1. sex survey pioneer
2. flexible survey formats
4. experimental method discovers this relationship type
6. requires postexperimental debriefing
7. vaginal blood volume measuring device

Practice Test

This test will work best to guide your learning if you take it as part of a final review session before an exam.

1. Sexology first became a field of scientific study during the
   a. late 1960's after Masters & Johnson's landmark study was published
   b. 20th century
   c. 19th century
   d. early 1700's

2. If a researcher wanted to know how many teenagers consumed alcohol or drugs prior to engaging in sexual activity, which research method would be best to use?
   a. case study
   b. survey
   c. direct observation
   d. experiment

3. Much of what is known about persons with sexual difficulties comes from
   a. experiments
   b. questionnaires
   c. case studies
   d. cross-sectional studies

4. A research team is conducting a survey on the marital adjustment of newlyweds. Which is the most representative sample?
   a. couples who established a bridal registry at a local department store
   b. volunteers who responded to a newspaper ad
   c. friends, neighbors, and co-workers of the research team
   d. couples who took out marriage certificates within the last year

5. Studies suggest that all of the following are characteristics of persons who volunteer for sex research except
   a. Volunteers are more sexually experienced
   b. Females are more likely to volunteer than males
   c. College students are more willing to volunteer
   d. Volunteers hold more positive attitudes toward sexuality

6. Which of the following is not associated with the survey research method?
   a. independent variable
   b. nonresponse
   c. questionnaire
   d. target population

7. Kinsey's studies on American sexuality were pioneering, but limited because his sample included
    a. a disproportionate number of better educated persons
    b. non-volunteers
    c. large numbers of rural dwellers
    d. mostly older adults

8. Readers of "Sports Illustrated" and "Maxim" magazines were asked to complete a survey regarding their attitudes toward extramarital sex, and mail the survey to an address listed in the magazine. Which of the following best describes a key problem of this survey?
    a. the artificial nature of the environment may adversely affect the responses
    b. problems with memory fallibility will contaminate the results
    c. demographic bias may adversely affect the study
    d. subjects' reactivity may positively sway the results

9. The National Health and Social Life Survey is considered noteworthy because
    a. large numbers of prostitutes and their customers agreed to participate
    b. it examined the sexual practices of teenagers
    c. a very high response rate was obtained
    d. new physiological recording devices were utilized

10. Direct observation is a highly desirable method for studying sexuality because the possibility of _____ is greatly reduced.
    a. demographic bias
    b. researcher interpretive bias
    c. data falsification
    d. self-selection

11. Case studies are of limited usefulness to sex research because
    a. they require rigid data gathering methods
    b. a controlled environment must be created
    c.   superificial information about behavior is often produced
    d. findings cannot be generalized to a larger population

12. Which of the following methods allows causal relationships to be discovered?
    a. case study
    b. survey
    c. experimental method
    d. direct observation

13. A research team is investigating the sexual response of women with spinal cord injury to two types of erotica. One group of women reads a short story, whereas another group of women sees a short film clip. Measures of heart rate, blood pressure and vaginal blood volume are taken. What is the independent variable in this study?
    a. heart rate
    b. the type of erotica
    c. vaginal blood volume
    d. type of spinal cord injury

14. The penile strain gauge and the vaginal photoplethysmograph both measure
    a. strength of muscle contraction
    b. galvanic response
    c. body temperature in the pelvic area
    d. sexual arousal

15. Which of the following is NOT an advantage of computer-assisted self-interviews (CASI)?
    a. respondents do not have to be literate
    b. CASI is a less threatening way to report sensitive behaviors
    c. normative behaviors may be underreported
    d. question presentation can be standardized for all respondents

16. Ethical guidelines for doing sex research with humans require that
    a. no pressure or coercion be applied
    b. subjects have the right of refusal
    c. informed consent be obtained
    d. all of the above are true

17. Several feminist sex researchers believe that traditional sex research is limited because
    a. lesbians have been studied more than gay men
    b. research is based upon a male model of sexuality
    c. qualitative data have been emphasized
    d. statistical methods have not been utilized

18. Surveys administered over the Internet may be especially useful because
    a. participants can be recruited from distant places
    b. it is easier to guarantee anonymity than with any other method
    c. demographic bias is greatly minimized
    d. response rates are much higher

19. Surveys in popular magazines should be viewed with skepticism because
    a. surveys are done primarily to sell a product
    b. sample sizes are large but biased
    c. scientific methodology is not typically used
    d. all of the above are true

20. Roberto reads a newspaper article which claims that sexual harassment and date rape are declining among college students. What question should Roberto ask to evaluate the legitimacy of the research?
    a. Does the article seem scientific?
    b. What are the credentials of the researchers?
    c. Did the reporter ask good questions of the researchers?
    d. Was the article easy to understand?

Answer Key – Chapter 2

<u>Concept-Checks.</u>

The Goals of Sexology
1. sexology
2. predicting, controlling
3. ethnographers
4. extramarital

Nonexperimental Research Methods

<u>Case Study</u>
1. small group
2. flexibility, in depth
3. generalize

<u>Survey</u>
1. sample, target population
2. interviews, questionnaires
3. representative
4. random
5. interviews; anonymity
6. flexible, rapport
7. nonresponse
8. self-selection
9. demographic bias
10. socially desirable
11. African-Americans
12. African-Americans
13. educational level
14. Hispanic, African-Americans
15. conservative

<u>Direct Observation</u>
1. Masters, Johnson
2. data falsification
3. observers

The Experimental Method
1. controlled
2. independent
3. dependent
4. independent, dependent
5. causal
6. artificiality

Technologies in Sex Research
1. subjective
2. penile strain gauge, penis circumference
3. penile plethysmograph
4. vaginal photoplethysmograph
5. privacy
6. literacy, face-to-face
7. video, screen
8. headphones, literate
9. data, anonymity
10. demographic, educated, affluent
11. e-mail
12. anonymity

Ethical Guidelines for Human Sex Research
1. coercion, harm
2. informed
3. deception
4. ethics

Feminist Theory and Sex Research
1. male, heterosexuality
2. quantitative

Popular Media and Sex Research
1. population
2. similar
3. scientific

Sexology in the New Millenium
1. interdisciplinary
2. sexual science

Matching

1.d   2.b   3.a   4.a   5.c   6.a   7.d   8.b   9.c   10.d

Crossword

Across
3. independent
5. Masters
8. representative
9. nonresponse
10. generalizability
11. target
12. feminism

Down
1. Kinsey
2. interviews
4. causal
6. deception
7. photoplethysmograph

Practice Test

1.c   2.b   3. c   4.d   5.b   6.a   7.a   8.c   9.c   10.c

11.d   12. c   13.b   14.d   15.c   16.d   17.b   18.a   19.d   20.b

Introduction

Distinctions are drawn between sex and gender; between biological and psychosocial influences on gender identity. Processes of typical and atypical prenatal development that affect gender identity are described. The impact of various familial, social, and cultural learning experiences on gender identity development are discussed. Variant gender identities are described as well as lifestyle options and treatment for those desiring it. Research on the socialization of gender roles is summarized, and the adverse impact of gender role expectations is discussed. Alternatives to traditional gender roles are discussed at the chapter's end.

Learning Objectives. In order to derive maximum benefit from these objectives, use these as soon as you begin reading the chapter. After you have completed reading and studying this chapter, you should be able to do the things listed below with ease, using only your memory.

1. Define the key terms and concepts listed in the margin of the text and be able to integrate them with all relevant material outlined below.

2. Distinguish between gender identity and gender role and provide examples of each.

3. List and describe the six different levels of gender-identity formation from a biological perspective.

4. Discuss some of the abnormalities that may occur in prenatal sex differentiation, making specific reference to the following:
   a. Turner's syndrome
   b. Klinefelter's syndrome
   c. androgen insensitivity syndrome
   d. fetally androgenized females
   e. DHT-deficient males

5. Explain how social-learning factors influence gender-identity formation.

6. Define the interactional model of gender-identity formation.

7. Discuss transsexualism, making specific references to the following:
   a. the characteristics of transsexualism
   b. various theoretical explanations regarding what causes gender dysphoria
   c. treatment options for people with gender dysphoria
   d. the various phases involved in sex reassignment surgery
   e. what studies have revealed regarding post-operative follow-up of the lives of transsexuals

8. Define and give examples of gender-based stereotypes.

9. Explain how parents, peers, schools, textbooks, television and religion contribute to the socialization of gender roles, making reference to relevant research.

10. List and describe five gender-role assumptions and explain how these stereotypes affect sexual attitudes and behaviors in men and women.

11. Define the term "androgyny" and discuss research comparing androgynous individuals to people who are gender-typed masculine or feminine.

Concept Map

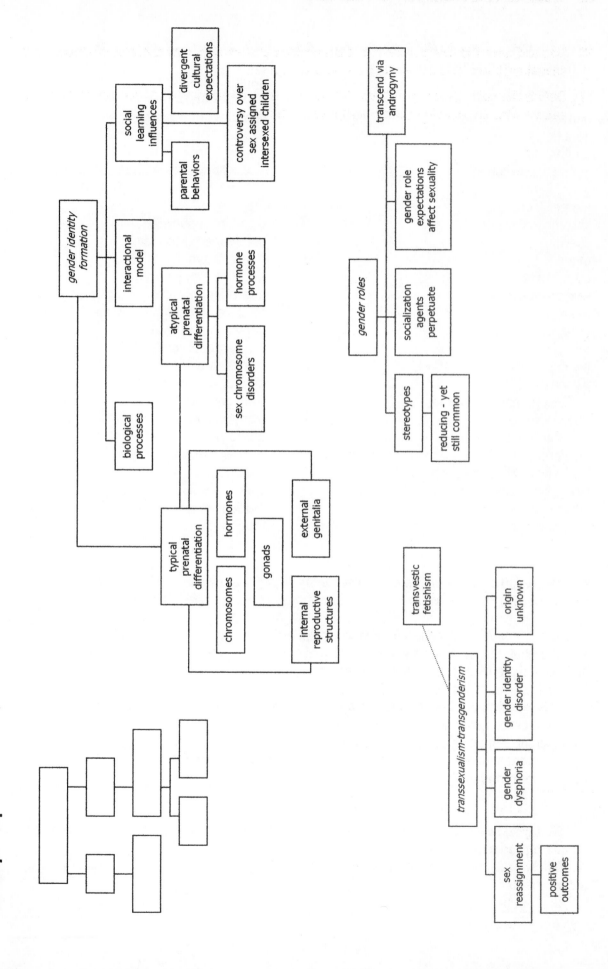

Key Terms . *Refer to the glossary or subject index in the back of your textbook for definitions and information.*

sex
gender
genetic sex
anatomical sex
gender assumptions
gender role
gender identity
chromosomal sex
sperm
ovum
autosomes
sex chromosomes
meiosis
gonads
testes
ovaries
estrogens
progestational compounds
androgens
Wolffian ducts
Mullerian ducts
Mullerian inhibiting substance
DHT (dihydrotestosterone)
labioscrotal swelling
genital tubercle

genital folds
hypothalamus
cerebral hemispheres
bed nucleus of stria terminalis (BST)
preoptic area (POA)
sexually dymorphic nucleus of
        the preoptic area (SND-POA)
intersexed
true hermaphrodite
pseudohermaphrodite
Turner's syndrome
Klinefelter's syndrome
androgen insensitivity syndrome (AIS)
fetally androgenized females (FAS)
DHT-deficient male
interactional model
transsexual
gender dysphoria
transgendered
transvestite
androgyny
gender identity disorder
stereotype
socialization
marianismo
machismo

Concept-Checks. *Complete this section by filling in each blank after you have studied the corresponding pages from the text. Answers are provided at the back of this chapter.*

Male and Female, Masculine and Feminine, pp. 46-47
1.   The qualities we associate with being male or female refer to _____ whereas our biological maleness of femaleness refers to _____.
2. Two features of biological sex include _____ and _____.
3. When we find out if someone is male or female, _____ lead us to expect that they will behave a certain way due to this maleness or femaleness.
4. A person's inner sense of maleness or femaleness refers to their _____.
5. The attitudes and behaviors that are considered suitable for males or females in a particular culture are termed _____.

Gender Identity Formation, pp. 47-53
1. Biological sex is determined by the male reproductive cell called _____ that fertilizes the female reproductive cell known as a(n) _____.
2. All chromosome pairs are matched except _____ which influence biological sex determination.

3. A male child with normal chromosomal sex has the _____ pattern whereas a female child has the _____ pattern.
4. The ovaries and the testicles comprise the _____ or sex glands.
5. Ovaries produce two groups of hormones: the _____ and the _____ compounds.
6. _____ are the hormones secreted by the testes.
7. At about _____ weeks past conception, internal reproductive organs begin to differentiate.
8. In a male fetus the _____ ducts develop into the vas deferens, seminal vesicles and ejaculatory ducts.
9. If androgens are not present the fetus will develop _____ structures.
10. In females the _____ ducts develop into the fallopian tubes, uterus, and the inner third of the vagina.
11. In order for the fetus' genitals to have a male appearance, _____ must be present.
12. Research has found that prenatal sex differentiation processes are partially responsible for sex differences in two major brain areas, the _____ and the _____.
13. The _____ and the _____ are two areas of the hypothalamus where sex differences have been identified.
14. Sex differences in verbal and spatial skills may be due, in part, to differences in the structure of cerebral _____.

Atypical Prenatal Differentiation, pp. 53-57
1. Individuals with ambiguous or contradictory sex characteristics have historically been called _____, though the term _____ is beginning to be used more frequently.
2. _____ are born with gonads that match their chromosomal sex, and have internal and external sex characteristics of both sexes.
3. In this very rare condition, _____ are born with the gonads of both sexes and have external and internal structures of both sexes.
4. The chromosome pattern of _____ identifies individuals with _____ syndrome.
5. Persons with Turner's syndrome typically have a _____ gender identity.
6. The XXY chromosome pattern is characteristics of individuals with _____ syndrome.
7. Three examples of disorders that affect prenatal hormone processes and produce intersexed persons include _____ females, _____ males and _____ syndrome.

Social Learning Influences on Gender Identity, pp. 57-62
1. Research has shown that _____ expectations influence the environments in which children are raised and the ways that parents respond to children beginning at birth.
2.   Most children have developed a firm sense of gender identity by _____ months of age.
3. In anthropologist Margaret Mead's classic work *Sex and Temperament in Three Primitive Societies,* the _____ people of New Guinea exhibited gender roles that were reversed from what most Americans consider typical.
4. Sexologist _____ and colleagues conducted studies of intersexed children who were assigned to a particular sex, providing some support for the role of social learning in forming gender identity.
5. Some long-term follow up studies of intersexed children have shown that _____ did not match assigned sex, questioning the notion that children are psychologically neutral at birth.

6. Intersexed activists have questioned the practice of operating on children who are unable to provide _____ consent prior to surgery.

7. Most theorists, researchers, and health care professionals support an _____ model of gender identity development.

Transsexualism and Transgenderism, pp. 62-67

1. An individual who feels imprisoned in the body of the wrong sex has the condition of gender _____.

2. A person whose body does not match their gender identity may be referred to as a(n) _____.

3. An individual may be considered _____ if their appearance or behaviors do not fall within the gender roles of a given society.

4. Some transgendered persons have no desire to seek _____ whereas many _____ wish to do so.

5. The term _____ is used to describe persons who cross-dress to achieve sexual arousal.

6. Most transsexuals have a _____ orientation and are biologically _____.

7. Current evidence regarding the causes of transsexualism is _____.

8. The key steps involved in undergoing sex reassignment are screening _____, adopting a lifestyle consistent with _____ _____, _____ therapy, and finally _____.

9. The majority of transsexuals who have experienced sex reassignment report _____ in their lives.

Gender Roles, pp. 67-74

1. When we fail to consider someone's individuality and make generalizations about them based on their membership in some group, we are using _____.

2. Most researchers agree that gender roles are learned through the process of _____.

3. Research studies have shown that parents tend to be more protective and restrictive of _____ whereas _____ are more likely to receive encouragement for self-assertion and restricting emotional expression.

4. Language helps build and maintain gender stereotypes as _____ talk more and use more speech than _____.

5. Peer groups continue traditional gender roles as _____ playmates are selected beginning in the preschool years.

6. Although schools and teachers seem to be acting in ways that reduce gender stereotyping in the classroom, _____ still portray girls and boys in a stereotypic manner.

7. The socialization agent of _____ is more frequently showing portrayals of gender equality, although recent research shows that gender role stereotyping is still the norm.

Gender-Role Expectations: Their Impact on Our Sexuality, pp. 74-77

1. Referring to a man who openly expresses his sexual interest as a "stud" and a woman who does so as a "slut" exemplifies the gender-role assumption of men as _____ and women as _____.

2. One outcome of the gender-role assumption of women as _____ and men as _____ is that men feel burdened and pressured to make the "first move" and women may be reluctant to assume an active role.

3. A woman may hesitate to suggest a variation in sexual activity with an other sex partner who is assumed to know more because of the gender-role assumption of men as
"_____."
4. Men may have greater difficulty being receptive during sexual activity because of the gender-role assumption of men as _____, and women as _____.
5. The "macho" conditioning of our society helps create the stereotype that men are _____ and_____ and that women are "naturally" more _____ and _____.

Transcending Gender Roles: Androgyny, pp. 77-78
1. A number of studies have shown that androgynous persons are more _____ in their behaviors and less limited by gender role stereotypes.
2. Androgynous persons have also been shown to have more _____ attitudes toward sexuality.

Crossword

<u>Across</u>
7. human sexuality "know-it-all"
8. experiences gender dysphoria
9. psychosocial meanings of biological sex
10. teachers are more tolerant of their bad behavior
11. some fetally androgenized females identify as this

<u>Down</u>
1. alternative term for hermaphrodite
2. researcher who studied sex-assigned intersexed children
3. dimension of biological sex that is easy to see
4. testes are a member of this group
5. sex of fetus if androgens absent
6. psychotherapy cannot change this aspect of gender

Practice Test

This test will work best to guide your learning if you take it as part of a final review session before an exam.

1. Five year old Jorge and his friends are playing "dress-up" and wearing women's clothing. When his playmates ask him if he is a boy or girl, Jorge emphatically replies, "I'm a boy!". Jorge's answer best reflects his
   a. gender assumptions
   b. gender identity
   c. gender role
   d. intersexed characteristics

2. When we say someone is female because she has a vulva and uterus, we are referring to
   a. gender role
   b. gender identity
   c. sex
   d. autosomal sex

3. If a sperm carrying an _____ sex chromosome fertilizes an egg carrying an _____ sex chromosome, a male fetus is produced.
   a. X; X
   b. X; Y
   c. Y; X
   d. Y; Y

4. The primary hormone products of the ovaries are _____ and _____ for the testes.
   a. estrogens; androgens
   b. estrogens; androgynous compounds
   c. progesterone; DHEA
   d. progesterone; androgynous compounds

5. The male gonads are called _____ and the females gonads are called _____.
   a. prostate glands; fallopian tubes
   b. seminal vesicles; ovaries
   c. Cowper's glands; Bartholin's glands
   d. testes; ovaries

6. In a male fetus that develops normally, the _____ ducts become the internal reproductive structures.
   a. Mullerian
   b. Wolffian
   c. ejaculatory
   d. Mullerian-inhibiting

7. The strongest support for sex differences in the brain comes from studies of the
   a. hippocampus
   b. nucleus accumbens
   c. hypothalamus
   d. homunculus

8. Which of the following is considered a form of atypical prenatal differentiation due to a disorder of the sex chromosomes?
   a. androgen insensitivity syndrome
   b. DHT-deficient males
   c. fetally androgenized females
   d. Klinefelter's syndrome

9. What conclusion can be reached regarding the biological basis of gender identity formation, based on studies done with intersexed children exposed to abnormal prenatal hormones?
   a. Gender identity is based upon chromosomal sex
   b. Gender identity is based upon the appearance of external genitalia
   c. Gender identity is based upon functional capacity of the gonads
   d. Studies provide contradictory evidence, so no firm conclusion can be reached

10. Most children have developed a firm gender identity by
    a. one year of age
    b. 18 months of age
    c. three years of age
    d. five years of age

11. Which of the following research findings does NOT support a social-learning view of gender identity formation?
    a. Some intersexed children did not adopt a gender identity consistent with their assigned sex
    b. Parents treat newborn boys and girls differently
    c. Mead's studies showed that different societies had different views about what is deemed masculine or feminine
    d. Girls are encouraged to be cooperative, whereas boys are encouraged to be aggressive

12. Standard protocols for the treatment of intersexed children are being questioned because of
    a. the difficulty of performing surgery on very young patients
    b. the number of new intersexed conditions being discovered
    c. the lack of long term outcome studies
    d. the growing acceptance of androgyny

13. Which of the following best describes a transsexual?
    a. An intersexed person who agrees to genital altering surgery
    b. Someone whose gender identity does not agree with their biological sex
    c. A person who is sexually attracted to a member of the same sex
    d. A person who cross-dresses in order to achieve sexual gratification

14. Transsexuals have a predominantly _____ orientation
    a. homosexual
    b. bisexual
    c. heterosexual
    d. psychosexually neutral

15. Transgenderists can be distinguished from transsexuals because transgenderists
    a. do not wish to change their bodies
    b. are more politically active
    c. have higher rates of mental illness
    d. are more likely to experience gender dysphoria

16. What statement best reflects current treatment options for transsexuals?
    a. Psychotherapy can help change gender identity
    b. Psychotherapy alone cannot change gender identity
    c. Biological alteration is only necessary if there is the possibility of suicide
    d. Biological alteration is required in order for successful adjustment to occur

17. Studies of transsexuals who have undergone sex reassignment surgery have shown that
    a. Adjustment is better for men becoming women
    b. Adjustment is better for women becoming men
    c. Adjustment is better when the period of living as the other sex is longer
    d. Adjustment is better for a substantial majority

18. Britta assumes that her new boyfriend will be able to fix her broken car, because she believes men are more mechanically inclined. Britta's behavior reflects
    a. gender stererotypes
    b. gender identity
    c. androgyny
    d. marianismo

19. Parents provide gender-role socialization by
    a. giving girl babies more attention
    b. encouraging assertive behavior in sons
    c. using different communication styles with sons and daughters
    d. all of the above

20. Peers influence the formation of traditional gender roles by
    a. offering a haven relatively free from gender role stereotypes
    b. providing and withholding social acceptance
    c. encouraging rebellion against parents' efforts to engrain stereotypes
    d. encouraging play in mixed-sex groups

21. Studies of television programming have demonstrated that
    a. most Sesame Street characters are female
    b. advertising features more girls than boys
    c. women are valued primarily for physical appearance
    d. traditional stereotypes dominate primarily in sitcoms

22. Which of the following groups tends to have the most egalitarian relations between men and women?
    a. African Americans
    b. Hispanic Americans
    c. White Americans
    d. Asian Americans

23. Even though Leticia loves her partner very much, she frequently denies that she has feelings of sexual arousal, preferring to think that she is just tense from all the stress she is under. Leticia's behavior illustrates the negative impact of which gender-role expectation?
    a. women as controllers, men as movers
    b. men as "sexperts"
    c. men as oversexed, women as undersexed
    d. men as initiators, women as controllers

24. Kyle feels compelled to make the first sexual advance with a new date, even though he'd really prefer to get to know someone better first, yet Kyle is concerned his date will think he's weird. Kyle's dilemma reflects which gender-role expectation?
    a. men as strong and unemotional, women as nurturing and supportive
    b. men as oversexed, women as undersexed
    c. men as movers, women as controllers
    d. men as "sexperts"

25. Baseball player Mark McGwire has cried at a press conference, hugged rival Sammy Sosa numerous times, expressing affection and admiration for this competitor. McGwire's behavior exemplifies
    a. androgyny
    b. misogyny
    c. misanthropism
    d. hegemony

Answer Key – Chapter 3

<u>Concept Checks</u>

Male and Female, Masculine and Feminine
1. gender; sex
2. biological ; anatomical
3. gender assumptions
4. gender identity
5. gender roles

Gender Identity Formation
1. sperm, ovum
2. sex chromosomes
3. XY; XX
4. gonads
5. estrogens; progestational
6. androgens
7. eight
8. Wolffian
9. female
10. Mullerian
11. DHT (dihydrotestosterone)
12. cerebral hemispheres; hypothalamus
13. BST (bed nucleus of the stria terminalus); POA (preoptic area)
14. hemispheres

Atypical Prenatal Differentiation
1. hermaphrodites, intersexed
2. pseudohermaphrodites
3. true hermaphrodites
4. XO; Turner's
5. female
6. Klinefelter's
7. fetally androgenized; DHT-deficient; androgen insensitivity

Social Learning Influences on Gender Identity
1. gender role
2. eighteen
3. Tchambuli
4. John Money
5. gender identity
6. informed
7. interactional

Transsexualism and Transgenderism
1. dysphoria
2. transsexual

3. transgendered
4. sex reassignment, transsexuals
5. transvestic fetishism
6. heterosexual, normal
7. inconclusive
8. interviews, gender identity, hormonal, surgery
9. improvement

Gender Roles
1. stereotypes
2. socialization
3. girls, boys
4. mothers, fathers
5. same sex
6. textbooks
7. television

Gender-Role Expectations: Their Impact on Our Sexuality
1. oversexed, undersexed
2. recipients, initiators
3. sexperts
4. movers, controllers
5. unemotional, strong, nurturing, supportive

Transcending Gender Roles: Androgyny
1. flexible
2. positive

Crossword Puzzle

Across
 7. sexpert
 8. transsexual
 9. gender
10. boys
11. tomboy

Down
1. intersexed
2. Money
3. genitals
4. gonads
5. female
6. identity

Practice Test

1. b 2. c 3. c 4. a 5. d 6. b 7. c 8. d 9. d 10. b 11. a 12. c 13. b
14. c 15. a 16. b 17. d 18. a 19. d 20. b 21. c 22. a 23. c 24. b 25. a

Chapter 4 – Female Sexual Anatomy and Physiology

Introduction

The genital self exam can begin the process of becoming more comfortable with our bodies, and is an important step toward taking charge of our sexual health. Both external and internal female structures and their associated functions are described in this chapter. The menstrual cycle and common problems are discussed. Key events during the transition from fertility to infertility in middle age are described. Gynecological health concerns, medical treatments, and self-help prevention methods are also discussed. The chapter closes with a description of the breasts, self-care methods and conditions affecting the breasts.

Learning Objectives. In order to derive maximum benefit from these objectives, use these as soon as you begin reading the chapter. After you have completed reading and studying this chapter, you should be able to do the things listed below with ease, using only your memory.

1. List the reasons for doing a genital self-exam.

2. Briefly describe the process of doing a genital self-exam.

3. Define the terms "gynecology" and "vulva".

4. Identify and briefly describe the following structures of the vulva: mons veneris, labia majora, labia minora, clitoris, vestibule, urethral opening, introitus and hymen, perineum.

5. Identify the location, structure, and function of the following: vestibular bulbs, Bartholin's glands, vagina, cervix, uterus, fallopian tubes, ovaries.

6. Explain when and for what purpose Kegel exercises were developed.

7. Describe the steps involved in practicing Kegel exercises, and explain the benefits of doing these exercises.

8. Discuss the source and function of vaginal lubrication during sexual arousal.

9. List several factors that may inhibit vaginal lubrication, and explain how those situations might be remedied.

10. Identify the location and function of the Grafenberg spot.

11. Describe what function vaginal secretions serve.

12. Describe the chemical balance of the vagina, and discuss ways in which this balance may be altered.

13. Discuss the following in reference to urinary tract infections: incidence of, causes of, symptoms of, preventative measures.

14. Define vaginitis and discuss the following in relation to it: symptoms, factors increasing the susceptibility to vaginitis, ways to help prevent vaginitis.

15. Discuss the following in relation to a Pap smear: what purpose it serves, how it is done, how often it should be done, what steps may be taken if the results of a Pap smear are not normal, certain subgroups of women who are less likely to have routine Pap smears.

16. Describe which women may be at higher risk of cervical cancer, how common it is, and discuss available treatment options for women who receive this diagnosis.

17. Define the following terms: hysterectomy, oophorectomy.

18. Describe how a hysterectomy may affect a woman sexually, physically and emotionally.

19. Describe the controversy surrounding breast implants.

20. Discuss the following in relationship to the breasts: structure and function of, self-exam — when, how and why, mammography, three types of breast lumps that may occur, breast cancer and treatment alternatives available for women who are diagnosed with it, high and low risk factors for breast cancer.

21. Discuss the following in regard to menstruation: attitudes toward it in American society; when it typically begins; the extent to which young women and men are informed about it; the length of the menstrual cycle; menstrual synchrony; the relationship among the hypothalamus, pituitary gland and adrenal glands; the proliferative, secretory and menstrual phases of the menstrual cycle; sexual activity and the menstrual cycle; premenstrual syndrome; primary and secondary dysmenorrhea; primary and secondary amenorrhea; self-help for menstrual problems; toxic shock syndrome.

22. Describe symptoms of and treatment for Premenstrual Dysphoric Disorder.

23. Describe three types of genital mutilation, the reasons for doing it, the health consequences that may result, and the current controversy that surrounds it.

24. Explain how some other cultures have viewed menstruation, including American culture.

25. Define menopause as it relates to the climacteric.

26. Describe the physiosexual changes that women experience during menopause.

27. Define hormone-replacement therapy and explain its advantages and potential risks.

Concept Map

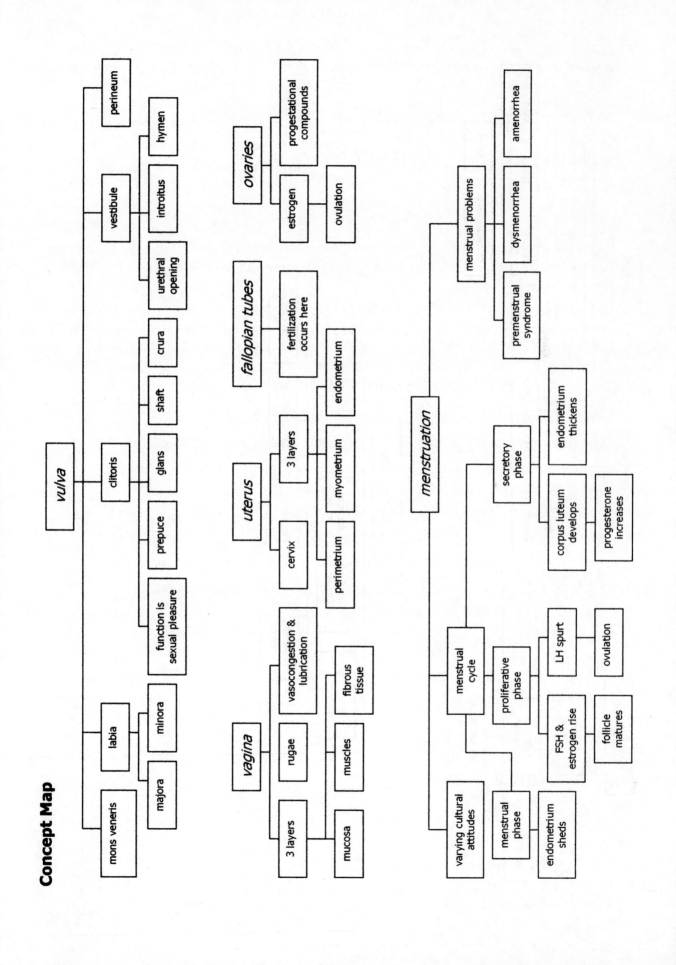

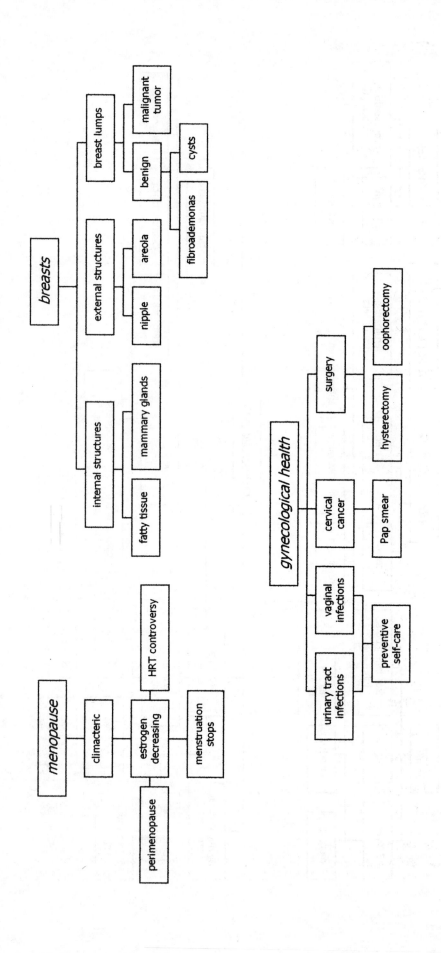

Key Terms. *Refer to the glossary or subject index in the back of your textbook for definitions and information.*

gynecology
vulva
mons veneris
labia majora
labia minora
prepuce
shaft
glans
crura
smegma
cavernous bodies
vestibule
circumcision
clitoridectomy
genital infibulation
urethra
intoitus
hymen
perineum
vestibular bulbs
Bartholin's glands
vagina
mucosa
rugae
Kegel exercises
vasocongestion
Grafenberg spot
douching
speculum
cervix

os
cervical mucus
uterus
perimetrium
myometrium
endometrium
fallopian tubes
fimbriae
ectopic pregnancy
ovaries
ovulation
menstruation
menarche
menstrual synchrony
follicle-stimulating
    hormone (FSH)
follicle
luteinizing hormone (LH)
corpus luteum
negative feedback
    mechanism
menstrual phase
proliferative phase
mittelschmerz
secretory phase
premenstrual syndrome
(PMS)
premenstrual dysphoric
disorder (PMDD)
dysmenorrhea

primary dysmenorrhea
secondary dysmenorrhea
prostaglandins
endometriosis
amenorrhea
primary amenorrhea
secondary amenorrhea
toxic shock syndrome
    (TSS)
climacteric
perimenopause
menopause
hormone replacement
    therapy (HRT)
vaginitis
pap smear
hysterectomy
oophorectomy
secondary sex
    characteristics
mammary glands
nipple
areola
mammography
fibroadenomas
fibrocystic disease
malignant tumor
mastectomy
lumpectomy

Concept-Checks. *Complete this section by filling in each blank after you have studied the corresponding pages from the text. Answers are provided at the back of this chapter.*

Genital Self Exam, pp.82-83
1. A self exam may help us feel more comfortable with our bodies and also supplements regular medical _____.

The Vulva, pp. 83-87
1. The _____ covers the pubic bone and is part of the external female genital structures known as the _____.

2. The labia _____ are covered with hair and surround the labia _____ , which are hairless.

3. A hood covers the _____ , whose only function is to provide pleasure.

4. A cheesy-like substance called _____ may form under the prepuce or hood.

5. The crura, _____ and _____ make up the clitoris.

6. During sexual arousal the _____ bodies of the clitoris swell with blood.

7. Studies have shown that women prefer clitoral stimulation over vaginal insertion during masturbation because of the high concentration of _____ _____ in the clitoris.

8. The urinary and vaginal openings lie within the _____ , an area of the vulva inside the labia minora.

9. The _____ refers to the opening of the vagina.

10. The _____ partially covers the vaginal opening and is thought to have no known function.

11. Nerve endings are present in the skin of the _____ which extends from the vagina to the anus.

12. The controversial practice of _____ _____ _____ continues as proponents believe the practice insures a girl's virginity whereas others are concerned about the health complications of the practice.

Underlying Structures, pp. 87-88

1. A vast network containing the _____ bulbs and _____ glands lies underneath the vulva.

2. An multidirectional array of _____ _____ muscles also lies beneath the vulva.

Internal Structures, pp. 88-93

1. The multi-layered _____ is a flexible canal that extends 3-5 inches in an upward angle toward the back.

2. When a finger is inserted into the vagina, a layer of _____ is felt as well as folded walls called _____ .

3. The walls of the vagina produce _____ which provide a proper chemical balance and lubrication during sexual arousal.

4. The musculature of the vagina is concentrated in the outer _____ , whereas the inner _____ can greatly expand.

5. Urinary control and increased sensation may result from regularly doing _____ exercises as pelvic floor muscles become stronger.

6. Vaginal lubrication during sexual arousal results from the process of _____ , with blood collecting in the pelvic area.

7. The front wall of the vagina contains the _____ spot, which is believed to be a female counterpart to the male prostate gland.

8. Activities such as _____ and using feminine hygiene sprays can alter the normal chemical balance of the vagina, producing vaginal problems.

9. The small end of the uterus is called the _____ and is located at the back of the vagina.

10. Sperm enter the uterus by swimming through the _____ , the narrow opening of the cervix.

11. The uterus is a _____ shaped organ that contains _____ layers.

12. When an egg leaves the ovary it travels down the _____ tubes which project from the _____ .

13. If a fertilized ovum implants outside the uterus, a(n) _____pregnancy results.
14. The female gonads or _____ are connected to the pelvic wall and uterus by ligaments.
15. When an egg matures and is released from the ovary, _____ is said to occur.

Menstruation, pp. 93-101

 1. Controversy exists regarding attitudes toward _____, where _____ lining sheds if conception does not occur.
2. First menstruation or _____ typically begins between the ages of _____ and 15.
3. The length of the menstrual cycle is measured from the beginning of the _____ day of flow to the day before the next flow begins.
4. The _____ stimulates the pituitary gland to release hormones that act on the ovaries.
5. The pituitary gland releases _____ which stimulates the ovaries to produce estrogen and causes ova in follicles to mature.
6. To produce ovulation and formation of the corpus luteum, _____ is secreted by the pituitary gland.
7. The corpus luteum secretes the hormone _____.
8. Menstruation occurs during the _____ phase of the menstrual cycle.
9. Menstruation is triggered by a drop in the levels of _____ and _____.
10. Production of follicle stimulating hormone (FSH) and ripening of ovarian follicles occur during the _____ phase of the menstrual cycle.
11. Luteinizing hormone (LH) production continues, the corpus luteum develops, and uterine lining thickens during the _____ phase of the menstrual cycle.
12. Premenstrual syndrome is used to describe the _____ and _____ symptoms that occur before menstruation.
13. Only 5% of women have symptoms severe enough to be diagnosed with _____ _____ disorder.
14. Primary _____ refers to pain and discomfort during menstruation and is usually caused by overproduction of _____ which cause the muscles of the uterus to contract.
15. Painful menstruation, pain during intercourse, and low backache may be caused by _____, in which the uterine lining implants outside the uterus in the abdominal cavity.
16. Pregnancy, menopause, and anorexia nervosa are common causes of _____ , or the absence of menstruation.
17. Using regular absorbency tampons may help reduce the risk of _____ _____syndrome, a rare disease that occurs most frequently in menstruating women.

Menopause, pp. 101-104

1. Irregular menstrual cycles are characteristic of _____ , the period prior to the cessation of menstruation.
2. When menstrual periods completely stop, _____ occurs.
3. Symptoms of menopause are primarily caused by a decline in _____.
4. The transition from fertility to infertility in women and men is termed the _____.
5. Hormone replacement therapy (HRT) may involve taking supplemental estrogen, _____, and possibly _____.
6. The estrogen in HRT may reduce hot flashes, _____ (abnormal bone loss) and may provide protection against _____ disease.
7. Estrogen also helps maintain _____ and _____ tissues.

8. Testosterone may be included as part of HRT in order to help with sexual _____ and _____.

9. Progestins are often combined with estrogens in HRT in order to reduce _____ cancer.

10. Research is unclear whether HRT is associated with an increase or decrease in _____ cancer risk.

Gynecological Health Concerns, pp. 104-108

1. Frequent need to urinate, burning sensations during urination, blood or pus in the urine and low back pain are all symptoms of _____ _____ infections.

2. Wiping from _____ to_____ after urination and bowel movements, drinking plenty of fluids, and urinating as soon as the urge is felt may help prevent urinary tract infections.

3. Common symptoms of _____ include irritation or itching of the vulva and vagina, unusual discharge, or unpleasant odor.

4. Wearing _____ underpants and using _____ if your partner is not monogamous may prevent the occurrence of vaginitis.

5. During a _____ smear a sample of cells is taken from the _____ in order to detect cancer.

6. Among women who are less likely to undergo screening for cervical cancer are _____ , _____ _____ women and poor women.

7. A greater risk of cervical cancer is associated with having _____ _____, _____ male sex partners, and exposure to cigarette smoke.

8. A(n) _____ refers to surgical removal of the ovaries, whereas a(n) _____ refers to surgical removal of the uterus.

The Breasts, pp. 108-114

1. The interior of the breast is primarily made of _____ tissue and _____ glands.

2. Since developed breasts distinguish physically mature women from men, breasts are considered a(n) _____ sex characteristic.

3. Differences in the size of breasts result from varying amounts of _____ tissue.

4. The _____ is located within the center of the dark, circular area known as the _____.

5. The best time to conduct a breast self exam is following _____.

6. In order to screen for breast cancer, _____is used to take a highly sensitive X-ray of the breasts.

7. Fibroadenomas and _____ are common types of noncancerous breast lumps.

8. Breast cancer currently affects one in _____ North American women.

9. _____ factors account for more of the share of breast cancer risk than genetic factors.

10. Surgical removal of all or part of a breast is called _____ .

Crossword

Across
3. this substance decreases during perimenopause
4. "pleasure is my only purpose"
6. cotton underwear prevents this discomfort
7. mucus maker that feels like the tip of your nose
8. nonmusical structure with a major and minor form
9. moist liner of the vagina

11. partially open vaginal cover

Down
1. for some Native Americans this is a woman's most powerful time
2. lies between the vagina and anus
5. active self-help remedy for menstrual problems
6. shown at Judy Chicago's Dinner Party
10. number of phases of the menstrual cycle

Matching

Identify the parts of the female anatomy as marked below. Answers may be found at the end of the chapter.

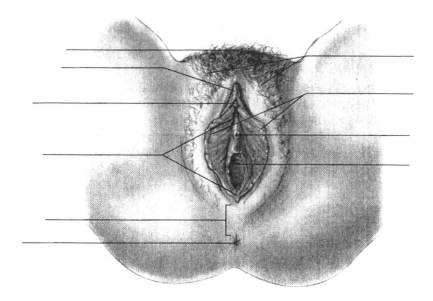

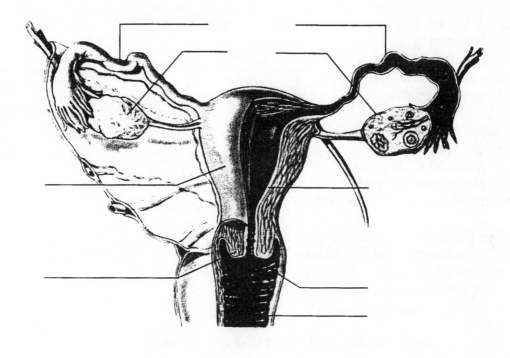

Practice Test

This test will work best to guide your learning if you take it as part of a final review session before an exam.

1. Which of the following does not make up part of the vulva?
   a. Grafenberg spot
   b. clitoris
   c. mons veneris
   d. urethral opening

2. Which structures are part of the clitoris?
   a. glans, shaft, hood
   b. glans, shaft, introitus
   c. glans, fimbriae, shaft
   d. shaft, hood, vestibular bulbs

3. The primary function of the clitoris is
   a. covering the urethral opening
   b. supplying the labia minora with blood
   c. secreting lubrication
   d. providing sexual pleasure

4. The _____ are hairless and contain sweat and oil glands.
   a. labia majora
   b. labia minora
   c. crura
   d. cavernous bodies

5. Smegma may be found
   a. along the areola
   b. along the rugae
   c. under the clitoral hood
   d. inside the vagina

6. Which of the following statements about the vagina is false?
   a. The vagina is about 3 to 5 inches in length when a woman is unaroused.
   b. The vagina contains folded walls.
   c. The greatest degree of musculature is found in the inner third.
   d. Lubrication is produced by the vaginal walls.

7. The vaginal opening may be partially covered by the
   a. Skene's glands
   b. hymen
   c. pubic symphysis
   d. seminal sheath

8. Kegel exercises may increase sensation and promote urinary control by
   a. strengthening the pelvic floor muscles
   b. contracting the clitoris
   c. stimulating the production of prostaglandins
   d. inhibiting the production of anti-diurectic hormone

9. Which of the following is false regarding vaginal secretions?
   a. They are normally rather acid.
   b. They are typically white or yellowish.
   c. The scent varies with a woman's cycle.
   d. The chemical balance is best maintained by regular douching.

10. Which of the following is not associated with the cervix?
    a. os
    b. triangular and soft
    c. Pap smear
    d. mucus secreting glands

11. This structure has a layer of muscle and is suspended in the pelvic cavity by ligaments.
    a. fallopian tubes
    b. ovaries
    c. fimbriae
    d. uterus

12. Fertilization occurs
    a. in the fallopian tubes
    b. in the uterus
    c. in the cervical os
    d. during mittelschmerz

13. Which of the following statements regarding menstruation is true?
    a. Menstruation usually begins between 10 and 13 years of age.
    b. Menstrual cycle length typically spans 21 to 50 days.
    c. The amount of menstrual flow may vary from month to month.
    d. Menstrual synchrony has yet to be observed in humans.

14. When the pituitary releases _____ the ovaries increase estrogen production and ova begin to mature.
    a. GnRH
    b. FSH
    c. LH
    d. Prolactin

15. What is the correct ordering of the phases of the menstrual cycle?
    a. proliferative phase, secretory phase, menstrual phase
    b. secretory phase, menstrual phase, proliferative phase
    c. menstrual phase, proliferative phase, secretory phase
    d. secretory phase, proliferative phase, menstrual phase

16. Ovulation
    a. is triggered by a sudden spurt of LH
    b. occurs 14 days before the onset of the next menstrual period
    c. may be accompanied by discomfort in the lower abdomen
    d. all of the above are true

17. During the secretory phase of the menstrual cycle the corpus luteum
    a. secretes progesterone
    b. produces LH
    c. signals the pituitary to make oxytocin
    d. promotes degeneration of the myometrium

18. What can be concluded about studies which have examined sexual behavior and the menstrual cycle?
    a. Sexual activity peaks near ovulation
    b. Sexual acitvity rises during menstruation
    c. Great individual variation is shown, so observing your own patterns is suggested
    d. Little variation occurs in sexual behavior throughout the cycle

19. Possible causes of dysmenorrhea include all of the following except
    a. reduced FSH levels
    b. pelvic inflammatory disease
    c. endometriosis
    d. excess production of prostaglandins

20. All of the following are associated with amenorrhea except
    a. pregnancy
    b. being obese
    c. being an athlete
    d. anorexia nervosa

21. Premenstrual syndrome may produce all of the following experiences except
    a. increased weight loss
    b. breast pain
    c. irritability
    d. "tight-jeans" syndrome

22. In women the climacteric is associated with a range of symptoms produced by
    a. declining estrogen levels
    b. increased testosterone production
    c. changes in free fatty acids in the blood
    d. decreased cortisol sensitivity

23. Which statement best reflects current views regarding Hormone Replacement Therapy?
    a. Women should begin HRT when perimenopause is first noticed.
    b. Testosterone supplementation should be part of HRT for most women.
    c. Women should consider the benefits and risks of HRT by discussing the matter with a health care provider.
    d. Progesterone supplementation is not required for women with a uterus.

24. A woman may reduce the chance of contracting a urinary tract infection by
    a. douching after menstruation
    b. urinating as soon as she feels the urge
    c. wiping from back to front
    d. using petroleum jelly during intercourse

25. The risk of vaginitis increases if a woman
    a. is using birth control pills
    b. wears cotton underpants
    c. uses mild soap when washing
    d. eats a low carbohydrate diet

26. A woman should begin having Pap smears
    a. when she starts menstruating
    b. when she notices pelvic pain
    c. when she is 18 or begins having intercourse
    d. when she shows secondary sex characteristics

27. A woman who smokes and has multiple male sexual partners is at increased risk of developing
    a. fibrocystic disease
    b. ectopic pregnancy
    c. endometriosis
    d. cervical cancer

28. Which of the following is not true regarding hysterectomy?
    a. It is the second most common surgical procedure for women.
    b. It is used to treat cervical and uterine cancer.
    c. It may affect sexual response.
    d. The uterus and ovaries are removed.

29. Breast size is primarily influenced by
    a. the size of the mammary glands
    b. the amount of muscle tissue on the chest wall
    c. the number of milk ducts
    d. the amount of fatty tissue surrounding the glands

30. Most breast lumps are not malignant tumors and may instead be a(n)
    a. cyst or fibroadenoma
    b. axillary adhesion
    c. fibroidal mass
    d. mammary body

31. Which of the following statements regarding breast cancer risk is false?
    a. Approximately one in nine North American women is affected.
    b. Environmental factors account for two times as much risk as genes.
    c. Sedentary lifestyle does not seem to increase risk.
    d. The risk of breast cancer rises with age.

Answer Key – Chapter 4

<u>Concept Checks</u>

The Genital Self Exam
1. care

The Vulva
1. mons veneris, vulva
2. majora, minora
3. clitoris
4. smegma
5. glans, shaft
6. cavernous
7. nerve endings
8. vestibule
9. introitus
10. hymen
11. perineum
12. female genital mutilation

Underlying Structures
1. vestibular, Bartholin's
2. pelvic floor

Internal Structures
1. vagina
2. mucosa
3. secretions (or lubrication)
4. third, two-thirds
5. Kegel
6. vasocongestion
7. Grafenberg
8. douching
9. cervix
10. os
11. pear, three
12. fallopian tubes, uterus
13. ectopic
14. ovaries
15. ovulation

Menstruation
1. menstruation, uterine (or endometrial)
2. menarche
3. first
4. hypothalamus

5. FSH
6. LH
7. progesterone
8. menstrual
9. estrogen, progesterone
10. proliferative
11. secretory
12. physical, psychological
13. premenstrual dysphoric disorder (PMDD)
14. dysmenorrhea
15. endometriosis
16. amenorrhea
17. toxic shock

Menopause
1. perimenopause
2. menopause
3. estrogen
4. climacteric
5. progesterone, testosterone
6. osteoporosis, heart
7. vaginal, urethral
8. desire, response
9. endometrial
10. breast

Gynecological Health Concerns
1. urinary tract
2. front, back
3. vaginitis
4. cotton, condoms
5. Pap
6. lesbians, Native American
7. genital warts, multiple
8. oophorectomy, hysterectomy

The Breasts
1. fatty, mammary
2. secondary
3. fatty
4. nipple, areola
5. menstruation
6. mammography
7. cysts
8. nine
9. environmental
10. mastectomy

Crossword Puzzle

<u>Across</u>
  3. estrogen
  4. clitoris
  6. vaginitis
  7. cervix
  8. labia
  9. mucosa
 11. hymen

<u>Down</u>
  1. menstruation
  2. perineum
  5. exercise
  6. vulva
 10. three

Matching

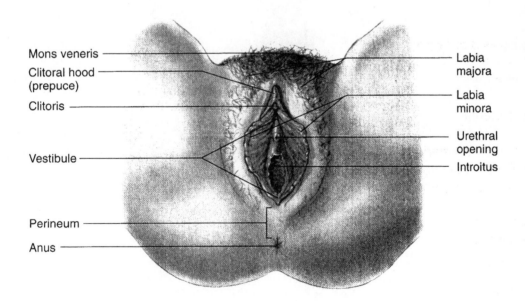

Mons veneris — Labia majora

Clitoral hood (prepuce) — Labia minora

Clitoris — Urethral opening

Vestibule — Introitus

Perineum

Anus

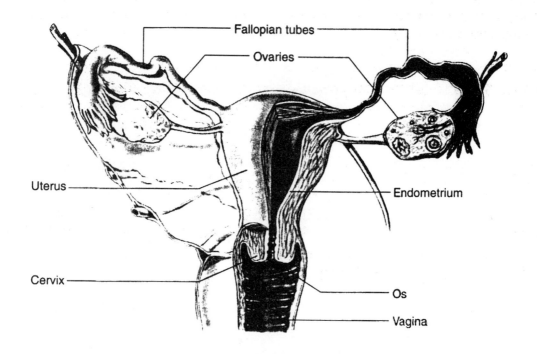

Practice Test

1. a 2. a 3. d 4. b 5. c 6. c 7. b 8. a 9. d 10. b 11. d 12. a 13. c 14. b
15. c 16. d 17. a 18. c 19. a 20. b 21. a 22. a 23. c 24. b 25. a 26. c
27. d 28. d 29. d 30. a 31. c

Introduction

Structures of internal and external male sexual anatomy are described. Their roles in sperm, hormone, and semen production are explained. Mechanisms of erection and ejaculation are discussed, as are psychosocial aspects of these functions. Concerns and controversies regarding penis size and circumcision are addressed. Common male genital health concerns and treatments are discussed in a manner which encourages men to take a more active role in maintaining their sexual health.

Learning Objectives. In order to derive maximum benefit from these objectives, use these as soon as you begin reading the chapter. After you have completed reading and studying this chapter, you should be able to do the things listed below with ease, using only your memory.

1. Describe the structure and function of the following parts of the male sexual anatomy: the penis, the scrotum, the testes, the vas deferens, the seminal vesicles, the prostate gland, the Cowper's glands, semen.

2. Describe how Kegel exercises are done, and give three possible benefits of doing them.

3. Define cryptorchidism, including its incidence and how it is treated.

4. Discuss the possible relationship between heat and sperm production.

5. Define the cremasteric reflex, and discuss what types of situations may provoke this response.

6. Explain how to conduct a male genital self-exam.

7. Explain how and where sperm production and storage takes place.

8. Discuss in detail the physiological processes involved in erection and ejaculation.

9. Explain why penis size has historically been so important, and how that has affected men's masculinity and/or self-image. Describe the physiological facts of sexual interaction and penis size.

10. Define circumcision and discuss recent research regarding its necessity.

11. Discuss various cultural beliefs and practices regarding male genital modification and mutilation, referring specifically to the following: under what circumstances it is practiced; advantages and disadvantages of these procedures; how these procedures relate to sexual pleasure and function; cross-cultural beliefs and practices.

12. Discuss health care concerns regarding the penis.

13. Discuss benefits and costs of circumcision and recent AAP recommendations regarding circumcision.

14. Describe the incidence of, symptoms of and treatment alternatives for penile and testicular cancer, prostatitis and benign prostate hyperplasia.

15. Describe recent advances in treatment and management of prostate cancer.

Concept Map

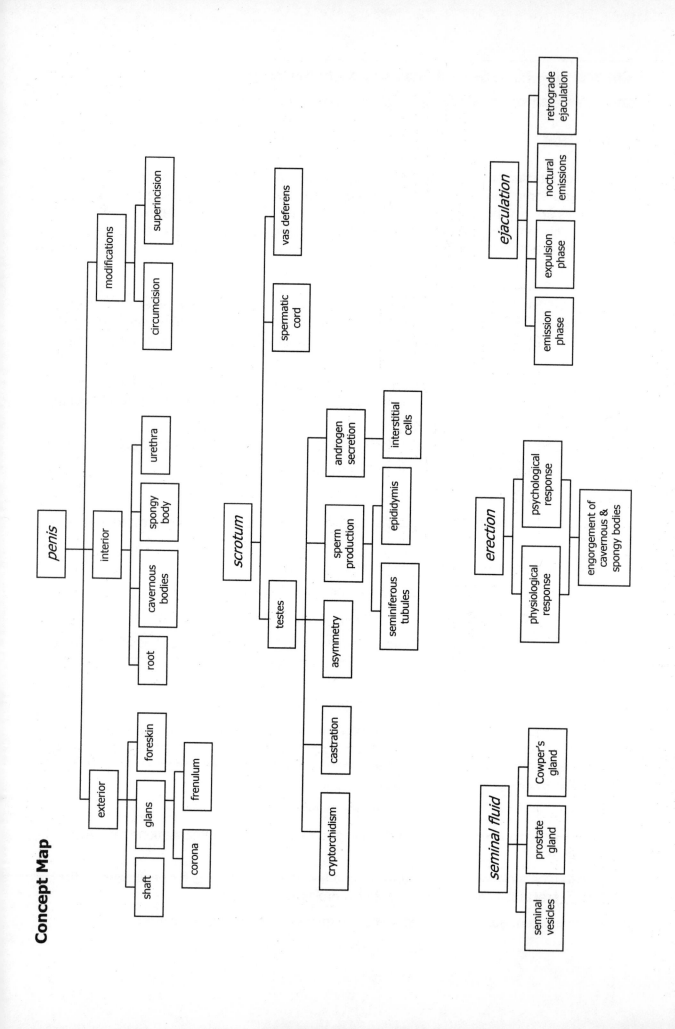

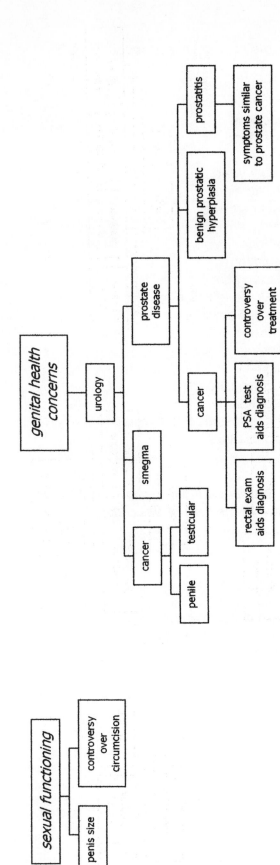

Key Terms. *Refer to the glossary or subject index in the back of your textbook for definitions and information.*

penis
root
shaft
glans
cavernous bodies
spongy body
foreskin
circumcision
bris
superincision
corona
frenulum
scrotum
testis
spermatic cord
tunica dartos
cremasteric reflex
inguinal canal
cryptorchidism
seminiferous tubules

interstitial cells
epididymis
vasectomy
ejaculatory duct
urethra
seminal vesicles
prostate gland
Cowper's gland
semen
erection
ejaculation
emission phase
retrograde ejaculation
nocturnal emissions
phimosis
urology
smegma
testicular cancer
prostatitis
benign prostatic hyperplasia
prostate cancer

Concept-Checks. *Complete this section by filling in each blank after you have studied the corresponding pages from the text. Answers are provided at the back of this chapter.*

Sexual Anatomy
The Penis, pp. 118-121
1. The exterior of the penis contains the shaft and _____.
2. The penis is connected to the body by the _____.
3. The interior of the penis contains two _____ bodies and one _____ body.
4. In an uncircumcised male, the _____ covers the glans of the penis.
5. Two areas of the glans that are especially sensitive to stimulation are the _____ and the _____.
6. If Kegel exercises are done regularly, increased sensation during sexual arousal, stronger _____ and better _____ control may result.
7. Three means of genital modification include circumcision, _____, and _____.

The Scrotum and the Testes, pp. 121-124
1. Each testis is suspended by the _____ cord within the pouch of skin called the _____.
2. During sexual arousal, when strong emotion is experienced or when the scrotum is cooled, the testicles move _____ to the body.
3. During fetal development the testes travel to the outside of the body through the _____ _____.

4. _____ results when the testes fail to descend, and may increase the risk of infertility, testicular cancer, and _____.

5. Research has indicated that _____ self-examination is seldom taught in health classes or performed.

6. In most men the testicles are _____ and excessive masturbation has been incorrectly identified as a cause.

7. Sperm are initially produced in highly coiled structures called _____ _____.

8. Males may continue to produce sperm until _____.

9. The _____ _____ manufacture much of a man's androgen.

10. Sperm complete the process of maturation while residing in the C-shaped _____.

The Vas Deferens, Seminal Vesicles, Prostate and Cowper's Glands, Semen , pp. 124-127

1. After sperm leave the epididymis they enter the _____ _____.

2. The vas deferens is severed during a _____, a male sterilization procedure.

3. The majority of seminal fluid is produced by the _____ _____.

4. The remainder of seminal fluid is produced by the walnut-shaped _____ _____.

5. Small drops of fluid that may appear at the tip of the penis in a sexually aroused man are produced by the _____ _____.

6. Cowper's gland secretions may contain _____, therefore the withdrawal method is not a very effective means of birth control.

7. The amount of seminal fluid may be affected by the length of time since last ejaculation, the duration of _____, and _____.

8. The products in semen are not harmful if swallowed, yet _____ may be transmitted from the semen to open sores or bleeding gums.

Male Sexual Functions, pp. 127-129

1. Erections are produced when the three chambers of the penis become engorged with _____.

2. The ability to have erections is present at _____.

3. In some respects an erection is merely a physiological response, yet research shows that the _____ also influences erections.

4. Erections may occur in _____ situations, such as when exercising or defecating.

5. The sensation that orgasm is inevitable occurs during the _____ phase of ejaculation.

6. During the _____ phase of ejaculation, semen is expelled from the penis.

7. Semen is released from the body by a series of _____ _____.

8. When semen is expelled into the bladder instead of outside the body, _____ ejaculation occurs.

9. Another name for a "wet dream" is _____ _____.

Some Concerns About Sexual Functioning, pp. 129-133.

1. Both the ancient and modern world have been concerned with penis _____.

2. Many men associate penis size with _____ and self image.

3. The textbook authors do not provide information about variations in penis size because they believe such information is _____.

4. During erection smaller flaccid penises increase _____ in size relative to larger flaccid penises.

5. Research has demonstrated that penis size is not related to length of fingers, race, body shape or _____.

6. When circumcision is performed, the _____ of the penis is removed.
7. Current medical evidence regarding the view that circumcision is necessary for proper hygiene has produced _____ results.
8. Currently the American Academy of Pediatrics (AAP) is _____ _____ to the practice of circumcision, through historically the AAP's position has been modified many times.

Male Genital Health Concerns, pp. 133-139
1. The field of medicine that specializes in male reproductive health and urinary tract diseases is called _____.
2. Secretions from the glands of the foreskin may combine with dead skin cells to form _____, which may result in irritaton, unpleasant odor, and an increased risk of infection.
3. A small sore on the penis may be a sign of _____, a rare condition that may destroy the entire penis.
4. _____ cancer is one of the most common malignancies among men aged 15-34.
5. A large percentage of men over 50 are likely to experience benign prostatic hyperplasia, because the prostate _____ in size.
6. Inflammation of the prostate, or _____ may be effectively treated with antibiotics.
7. _____ cancer is the second most common cancer among men.
8. Decreased _____ flow, pelvic pain, and low back pain are early symptoms of both _____ cancer and prostatitis.
9. The _____ _____ exam and the PSA test are used to diagnose prostate cancer.
10. At this point in time there is considerable _____ regarding the optimal treatment of early-stage prostate cancer.

Crossword

Across

1. site for a vasectomy
3. removed in circumcision
6. cover of the testes
8. exercise which may improve sexual function
10. ejaculation is not the same as this experience
11. singular maker of sperm and hormones

Down

2. sperm continue to mature here
4. makes up only 1% of the ejaculate
5. second most common cancer in men
7. erection producing fluid
9. penis area with many nerve endings

Matching

Identify the parts of the male anatomy as marked below. Answers may be found at the end of the chapter.

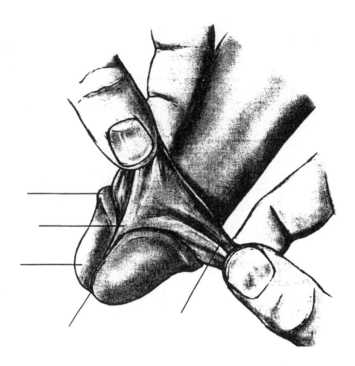

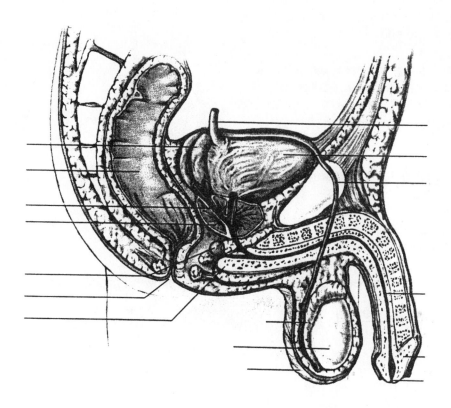

Practice Test

This test will work best to guide your learning if you take it as part of a final review session before an exam.

1. The interior of the penis contains
   a. the cavernous bodies and spongy body
   b. an extensive network of muscle tissue
   c. a cylinder-shaped piece of cartilage
   d. all of the above

2. The exterior of the penis includes the
   a. glans, shaft, and vas deferens
   b. crura, shaft, and glans
   c. foreskin, glans, and shaft
   d. corona, root, and ureter

3. The glans contains two areas that are quite responsive to stimulation. These are the
   a. corona and crura
   b. foreskin and frenulum
   c. meatus and ampulla
   d. corona and frenulum

4. Male genitals have been altered using all of the following procedures except
   a. castration
   b. infibulation
   c. superincision
   d. circumcision

5. Which of the following is not one of the benefits of doing Kegel exercises?
   a. increased pelvic sensation
   b. increased ejaculatory control
   c. more rapid erection
   d. stronger orgasm

6. Which of the following structures is not associated with the scrotum?
   a. testis
   b. spermatic cord
   c. seminal vesicles
   d. interstitial cells

7. The testicles may be drawn closer to the body when
   a. the scrotum is cooled
   b. straining during a bowel movement
   c. experiencing sudden fear
   d. all of the above

8. The two major functions of the testes are
   a. controlling ejaculation and producing seminal fluid
   b. producing male sex hormones and making sperm
   c. making sperm and initiating the erectile response
   d. manufacturing seminal fluid and urine

9. Sperm are produced in tightly coiled structures called the
   a. seminiferous tubules
   b. seminal vesicles
   c. vas deferencs
   d. epididymis

10. Most of a man's androgen is made in the
    a. adrenal glands
    b. interstitial cells
    c. Cowper's gland
    d. prostate gland

11. During a vasectomy a section of the _____ is removed, resulting in sterilization.
    a. vas deferens
    b. spongy body
    c. urethra
    d. spermatic cord

12. The majority of the seminal fluid is produced by the
    a. seminal vesicles
    b. seminiferous tubules
    c. prostate gland
    d. Leydig's cells

13. Which walnut-shaped structure at the base of the bladder may cause problems with urination when enlarged?
    a. ejaculatory ducts
    b. urethral bulb
    c. seminal vesicles
    d. prostate gland

14. The fluid from this gland is often confused with semen and may contain live sperm.
    a. ejaculatory gland
    b. Cowper's gland
    c. prostate gland
    d. ampulla gland

15. Sperm comprise ____ percent of total semen volume.
    a. 1%
    b. 10%
    c. 46%
    d. about 63%

16. Which of the following influences the amount of seminal fluid?
    a. type of sexual activity that leads to ejaculation
    b. exposure of the testicles to warmer temperatures
    c. length of time since the last ejaculation
    d. presence of bioflavinoids in the diet

17. In order for the penis to become erect, which of the following must occur?
    a. swelling of the penis bone
    b. stiffening of the spermatic cord
    c. blood must accumulate in the cylinders of the penis
    d. activation of the penis muscle fibers must exceed threshold

18. The first phase of ejaculation is _____ whereas the second is called
    a. intromission; expulsion
    b. expulsion; intromission
    c. expulsion; emission
    d. emission; expulsion

19. Research has shown that penis size appears to be related to
    a. age at puberty
    b. height
    c. set point weight
    d. none of the above

20. Which of the following is not an argument against routine circumcision?
    a. the procedure is traumatic for infants
    b. penile cancer rates are the same for circumcised and uncircumcised men
    c. sexual function may be altered by the removing the foreskin
    d. the foreskin may serve a function not known at this time

21. Proponents of circumcision cite all of the following as reasons to continue circumcision except
    a. female partners of uncircumcised men have increased risk of cervical cancer
    b. organisms living under the foreskin may cause vaginal infections in women who are partners of uncircumcised men
    c. few health risks are associated with circumcision
    d. uncircumcised men are at greater risk of contracting HIV

22. Luis has been experiencing pain in his penis when urinating and has an aching lower back. What type of health care provider would be best for him to see?
    a. internist
    b. proctologist
    c. endomologist
    d. urologist

23. Cleaning under the foreskin may remove _____, which may cause irritation, unpleasant odor, or infection.
    a. condyloma accuminata
    b. smegma
    c. sebaceous cysts
    d. urethral granuloma

24. Symptoms of prostatitis and prostate cancer include all of the following <u>except</u>
    a. lower back pain
    b. difficulty urinating
    c. pelvic pain
    d. a mass in the testicle

25. Men are hesitant to have rectal examinations because
    a. of discomfort about homosexual overtones if the doctor is male
    b. they fear of the examination's results
    c. they anticipate that treatment will impair sexual functioning
    d. all of the above

Answer Key – Chapter 5

<u>Concept Checks</u>

Sexual Anatomy

The Penis
1. glans
2. root
3. cavernous, spongy
4. foreskin
5. corona, frenulum
6. orgasms, ejaculatory
7. superincision, castration

The Scrotum and Testes
1. spermatic
2. closer
3. inguinal canal
4. cryptorchidism
5. testicular
6. asymmetrical
7. seminiferous tubules
8. death
9. interstitial cells
10. epididymis

The Vas Deferens, Seminal Vesicles, Prostate and Cowper's Glan, Semen
1. vas deferens
2. vasectomy
3. seminal vesicles
4. prostate gland
5. Cowper's gland
6. sperm
7. arousal, age
8. HIV

Male Sexual Functions
1. blood
2. birth
3. mind
4. nonsexual
5. emission
6. expulsion
7. muscular contractions
8. retrograde
9. nocturnal emission

Some Concerns About Sexual Functioning
1. size
2. masculinity
3. unimportant
4. more
5. height
6. foreskin
7. mixed
8. moderately opposed

Male Genital Health Concerns
1. urology
2. smegma
3. cancer
4. Testicular
5. enlarges
6. prostatitis
7. Prostate
8. urine
9. digital rectal
10. controversy

Crossword Puzzle

Across
1. vasdeferens
3. foreskin
6. scrotum
8. Kegel
10. orgasm
11. testis

Down
2. epididymis
4. sperm
5. prostate
7. blood
9. glans

Matching

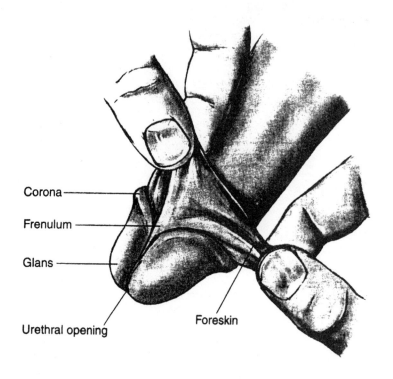

Corona

Frenulum

Glans

Urethral opening

Foreskin

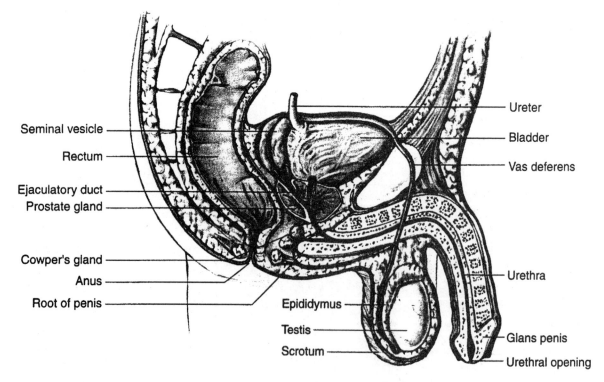

Seminal vesicle

Rectum

Ejaculatory duct

Prostate gland

Cowper's gland

Anus

Root of penis

Epididymus

Testis

Scrotum

Ureter

Bladder

Vas deferens

Urethra

Glans penis

Urethral opening

Practice Test

1. a   2. c   3. d   4. b   5. c   6. c   7. d   8. b   9. a   10. b   11. a   12. a   13. d
14. b   15. a   16. c   17. c   18. d   19. d   20. b   21. c   22. d   23. b   24. d   25. d

Chapter 6 – Sexual Arousal and Response

Introduction

Recognizing that human sexuality is influenced by both psychosocial and biological factors, the authors focus upon biological aspects of sexual arousal and response. The role of hormones, the brain, our sensory systems, foods and drugs in sexual arousal are analyzed. Human physiological sexual response is discussed, as are typical changes in response associated with aging. Key differences between the sexes are noted as the chapter concludes.

Learning Objectives. *In order to derive maximum benefit from these objectives, use these as soon as you begin reading the chapter. After you have completed reading and studying this chapter, you should be able to do the things listed below with ease, using only your memory.*

1. Explain the role of hormones in male sexual behavior, including the following: definition of androgens and their source; how testosterone affects male sexuality; definition of orchidectomy and what research has revealed regarding the effects of this procedure on sexual functioning; definition of antiandrogens and what research has demonstrated regarding the use of antiandrogens in the treatment of sex offenders; definition of hypogonadism and how research on this condition has contributed to our understanding of the relationship between androgens and sexual motivation

2. Explain the role of hormones in female sexual behavior, making specific reference to estrogens and testosterone, and citing relevant research studies.

3. Discuss the amount and type of testosterone that is necessary for hormonal sexual functions in men and women.

4. Discuss the signs of testosterone deficiency and issues involved in seeking testosterone replacement therapy.

5. Discuss the role of the brain in sexual arousal.

6. Describe the role of the following senses in sexual arousal: touch, vision, smell, taste and hearing.

7. Assess each of the following in regard to their aphrodisiac effects: various foods (oysters, eggplant, etc.), alcohol, amphetamines, barbiturates, cantharides, cocaine, psychedelic drugs, marijuana, amyl nitrate, L-dopa, yohimbine hydrochloride, Libido.

8. List at least seven substances that inhibit sexual behavior (anaphrodisiacs).

9. Describe the influence of pheromones on sexual response in humans and animals.

10. Describe Kaplan's three-stage model of sexual response.

11. List the four phases of Masters and Johnson's sexual response cycle and briefly describe the physiological changes that occur in each stage for women and men.

12. Discuss how female orgasmic response has been analyzed and explained over time, beginning with Freud's interpretation.

13. Define the Grafenberg spot and explain the controversy surrounding it.

14. Describe changes in the sexual response cycle of women as they age.

15. Describe changes in the sexual response cycle of men as they age.

16. Identify at least three significant differences in sexual response between men and women.

17. Discuss sexual arousal from a cross-cultural perspective, citing specific examples.

Concept Map

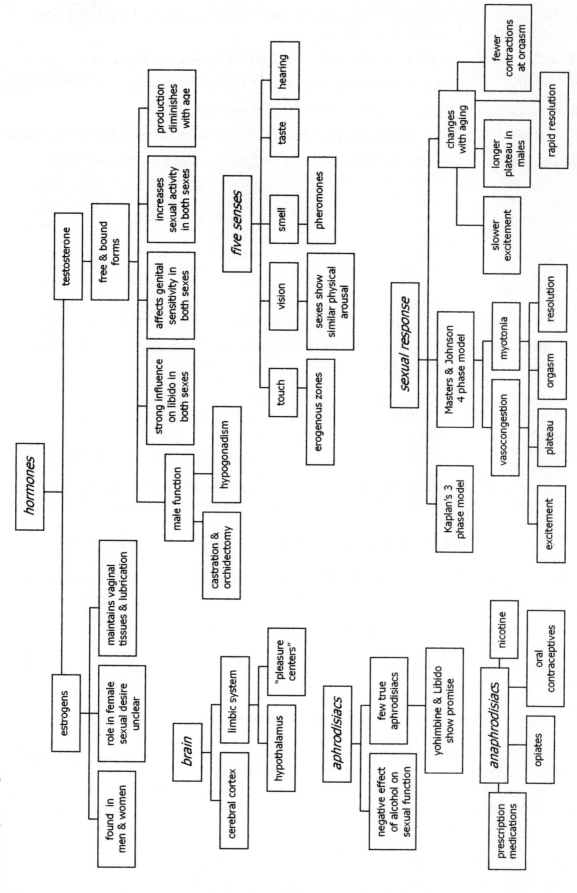

Key Terms. *Refer to the glossary or subject index in the back of your textbook for definitions and information.*

castration
orchidectomy
hypogondadism
bound testosterone
free testosterone
testosterone replacement therapy
cerebral cortex
limbic system
erogenous zones
primary erogenous zones
secondary erogenous zones
pheromones
aphrodisiac
anaphrodisiac

Kaplan's three stage model
Masters and Johnson's four phase model
vasocongestion
myotonia
excitement phase
sex flush
plateau phase
orgasmic platform
orgasm
Grafenberg spot
resolution
refractory period
multiple orgasms

Concept-Checks. *Complete this section by filling in each blank after you have studied the corresponding pages from the text. Answers are provided at the back of this chapter.*

The Role of Hormones in Sexual Arousal, pp. 142-146

1. Ninety-five percent of a man's androgens are produced by the _____, with the remainder being made by the _____ _____.

2. A woman's _____ and _____ _____ manufacture androgens in nearly equal amounts.

3. The testes produce estrogens but in _____ quantities than in a woman's body.

4. A man with low testosterone is physically capable of having an erection, yet he may have little sexual _____.

5. If a man's testicles have been surgically removed, in medical terms he has had a(n) _____.

6. Surgically castrated men frequently exhibit a _____ in sexual interest and activity.

7. Drugs such as Depo-Provera are classified as _____ and reduce the levels of testosterone present in the bloodstream.

8. If a man experiences testosterone deficiency due to disease of the endocrine system, he has the medical condition called _____.

9. Estrogens influence female sexual behavior by providing a general sense of well being, by maintaining the thickness and elasticity of the _____, and by contributing to vaginal _____.

10. Research findings on the role of estrogens in female sexual desire are _____ at this time.

11. Numerous research studies have shown that _____ influences sexual desire, genital sensitivity, and frequency of sexual activity among women.

12. Total testosterone is comprised of two forms, free and _____.

13. Women may make less testosterone than men, yet a woman's body cells are more _____ to testosterone.

14. _____ testosterone may be abnormally low in people with a low sex drive, even though total testosterone is within normal limits.

15. Males typically experience a _____ reduction in total testosterone as they age, whereas women are more likely to have a _____ reduction in total testosterone with aging.

16. Symptoms of testosterone deficiency include reduction in sexual desire, reduced _____ of the genitals, reduced sexual arousability, diminished energy levels and mood, increased _____ mass, decreased bone mineral density, _____ body hair, and decreased muscle _____ and strength.

17. Currently it is easier for _____ to receive medical advice about testosterone replacement therapy.

The Brain and Sexual Arousal, pp. 147-149

1. Events like sexual fantasy are produced by the _____ _____ of the brain.

2. The _____ system of the brain contains many structures that play an important role in sexual behavior.

3. According to several studies, when the _____ is surgically destroyed or stimulated, sexual behavior is altered.

4. _____ is a behavior that is nearly universal in Western cultures, yet rare in many other parts of the world.

5. Although oral sex is a common activity in the South Pacific, industrialized Asia, and much of the Western world, in southern _____ it is viewed as unnatural.

6. Unlike America, many societies do not consider bare _____ to be erotic.

The Senses and Sexual Arousal, pp. 149-154

1. Body areas that are especially responsive to tactile stimulation are called _____ _____.

2. The breasts, buttocks, and inner thighs are rich in nerve endings and are therefore termed _____ erogenous zones.

3. Selma has learned to enjoy the way her lover caresses her toes and fingers when they make love, so it seems that Selma has developed _____ erogenous zones.

4. Women viewing visual erotica have shown _____ responses to men when sexual arousal is measured physiologically.

5. If women's responses to visual erotica are measured using self reports, women are _____ inclined than men to report feeling aroused.

6. During their fertile periods females of many species produce invisible substances called _____ which can be detected by the sense of smell.

7. Current evidence indicates that humans _____ secrete pheromones, yet their role as a sexual attractant remains undetermined.

8. The sense of taste plays a _____ role in sexual arousal.

9. Regarding the role of hearing in sexual arousal, one study reported that men's silence during lovemaking _____ their female partner's sexual arousal.

Aphrodisiacs and Anaphrodisiacs in Sexual Arousal, pp. 154-158

1. Substances that purportedly increase sexual desire or increase capacity for sexual activities are called _____.

2. Although _____ is commonly considered a stimulant, it actually depresses the activity of the higher brain centers and the central nervous system.

3. Several studies have shown that with increasing levels of alcohol consumption people experience _____ sexual arousal, pleasurability, and orgasm intensity.
4. Research investigations have also demonstrated a _____ relationship between alcohol use and the tendency to engage in sexual practices that increase the risk of contracting serious disease.
5. *Yohimbine hydrochloride* may have true aphrodisiac properties as it generates intense sexual arousal and performance in _____ , yet results with _____ are still inconclusive.
6. A team of Norwegian investigators has shown that the commercial product _____ may be a true aphrodisiac for humans, yet other studies need to be done by research teams without a commercial interest in the product.
7. Substances that reduce sexual behavior or interest are called _____ .
8. Common anaphrodisiacs include birth control pills, blood pressure medicines, tranquilizers, psychiatric medications, opiates and _____ , the most widely used anaphrodisiac which constricts the blood vessels and reduces testosterone levels.

Sexual Response, pp. 158-168
1. Helen Singer Kaplan's model of sexual response include the stages of _____ , _____ , and orgasm.
2. Master's and Johnson's four stage model is composed of four stages: _____ , _____ , orgasm, and _____ .
3. When body tissues becoming engorged with blood, _____ has occurred.
4. Facial grimaces and spasms of the hands or feet are examples of _____ , which results from an increase in muscle tension.
5. The phases of the sexual response cycle follow the _____ basic pattern regardless of the method of stimulation.
6. A study of men's and women's subjective descriptions of orgasm found them to be _____ .
7. Freud believed that a _____ orgasm was more mature than a _____ orgasm, a belief later found to be physiologically incorrect.
8. Josephine and Irving Singer contend that emotional satisfaction must be considered when studying female orgasm, so they distinguish between a vulval and _____ orgasm.
9. The Grafenberg spot is located along the anterior wall of the _____ .
10. Women do not typically experience a _____ period during the resolution phase, therefore they can more readily experience multiple orgasms.
11. The length of the refractory period depends on _____ , frequency of previous sexual activity, and emotional closeness and desire for a man's partner.

Aging and the Sexual Response Cycle, pp. 169-171
1. As women age vaginal lubrication begins more _____ and the amount of vaginal lubrication is _____ .
2. A study comparing pre- and post-menopausal women found that these two groups reported _____ levels of sexual activity and enjoyment.
3. Since diminished estrogen levels change vaginal tissues, some women find that _____ becomes uncomfortable.
4. The number of uterine and orgasmic platform contractions during _____ decreases in older women.
5. In one study, the majority of older women reported that their frequency of _____ was the same as when they were younger.

6. The resolution phase occurs more _____ in older women.
7. The rate of erectile response typically _____ in older men, causing many men to fear they are impotent, even though this altered response pattern is normal.
8. Complete erection is usually not experienced until late in the _____ phase.
9. Older men typically exhibit better _____ control , resulting in a prolonged opportunity to enjoy sexual activity prior to ejaculation.
10. Many older men notice a _____ in the intensity of orgasm.
11. The refractory period often gradually _____ as men age.

Some Differences Between the Sexes in Sexual Response, pp. 171–173
1. Women tend to show greater _____ in their sexual response patterns than men.
2. Most women have the capacity for multiple orgasms, yet only a _____ portion experiences them.
3. Women who are _____ and women who have sex with other women are more likely to experience multiple orgasms.
4. The experiences of men who have multiple orgasms illustrates that lovemaking need not stop after _____.

Matching

Match each physiological change with the phase of the sexual response cycle in which it occurs. Please remember that an answer may be used more than once.

a. excitement
b. plateau
c. orgasm – female

d. emission phase of orgasm - male
e. expulsion phase of orgasm - male
f. resolution phase

_____ 1. uterus contracts

_____ 2. testes return to unstimulated size

_____ 3. labia minora increase in size

_____ 4. vaginal walls make lubrication

_____ 5. erection loss begins

_____ 6. Cowper's gland secretion may be noticed

_____ 7. labia majora move away from vaginal opening

_____ 8. orgasmic platform rhythmically contracts

_____ 9. testes completely elevate

_____ 10. scrotum keeps its thickened and tense state

_____ 11. partial to full erection occurs

_____ 12. clitoris withdraws under hood

_____ 13. areola increases in size

_____ 14. seminal vesicles and prostate contract

_____ 15. clitoris and labia return to unaroused state

_____ 16. orgasmic platform develops

_____ 17. testes begin to increase in size

_____ 18. refractory period occurs

_____ 19. rectal sphincter and penile urethra contract

_____ 20. breast size decreases

Crossword

<u>Across</u>
5. liquid promoter of high risk sexual behavior
7. this period is absent in women
8. nonpenile area of erection in both sexes
10. zone rich in nerve endings
11. hormonal arouser of ardor
12. rat aphrodisiac

<u>Down</u>
1. fantasy maker of the brain
2. smelly sexual attractant
3. erection inducer
4. smokeable reducer of sexual motivation
6. shortest phase of the sexual response cycle
9. longer response phase in older men associated with ejaculatory control

Practice Test

This test will work best to guide your learning if you take it as part of a final review session before an exam.

1. Estrogen is produced
   a. in both men and women
   b. only during a woman's reproductive years
   c. primarily by the adrenal glands in women
   d. primarily by the Cowper's gland in men

2. Which statement about testosterone and male sexual function is true?
   a. Sexual behavior completely stops after castration
   b. Antiandrogens stop sexual behaviors motivated by anger or the desire to control
   c. Sexual interest declines when testosterone levels decrease
   d. If sexual interest and activity decline due to hypogonadism, the decline is permanent

3. Current research demonstrates clearer and stronger evidence regarding the role of
   _____ in female sexuality.
   a. progesterone
   b. estrogen
   c. adrenaline
   d. testosterone

4. Women who receive testosterone replacement therapy show
   a. increased genital sensitivity
   b. inceased sexual desire
   c. more frequent sexual activity
   d. all of the above

5. Which form of testosterone plays the greatest role in libido?
   a. bound
   b. free
   c. total
   d. alpha-androstenal

6.   Testosterone deficiency is characterized by all of the following except
   a. reduced genital and breast sensitivity
   b. increased body hair
   c. lowered sexual desire
   d. diminished energy levels

7. Stimulation of the _____ has resulted in increased sexual activity in rats and
   feelings of sexual arousal in humans.
   a. hippocampus
   b. hypothalamus
   c. cerebral cortex
   d. histamine blocking system

8. When women view visual erotica, ratings of sexual arousal are likely to be higher when
   a. old style "porn" films are used
   b. arousal is measured using physiological recording devices
   c. arousal is measured by self reports
   d. films are made by female directors

9. Current research evidence seems to indicate that humans do secrete _____, yet it is still uncertain if they influence sexual behavior.
   a. pheromones
   b. olfactory hormones
   c. libidinial compounds
   d. vomeronasal enhancers

10. Which of the following seems to have true aphrodisiac qualities?
    a. alcohol
    b. Spanish fly
    c. rhinoceros horn
    d. yohimbine

11. Blood pressure medicines and psychiatric medications may
    a. increase vasocongestion
    b. promote a stronger orgasmic response
    c. impair erectile function
    d. elevate sexual desire

12. Nicotine affects sexual behavior by
    a. promoting feelings of relaxation through reduction of central nervous system activity
    b. slowing vasocongestion
    c. elevating testosterone levels
    d. increasing sexual desire

13. Which phase of sexual response is found only in Kaplan's model?
    a. excitement
    b. desire
    c. plateau
    d. refractory period

14. Which of the following is the best example of vasocongestion?
    a. orgasmic platform contractions
    b. spasms of the hands or feet
    c. facial grimaces
    d. vaginal lubrication

15. The correct order of Masters and Johnson's model is
    a. plateau, excitement, orgasm, resolution
    b. excitement, orgasm, plateau, resolution
    c. excitement, plateau, orgasm, resolution
    d. excitement, orgasm, resolution, plateau

16. A sex flush may appear during all of the following phases of the sexual response cycle except
    a. excitement
    b. orgasm
    c. resolution
    d. plateau

17. Which statement regarding the orgasmic platform is true?
    a. It forms in the upper two-thirds of the vagina
    b. It is present primarily in multi-orgasmic women
    c. It develops during the plateau phase
    d. It is a diving event that will debut in the 2004 Olympics

18. The rectal sphincter contracts
    a. primarily in homosexual men
    b. in both women and men during orgasm
    c. in men only during orgasm
    d. during orgasm only if anal intercourse has occurred

19. The testes become completely engorged and elevated during
    a. plateau
    b. orgasm
    c. excitement
    d. the expulsion phase of orgasm

20. Which statement about female orgasm is true?
    a. Vaginal orgasms are more mature than clitoral orgasms
    b. Clitoral orgasms are more mature than vaginal orgasms
    c. Uterine orgasm may result from clitoral stimulation
    d. There is only one kind of orgasm, physiologically speaking

21. Orgasms that result from stimulation of the Grafenberg spot
    a. may result in the ejaculation of fluid from the urethra
    b. are similar to vulval orgasms
    c. are similar to uterine orgasms
    d. are psychologically similar to blended orgasms

22. The period of time following orgasm when no additional stimulation will produce orgasm is called the
    a. refractory period
    b. resolutory period
    c. erectile inhibition interval
    d. remission period

23. Which statement regarding older women and sexual response is false?
    a. vaginal lubrication occurs more slowly
    b. sexual enjoyment declines
    c. vaginal mucosa becomes thinner
    d. resolution occurs more rapidly

24. Which of the following is true regarding older men and sexual response?
    a. resolution occurs more slowly
    b. orgasm becomes more intense
    c. ejaculatory control may improve
    d. erection occurs as rapidly as when younger

25. Which statement regarding multiple orgasms is true?
    a. The majority of women regularly experience multiple orgasms
    b. The majority of women are capable of having multiple orgasms
    c. Men cannot experience multiple orgasms
    d. Kinsey's subjects reported the highest rates of multiple orgasms

Answer Key – Chapter 6

Concept Checks

The Role of Hormones in Sexual Behavior
1. testes; adrenal glands
2. ovaries; adrenal glands
3. smaller
4. interest
5. orchidectomy
6. decrease
7. antiandrogens
8. hypogonadism
9. vagina; lubrication
10. unclear
11. testosterone
12. bound
13. sensitive
14. free
15. gradual; rapid
16. sensitivity; fat; decreased; mass
17. men

The Brain and Sexual Arousal
1. cerebral cortex
2. limbic
3. hypothalamus
4. kissing
5. Africa
6. breasts

The Senses and Sexual Arousal
1. erogenous zones
2. primary
3. secondary
4. similar
5. less
6. pheromones
7. do
8. minor
9. hindered

Aphrodisiacs and Anaphrodisiacs in Sexual Arousal
1. aphrodisiacs
2. alcohol
3. reduced
4. strong
5. rats; humans

5. rats; humans
6. Libido
7. anaphrodisiacs
8. nicotine

Sexual Response
1. desire, excitement
2. excitement, plateau, resolution
3. vasocongestion
4. myotonia
5. same
6. indistinguishable
7. vaginal; clitoral
8. uterine
9. vagina
10. refractory
11. age

Aging and the Sexual Response Cycle
1. slowly; reduced
2. similar
3. intercourse
4. orgasm
5. orgasm
6. rapidly
7. slows
8. plateau
9. ejaculatory
10. decrease
11. lengthens

Some Differences Between the Sexes in Sexual Response
1. variability
2. small
3. lesbians
4. ejaculation

Matching

1. c 2. f 3. a 4. a 5. f 6. b 7. a 8. c 9. b 10. b 11. a 12. b
13. b 14. d 15. f 16. b 17. a 18. f 19. e 20. f

Crossword Puzzle

Across
5. alcohol
7. refractory
8. nipples
10. erogenous
11. testosterone
12. yohimbine

Down
1. cerebralcortex
2. pheromones
3. vasocongestion
4. nicotine
6. orgasm
9. plateau

Practice Test

1. a 2. c 3. d 4. c 5. b 6. b 7. b 8. b 9. a 10. d 11. c 12. b
13. b 14. d 15. c 16. c 17. c 18. b 19. a 20. d 21. a 22. a 23. b
24. c 25. b

Introduction

Social scientists and sex researchers have begun to study love, a domain once considered off-limits to scientific inquiry. Various theoretical models of love are presented in the chapter, as well as research studies that examine the usefulness of these models. The complexity of falling in love is explored as the authors integrate current research findings with practical application of those findings to our lives. Suggestions for building healthy and loving sexual relationships, and maintaining those relationships over time are discussed.

Learning Objectives. *In order to derive maximum benefit from these objectives, use these as soon as you begin reading the chapter. After you have completed reading and studying this chapter, you should be able to do the things listed below with ease, using only your memory.*

1. Explain how Zick Rubin attempted to measure love, including a list and description of the three components of his love scale and what his findings revealed.

2. Describe the characteristics of passionate love.

3. Describe the characteristics of companionate love.

4. Explain Sternberg's triangular theory of love.

5. List and describe six styles of loving as proposed by John Lee.

6. Discuss the factors that affect with whom we fall in love, making specific reference to the following: the chemistry of love; proximity; similarity; reciprocity; physical attraction.

7. Discuss sociobiological accounts of gender differences in mate selection.

8. Describe the role self-love plays in the development of intimacy.

9. List and describe each of the following phases of a relationship as it develops and becomes more intimate: inclusion; response; care; trust; affection; playfulness; genitality.

10. Discuss what research findings reveal regarding how women and men, both heterosexual and homosexual, perceive the relationship between love and sex.

11. Discuss strategies for determining personal values and guidelines regarding sexual expression.

12. Define jealousy, and discuss the role it plays in love relationships and how to manage jealous feelings.

13. Summarize research findings regarding sex differences in jealousy.

14. Discuss some of the factors that contribute to maintaining relationship satisfaction over time.

15. Discuss differences in love and marriage in collectivist vs. individualistic cultures.

16. From a cross-cultural perspective, discuss men's and women's preferences in mate selection.

17. Describe research findings that clarify whether romantic love is a universal experience.

Concept Map

falling in love

- proximity
  - reciprocity
- amphetamine-like neurotransmitters
  - similarity
- physical attractiveness
  - important only in early stages
  - more valued by men

types of love

- passionate
- companionate

Sternberg's Triangular Theory
- 8 varieties of love
  - passion
  - intimacy
  - commitment

Lee's Styles
- romantic
- altruistic
- game playing
- pragmatic
- possessive
- companionate

developing intimacy

- self love is foundation
- phases of relationship growth
  - inclusion
  - trust
  - response
  - affection
  - care
  - playfulness
  - genitality

issues in loving relationships

- relationship between love & sex
  - gender differences exist
  - gays & lesbians like heterosexuals
- sex & relationships on your terms
  - know what you want
    - explore friendships without sex
  - say "not yet" to sexual relationship
    - social expectations of instant sex oppose research findings
  - ending relationships compassionately
    - communicate with clarity
  - managing rejection
    - unrequited love is common experience
    - self-worth not dependent on other's approval

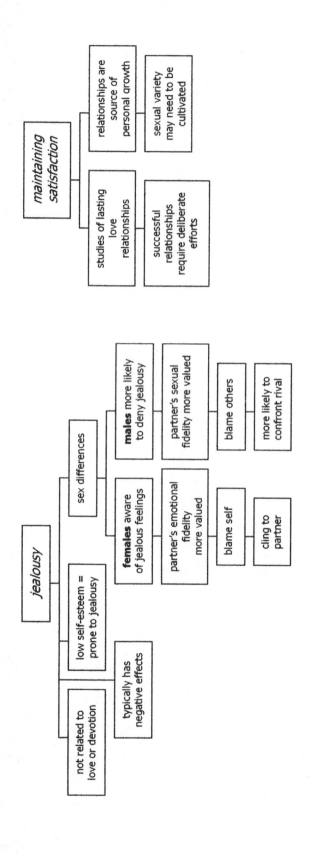

jealousy

- not related to love or devotion
- low self-esteem = prone to jealousy
  - typically has negative effects
- sex differences
  - **females** aware of jealous feelings
    - partner's emotional fidelity more valued
      - blame self
      - cling to partner
  - **males** more likely to deny jealousy
    - partner's sexual fidelity more valued
      - blame others
      - more likely to confront rival

maintaining satisfaction

- studies of lasting love relationships
  - successful relationships require deliberate efforts
- relationships are source of personal growth
  - sexual variety may need to be cultivated

Key Terms   *Refer to the glossary or subject index in the back of your textbook for definitions and information.*

attachment
caring
intimacy
passionate love
companionate love
passion
intimacy
commitment
collectivist culture
individualistic culture
friendship
infatuation
empty love
fatuous love
romantic love
consummate love
game-playing love
possessive love
altruistic love

pragmatic love
neurotransmitters
phenylethylamine
proximity
mere exposure effect
similarity
reciprocity
physical attractiveness
self-love
inclusion
response
care
trust
affection
playfulness
genitality
unrequited love
jealousy

Concept-Checks.   *Complete this section by filling in each blank after you have studied the corresponding pages from the text. Answers are provided at the back of this chapter.*

What is Love; Types of Love pp. 178-185
1. Zick Rubin's questionnaire measured three aspects of love: _____, caring, and
_____.
2. According to Rubin's scale, _____ lovers spent more time staring into each other's eyes than _____ lovers.
3. A state of extreme absorption and desire for another accompanied by feelings of sexual desire, elation and anxiety describes _____ love.
4. The duration of passionate love is typically _____.
5. Research by anthropologists Jankowiak and Fisher has shown that _____ love was present in the majority of societies studied.
6. Friendly affections and deep attachment stemming from familiarity with a loved one describe _____ love.
7. Robert Sternberg proposed that love has three aspects: passion, _____ and
_____.
8. In Sternberg's framework, infatuation is the presence of passion without _____ or commitment.
9. When all three of Sternberg's components are present, _____ love is experienced.
10. A study comparing individualistic and collectivist cultures demonstrated that students in _____ cultures would be less likely to marry someone they did not love.
11. Someone who prefers that love relationships be causal and transitory has a _____ love style, according to sociologist John Lee.

12. _____ love reflects Lee's style of love where there is a desire to give to another without expectation of reciprocity.

13. Sam fell in love with Brad because Sam believes that his life partner should be chosen in a businesslike manner, so it seems that Sam is influenced by Lee's _____ style of loving.

14. Research with the Hendricks' Love Attitude Scale has shown that _____ and _____ loving styles are positively associated with relationship satisfaction for all life ages.

Falling in Love: Why and With Whom? pp. 185-190

1. The elation and euphoria of love is has its chemical basis in neurotransmitters such as norepinephrine, _____ , and phenylethylamine (PEA) which are all similar to amphetamine drugs.

2. The inability of the brain to produce enough _____ to meet demand has been proposed as one explanation for the fading of love's "high".

3. The mere exposure effect helps us to understand why we are attracted to people who live in close _____.

4. The National Health and Social Life Survey found that people were most likely to meet sex partners in locations reflecting _____ interests.

5. Other National Health and Social Life Survey results have shown that people form intimate relationships with people of _____ race and ethnicity.

6. The principle of _____ accounts for the fact that people tend to respond in kind when we convey liking and affection.

7. Research by Langlois has revealed that _____ demonstrated a preference for beauty even before learning cultural standards of attractiveness.

8. Cross cultural studies have shown that heterosexual males placed greater importance on _____ and _____ _____ when choosing a mate.

9. According to research by Buss, females preferred mates who were _____, had good financial prospects, and were _____ and industrious.

10. Physical attractiveness becomes _____ important as a relationship progresses.

The Development of Intimacy, pp. 190-192

1. Healthy and satisfying intimate relationships are built upon a foundation of _____, a sense of respect, caring, and concern for ourselves.

2. The authors propose a scheme for understanding the phases of relationship growth that begins with _____, when we meet another.

3. The phase of _____ determines if the relationship continues, and _____ ensues if we express a heartfelt concern for the other's welfare.

4. In order for relationship growth to continue _____ must be developed, followed by _____, or the expression of feelings of warmth and attachment.

5. The relationship has entered the phase of _____ when partners exhibit delight, pleasure, and expansive laughter.

6. The final phase of relationship development is _____, where the partners expand the relationship to include genital sex.

Issues in Loving Relationships, p.162-201

1. Studies have indicated that _____ find it easier to have sex without love than _____.

2. Two recent surveys suggest a _____ in men's and women's attitudes toward love and sex.

3. An essential ingredient in establishing a homosexual identity seems to be _____ someone of the same sex, rather than merely having sex with a same sex partner.

4. In addition to knowing what you want in life and sexual relationships, the authors suggest that you ask yourself if engaging in a sexual relationship will _____ positive feelings about yourself and your partner.

5. Saying "not yet" to a sexual relationship is supported by findings from the National Health and Social Life Survey, as people who had sex within a month of meeting were more likely to have _____ relationships.

6. The authors' experience with their students has shown that a majority of people prefer to be told in a _____ manner that the other does not desire to continue a relationship.

7. When someone does not reciprocate our feelings of love and attraction, _____ love may be experienced.

8. The authors remind us that being rejected usually is an expression of individual preference, not a _____ of us or our worth.

9. Feelings of jealousy are often rooted in fears of being _____ by one's partner, instead of arising from devotion.

10. Studies have shown that women are more envious of _____ and popularity, whereas men show the most envy toward _____ and fame.

11. People who have frequent feelings of insecurity and _____ are more likely to feel jealousy in relationships, according to several recent studies.

12. Research has also revealed that jealousy may trigger _____ in marriages and intimate relationships.

13. Cross cultural research shows that _____ are more likely to feel jealous over the emotional involvement of their partner with another, whereas _____ are more inclined to feel jealous about the sexual relationship their partner has with another.

Maintaining Relationship Satisfaction, pp. 201-204

1. A study of successful marriages found that they shared several qualities: having shared interests; both spouses having parents with _____ marriages; satisfaction with sexual _____; steady and adequate _____; and the couple was not pregnant when the marriage began.

2. Another study of 300 couples revealed that the most frequently cited reason for a happy marriage was viewing one's partner as a best _____.

3. Fewer than 10 percent of happily married couples indicated that good _____ relations helped keep their marriages intact.

Crossword

Across

     1. Erikson and the authors' prerequisite for a satisfying relationship
     3. high proximity place where many NHSLS participants met their mates
     5. triangular theory love component that peaks early in a relationship
     7. relationship growth phase that distinguishes sexual from nonsexual relationships
     10. Lee's loving type positively associated with relationship satisfaction over time
     11. over 90% of college students have had multiple episodes of this love type

Down

     2. jealousy frequently triggers this in marriage
     3. partner in successful marriages have this attitude and personality type
     4. potential mate quality favored by men worldwide
     6. whirlwind type of love shared by lovers who meet on vacation in exotic locale
     8. target of male envy
     9. acronym for a "love" neurotransmitter

Practice Test

This test will work best to guide your learning if you take it as part of a final review session before an exam.

1. Which of the following is <u>not</u> an aspect of love measured by Zick Rubin's love scale?
   a. caring
   b. attachment
   c. concern
   d. intimacy

2. What quality did Rubin observe among "weak" lovers or those less deeply in love?
   a. more episodes of conflict
   b. less eye contact
   c. increased personal space
   d. poorer communication skills

3. Generalized physiological arousal and strong sexual desire are components of
   a. compassionate love
   b. companionate love
   c. paraphiliac love
   d. passionate love

4. According to Sternberg's triangular theory of love, _____ declines in a relationship whereas _____ builds gradually over time.
   a. passion; intimacy
   b. infatuation; philia
   c. passion; philia
   d. fatuous love; companionate love

5. Faye and Suzanne share a strong commitment to each other that they expressed in a holy union ceremony over 12 years ago. The passion in their relationship has slowly decreased over the years, nonetheless they still feel a deep emotional connection to each other. In Sternberg's framework this couple shows
   a. empty love
   b. consummate love
   c. romantic love
   d. companionate love

6. Ever since Thach met his new girlfriend at school, he feels that his life is like a roller coaster. He can't stop thinking about Anh and feels intensely jealous whenever he sees her talking to any other men. According to Lee, Thach's style of loving is
   a. romantic love
   b. altruistic love
   c. possessive love
   d. game playing love

7. Now that Erika is dating again, she is determined to find the very best looking man around, and she fantasizes about how she will enjoy sensual exploration of this handsome man's body after she finally meets him. Erika's behavior reflects Lee's _____ style of loving.
   a. possessive
   b. game-playing
   c. romantic
   d. pragmatic

8. The popular saying "love is a drug" has received some support through research, as studies have shown that when were are in love, the body makes _____ that are chemically similar to amphetamine drugs.
   a. neurotransmitters
   b. estrogens
   c. enzymes
   d. androgens

9. When our attraction to someone grows because we see them regularly and they become familiar it is called the
   a. social distance effect
   b. similarity effect
   c. familiarity gradient
   d. mere exposure effect

10. Which statement below best reflects the findings from two recent studies that examined partner choice and race?
   a. White Americans preferred white partners more than African Americans preferred African American partners
   b. Hispanic Americans preferred White partners more than any other group
   c. Asian Americans were the most likely to find partners outside their ethnic group
   d. People generally prefer to form partnerships with people of similar race and ethnicity

11. Several studies have demonstrated that _____ placed greater emphasis on a partner's physical attractiveness and _____ placed greater importance on a mate's financial status.
   a. men; women
   b. women; men
   c. men; men
   d. women; women

12. Returning someone's gaze with a smile and greeting is an example of the _____ phase of a relationship.
   a. inclusion
   b. response
   c. affection
   d. care

13. Which of the following is <u>not</u> consistent with the authors' conceptualization of self-love?
    a. respect
    b. interest
    c. conceit
    d. concern

14. Which of the following describes the final phase of relationship growth?
    a. feelings of exhilaration and abandon
    b. feelings of warmth and attachment
    c. holding the belief that a partner will act consistently
    d. expressing feelings through genital sex

15. Research has revealed that _____ find it easier than _____ to have sex without an emotional commitment.
    a. lesbians; gay men
    b. bisexuals; lesbians
    c. men; women
    d. women; men

16. A study of lesbians showed a preference to postpone sexual involvement with a partner until
    a. emotional intimacy is present
    b. they have know each other at least one month
    c. both have received STD screenings
    d. they have agreed to cohabitate

17. Findings from over 1800 married persons in the National Health and Social Life Survey demonstrated that _____ knew their spouse less than one month before having sex.
    a. 76%
    b. 51%
    c. 23%
    d. 10%

18. Citing their experience with their classes, the authors suggest which strategy to end a relationship?
    a. relay the information through a third party, in order to avoid hurting the other more
    b. write a letter and honestly share your feelings
    c. tell the other clearly and unmistakably that you don't wish to be involved
    d. avoid the other by failing to return phone calls

19. Several writers believe that jealousy is closely related to all of the following <u>except</u>
    a. feelings of love
    b. injured pride
    c. fear of abandonment
    d. fear of losing control

20. Men whose jealousy is aroused are more likely to
    a. deny their feelings
    b. confront a third party rival
    c. retaliate by seeking extrarelationship involvement
    d. all of the above are true

21. Jealous women are more inclined to
    a. be more concerned about a partner's sexual fidelity than emotional involvement
    b. blame themselves
    c. suppress attempts to provoke jealousy in their partner
    d. ignore their feelings

22. People who are more prone to feel jealous have
    a. parents who had distressed marriages
    b. higher distrust of others
    c. low self esteem
    d. feelings of guilt

23. When researchers reviewed studies on marital satisfaction they found that successful marriages had which of the following qualities?
    a. The parents of the partners had happy marriages
    b. The woman was not pregnant when they married
    c. Partners had similar interests and personalities
    d. all of the above are true

24. A study of over 300 happily married couples revealed that
    a. Fewer than 10% thought that good sexual relations kept their relationships together
    b. Most dated extensively prior to marriage
    c. Seeing one's partner as a best friend was not considered important by a majority
    d. Marriage encounter weekends gave their relationships added zest when needed

25. Which of the following best exemplifies a strategy suggested by the authors for adding sexual variety to a relationship?
    a. purchase sex toys at a boutique
    b. provoke a little jealousy in your partner
    c. make love in places other than the bed
    d. concern yourself with what is considered normal to keep a quest for variety healthful

Answer Key – Chapter 7

<u>Concept Checks</u>

What is Love; Types of Love
1. intimacy, attachment
2. strong, weak
3. passionate
4. brief
5. romantic
6. companionate
7. intimacy, commitment
8. intimacy
9. consummate
10. individualistic
11. game-playing
12. Altruistic
13. pragmatic
14. eros, agape

Falling in Love: Why and With Whom?
1. dopamine
2. neurotransmitters
3. proximity
4. similar
5. similar
6. reciprocity
7. infants
8. youth; physical attractiveness
9. older, ambitious
10. less

The Development of Intimacy
1. self-love
2. inclusion
3. response, care
4. trust, affection
5. playfulness
6. genitality

Issues in Loving Relationships
1. men, women
2. convergence
3. loving
4. enhance
5. brief
6. clear

7. unrequited
8. rejection
9. abandoned
10. attractiveness, wealth
11. inadequacy
12. violence
13. women, men

Maintaining Relationship Satisfaction
1. happy (or successful), sharing, income
2. friend
3. sexual

Crossword Puzzle

Across
 1. selflove
 3. school
 5. passion
 7. genitality
10. agape
11. unrequited

Down
2. violence
3. similar
4. youth
6. fatuous
8. wealth
9. PEA

Practice Test

1. c   2. b   3. d   4. a   5. d   6. c   7. c   8. a   9. d   10. d   11. a   12. b   13. c
14. d   15. c   16. a   17. d   18. c   19. a   20.d   21. b   22. c   23. d   24. a   25. c

Chapter 8 – Communication in Sexual Relationships

Introduction

Developing greater comfort with talking about emotionally involving issues, our bodies, and our personal needs is a significant step you can take toward building a healthy and satisfying sexual relationships. To help you begin this process, the chapter initially discusses some reasons why many of us experience difficulty communicating about sexual matters. Strategies that will enable you to start a conversation about sex are outlined and skills that make for good listening are discussed.   Effective methods for learning more about our partner's needs and ways to make requests are described and modeled, as are techniques for giving and receiving criticism in a constructive manner. The chapter concludes with a presentation of strategies to decline an offer to become sexually intimate, and the roles of nonverbal communication and impasses are discussed.

Learning Objectives. *In order to derive maximum benefit from these objectives, use these as soon as you begin reading the chapter. After you have completed reading and studying this chapter, you should be able to do the things listed below with ease, using only your memory.*

1.   Define mutual empathy and explain how it relates to effective sexual communication.

2.   Discuss how each of the following may hinder effective sexual communication:
     a. socialization
     b. language
     c. gender-based communication styles
     d. sexual anxiety

3.   Discuss three strategies that may be helpful to begin talking about sex.

4.   Identify and describe at least six characteristics of effective listening and feedback.

5.   List and expand upon four different strategies that could be used to discover what is pleasurable to your partner.

6.   Describe three aspects of communication to consider in learning to make sexual requests.

7.   Discuss seven aspects of communication to consider in order to give criticism effectively.

8.   Describe five strategies to consider in order to receive criticism effectively.

9.   Outline a three-step approach that can be used to effectively turn down offers for sexual involvement.

10. Discuss the effects of sending mixed messages and explain how to   respond if receiving them.

11. Articulate four aspects of nonverbal communication that play an important part in the process of communication.

12. Enumerate and discuss several strategies for dealing with an impasse that may occur in sexual communication.

13. Discuss ethnic differences in intimate communication among white Americans, African Americans, Hispanic Americans and Asian Americans.

14. Discuss normal male alexithymia and treatment strategies to address this issue.

Concept Map

mutual empathy

sexual communication is difficult
- socialization
- lack of vocabulary
- few positive role models
- ethnic differences in communication
- anxiety
- gender differences in communication

constructive criticism

giving:
- awareness of motivation
- avoid "why" questions
- right time & place
- express negative feelings appropriately
- temper criticism with praise
- limit complaints to 1 per session
- small steps toward change

receiving:
- empathize & paraphrase
- acknowledge & agree
- ask clarifying questions
- express feelings
- focus upon concrete future change

talking: getting started
- talking about talking
- reading & discussing
- sharing sexual histories

listening & feedback
- active vs. passive listening
- eye contact
- feedback in words
- support partner's efforts
- unconditional positive regard
- paraphrasing

nonverbal communication
- facial expression
- interpersonal distance
- touch
- sounds

discovering partner's needs

ask questions:
- yes/no format
- open-ended
- either/or format

- self-disclosure
- comparing notes
- giving permission

saying "no"
- avoid mixed messages

3 steps:
- express appreciation or validate
- say "no" unequivocally
- offer an alternative

making requests
- taking responsibility for your pleasure
- making specific requests
- "I" language

impasses
- validating
- take a break & resume

Key Terms . *Refer to the glossary or subject index in the back of your textbook for definitions and information.*

mutual empathy
active listening
passive listening
feedback
unconditional positive regard
paraphrasing
yes-or-no questions
open-ended questions

either/or questions
self-disclosure
normative male alexithymia
giving permission
"I" language
personal space
validating

Concept-Checks. *Complete this section by filling in each blank after you have studied the corresponding pages from the text. Answers are provided at the back of this chapter.*

The Importance of Communication, pp. 207-211
1. Effective sexual communication begins with _____ _____, the underlying belief that each partner cares for the other and that care is reciprocated.
2. Sexual communication may be difficult because of our _____ or the way were raised as children.
3. Few of us have been exposed to positive _____of persons discussing sex in a meaningful, open, and accepting fashion.
4. Lack of a suitable _____ of sex further compounds the difficulties we have communicating about sex.
5. African Americans and _____ Americans are more likely than _____ Americans and _____ Americans to believe that good communication is essential within sexually intimate relationships.
6. Conflict is more likely to be openly acknowledged and dealt with and among _____ Americans.
7. _____ Americans are especially likely to avoid direct confrontations and conflict due to the high value placed on harmony and the collective good.
8. Deborah Tannen's analysis of communication styles suggests that _____ use language in order to challenge others and remain "one-up" whereas _____ tend to use language as a way to promote closeness and intimacy.
9. Many persons experience anxiety when communicating about sex because talking about sex often involves taking _____.

Talking: Getting Started, p. 211
1. Since people often feel uncomfortable initiating a conversation about sex, the authors suggest using the strategy of _____, sharing why it may be difficult to talk about sex.
2. Other ways to begin talking about sex include _____ and discussing books or articles about sex; and sharing _____ _____.

Listening and Feedback, p. 212-213
1. _____ listeners do not make much eye contact and as a result we often think this type of listener does not care about us or our concerns.

2.. In contrast _____ listeners show their interest by nodding, using sympathetic facial expressions, asking relevant questions and comments.

3. Since a message's impact may not be the same as its intent, providing _____ helps prevent misunderstandings.

4. Telling our partner "Thanks for letting me know how you feel" helps support our partner's communication _____ and has the added benefits of encouraging mutual _____, and open, honest talk in the future.

5. When we let our partner know we will care for them no matter what they say or do, we are expressing _____ _____ _____.

6. Restating a speaker's message using our own words demonstrates the use of _____, and also offers an opportunity to clarify any misunderstandings that have developed.

Discovering Your Partner's Needs, pp. 213-218

1. "Yes-or-no" questions are a less effective because they give _____ opportunity to talk about an issue.

2. When we ask _____ questions we may learn much more about our partner because they have the freedom to share what they perceive to be important.

3. If our goal is to learn about a partner's preference among a few alternatives, _____ questions are often effective.

4. Sharing our thoughts and feelings about a topic involves the technique of _____-_____ , and may help "break the ice" for highly emotional or difficult topics.

5. A Canadian study of dating couples showed that self-disclosure enhanced _____ satisfaction.

6. The inability to put emotions into words is defined as _____, and is believed to be widespread among men due to gender socialization.

7. Mutual feedback results from _____ _____ after a shared activity and can also be used to discover our partner's feelings and reactions after sex.

8. Saying "I like it when you tell me how you want to be kissed. Please tell me more" is a form of _____ _____ and demonstrates that it is okay to keep talking.

Learning to Make Requests, pp. 218-220

1. The statement "If you love me, you'll know what I want" shows an unwillingness to take _____ for our own pleasure.

2. We are more likely to have a communication understood and to get what we ask when requests are _____.

3. When we use "_____" language we are recognizing our self-worth rather than being self-centered.

Giving and Receiving Criticism, pp. 220-226

1. Before beginning a conversation where we would like to express a complaint, it is important to be aware of our _____ .

2. If our motivation stems from a desire to hurt, humiliate, or blame, expressing a criticism will more likely be _____ than constructive.

3. In order for mutual empathy and effective communication to occur, it is important to choose the right _____ and place to give criticism.

4. The negative impact of criticism can be reduced when we temper criticism with _____.

5. Telling our partner "I really appreciate that you're trying to be less quiet when we make love. It means a lot to me" demonstrates that we are nurturing _____ steps toward change, since people rarely change ingrained habits overnight.

6. "Why" questions backfire and have destructive consequences because such questions often convey hidden _____ and represent attempts to avoid assuming _____ for our feelings and desires.

7. . Anger and other negative emotions may be expressed appropriately by using "_____" statements rather than "you" statements. which attempt to fix blame or defame someone's character.

8. One final strategy for delivering criticism involves limiting criticism to _____ complaint per discussion.

9. Receiving a criticism begins with _____ your partner's criticism, which conveys that you are trying to understand and empathize with your partner.

10. A second step is to _____ the criticism and find something, however small, that you feel you can agree with.

11. Asking _____ questions and _____ your feelings by talking about them, rather than blindly acting upon them continues the process of receiving criticism.

12. Focusing on _____ changes that you are willing to make provides appropriate closure to receiving criticism.

Saying No, pp. 226-228
1. A three step approach to saying, "No" involves expressing _____ for the invitation; saying no in a _____ and unmistakable manner; and offering an _____ if appropriate.

2. Saying "I don't want to get undressed" and then allowing a partner to unbutton our shirt is an example of a _____ message which often reflects underlying ambivalence about the matter at hand.

Nonverbal Sexual Communication, pp. 228-230
1. Aspects of nonverbal communication include facial expression, interpersonal _____, _____, and sounds.

2. _____ interpersonal distance typically indicates that someone likes another person and desires more intimate contact.

3. The absence of _____ during lovemaking may hinder a partner's sexual arousal.

Impasses, pp. 230
1. When we recognize the reasonableness of another persons' viewpoint – even though we may not agree -- we are engaged in the process of _____.

2. When impasse is reached, it may be a good idea for partners to take a _____ from each other and schedule another time to talk.

3. If an impasse cannot be resolved and the relationship suffers, a couple has the option of seeking professional _____.

Matching

Pair the phrase or statement below with the communication strategy it best exemplifies. Please be reminded that a letter may be used more than once.

a. talking about talking
b. mutual empathy
c. unconditional positive regard
d. paraphrasing
e. yes-or-no question
f. open-ended question

g. either/or question
h. self-disclosure
i. giving permission
j. "I" language
k. making a specific request
l. tempering criticism with praise

_____ 1. "I like it when you make sounds when we make love. Please make as much noise as you like! It's fine with me".

_____ 2. "Do you like it when I'm on top of you?"

_____ 3. " It seems like it was hard for you to tell me that. I want you to know I love you very much and will always stand by you"

_____ 4. "I love it when you kiss and nibble my ears, yet I don't feel as good when your tongue goes inside my ear"

_____ 5. "I feel rather nervous bringing this up, but I'd like to talk to you about birth control".

_____ 6. "Tell me how to stroke your penis".

_____ 7. "So, are you saying that you feel unloved when I don't kiss you goodbye in the morning?

_____ 8. "I feel lonely and used when you fall asleep so soon after we make love".

_____ 9. " Would you like to take a shower together or cuddle some more?"

_____ 10. "It is important to me that you know how I feel about my ex-partner's affair"

_____ 11. "I like it when you press my clitoris gently and make small circles. Please do that again."

_____ 12. "It's feels great to hear how much you care about me. I want you to know I feel the same way, too".

Crossword

Across
1. effective communication demands this listening type
5. unconditional _____ regard shows unwavering caring for a partner
7. mixing a complaint with this quality promotes constructive criticism
8. sending this message type may make a "no" seem like a "yes"
9. widespread form of male alexithymia
10. giving _____ may help a partner freely express their needs
12. creating your summarized version of a speaker's words

Down
2. mutual _____ forms the foundation for successful communication
3. comparing these nonmusical reactions provides feedback
4. icebreaker that involves some personal exposure
6. "Your viewpoint is reasonable, yet I don't agree"
11. blaming question type that creates defensiveness

Practice Test

This test will work best to guide your learning if you take it as part of a final review session before an exam.

1. Which statement below best reflects the concept of mutual empathy?
   a. Getting in touch with your partner's feelings
   b. Expressing your feelings no matter what they are
   c. Caring for another and knowing that such care is reciprocated
   d. Telling your partner you care about them no matter what they do or say

2. Obstacles to effective communication about sex include
   a. anxiety
   b. lack of a suitable language for sex
   c. ethnic group differences in intimate communication
   d. all of the above are true

3. Of the following strategies listed below, which is most effective in dealing with gender-based differences in communication?
   a. Males should suggest solutions to their female partner's problems
   b. Women should let men push them around, since it is natural for men to do so
   c. Males should refrain from seeking advice or looking vulnerable
   d. Women should tell their male partners that they need someone to just listen

4. _____ American couples and _____ American couples are least likely to discuss sex and relationship issues with a partner.
   a. African ; Asian
   b. Hispanic; Asian
   c. African; Hispanic
   d. Asian; white

5. Nhat tells his partner that he is afraid to discuss their sexual relationship out of fear of embarrassing or hurting his partner. Nhat is using the communication strategy of
   a. talking about talking
   b. mutual empathy
   c. sharing sexual histories
   d. paraphrasing

6. Providing attentive body language, sympathetic facial expressions, nodding, and asking questions are ways to demonstrate
   a. unconditional positive regard
   b. active listening
   c. comparing notes
   d. validating

7. Which of the following was <u>not</u> suggested as a method of providing feedback to a partner?
   a. paraphrasing
   b. self-disclosure
   c. unconditional positive regard
   d. supporting a partner's communication efforts

8. "What are some of the places where you'd like to make love?" is an example of a(n) _____ question.
   a. yes-or-no
   b. open-ended
   c. either/or
   d. mixed

9. Which question type provides the least opportunity to discuss an issue?
   a. either/or
   b. clarifying
   c. open-ended
   d. yes-or-no

10. Research has shown that when one partner begins self-disclosure the other partner
    a. is likely to reciprocate
    b. will respond in kind only if the topic of fantasies is being discussed
    c. should avert eye contract in order to establish positive regard
    d. may experience a reduction in relationship satisfaction

11. Normative male alexithymia may result in
    a. difficulty communicating intimate feelings
    b. channeling of vulnerable feelings into aggression
    c. sexual sharing being the only place where love is expressed
    d. all of the above may occur

12. Which statement best reflects taking responsibility for your own pleasure?
    a. "If you loved me, you'd know what I want".
    b. "If our relationship is healthy, we won't need to talk about sex".
    c. "It's not your fault if I don't climax. Sometimes it's difficult for me to relax".
    d. "It is my job to satisfy you".

13. Saying "I would like it if you stayed inside me longer" is more likely to be understood and heeded than "I wish we could do something different" because
    a. "I" language is being used
    b. a specific request has been made
    c. permission has been given
    d. a vague request communicates our desires more effectively

14. Expressing criticism is likely to be constructive when the motivation behind the criticism is
    a. to assert one's needs as primary in the relationship
    b. giving a partner a taste of their own medicine, so that empathy can be established
    c. getting even with your partner so that equilibrium may be restored
    d. a genuine desire to make a relationship better

15. Which of the following is out of place here among suggestions for giving criticism?
    a. withholding praise until criticism is received
    b. nurturing small steps toward change
    c. expressing negative emotions appropriately
    d. choosing the right time and place

16. "Why" questions should be avoided because
    a. they are vague
    b. it is important that a partner assume their fair share of the blame
    c. they promote defensiveness and rarely bring about positive change
    d. they represent simple, straightforward requests for information

17. Which of the following statements represents the best way to express negative emotions?
    a. "You never seem to want to touch me anymore."
    b. "You don't seem interested in sex any more".
    c. "I feel afraid for us when we go so long without sex".
    d. "You don't care about us and our problems".

18. Receiving a criticism in a way that can strengthen the relationship begins with
    a. Defending your position
    b. Empathizing with your partner's concern
    c. Immediately venting your feelings of frustration
    d. Withdrawing so that your and your partner can calm down and resume discussion later

19. The process of receiving criticism continues by
    a. finding something to agree with
    b. asking clarifying questions
    c. focusing on future changes that can be made
    d. all of the above are true

20. The three-step approach for "saying no" consists of all of the following except
    a. expressing appreciation for the invitation
    b. saying no in a clear, unmistakable manner
    c. encouraging the person to engage in self-disclosure
    d. offering an alternative

21. Which of the following best illustrates a mixed message?
    a. "I don't want to date you, I want a nonsexual friendship instead".
    b. "I'd like to make love, but I'd prefer to do so in the morning when I'm rested".
    c. Your partner says "Let's crawl in bed and make love after I check my e-mail" and then they spend so much time on line that you have fallen asleep on the sofa.
    d. "I don't want to hop into the shower. How about a dip in the jacuzzi?.

22.   Facial expression, personal space, touch and sounds refer to the _____ aspects of sexual communication.
    a. gendered
    b. nonverbal
    c. semiotic
    d. psychological

23. Impasses in communication may be bridged by
    a. validating
    b. continuing to talk until all concerns have been aired
    c. maintaining the reasonableness of your position until your partner yields
    d. letting negative emotions rise to the surface

Answer Key – Chapter 8

Concept Checks

The Importance of Communication
1. mutual empathy
2. socialization
3. models
4. language
5. white
6. white
7. Asian
8. men; women
9. risks

Talking: Getting Started
1. talking about talking
2. reading; sexual histories

Listening and Feedback
1. passive
2. active
3. feedback
4. efforts; mutual
5. unconditional positive regard
6. paraphrasing

Discovering Your Partner's Needs
1. little
2. open-ended
3. either/or
4. self-disclosure
5. sexual
6. alexithymia
7. comparing notes
8. giving permission

Learning to Make Requests
1. responsibility
2. specific
3. "I"

Giving and Receiving Criticism
1. motivation
2. destructive
3. time
4. praise
5. small

6. emotions; responsibility
7. "I"
8. one
9. paraphrasing
10. acknowledge
11. clarifying; expressing
12. future

Saying No
1. appreciation; clear; alternative
2. mixed

Nonverbal Sexual Communication
1. distance; touch
2. decreasing
3. sounds

Impasses
1. validation
2. break
3. counseling

Matching

1. i 2. e 3. c 4. l 5. a 6. f 7. d 8. j 9. g 10. h 11. k 12. b

Crossword Puzzle

Across
1. active
5. positive
7. praise
8. mixed
9. normative
10. permission
12. paraphrasing

Down
2. empathy
3. notes
4. selfdisclosure
6. validating

Practice Test

1. c 2. d 3. d 4. b 5. a 6. b 7. b 8. b 9. d 10. a 11. d 12. c 13. a
14. d 15. a 16. c 17. c 18. b 19. d 20. c 21. c 22. b 23. a

Chapter 9 – Sexual Behaviors

Introduction

The great range of ways our sexuality is expressed is profiled in this chapter. The practices of celibacy, fantasy, masturbation, kissing, touching, oral-genital sex, anal stimulation, and coitus are examined through the lenses of gender, sexual orientation, ethnicity, educational attainment, religious and economic background. The authors bring to bear their clinical experience, sexuality research, and anecdotes from their files to enrich our exploration of the diversity of sexual behavior.

Learning Objectives. *In order to derive maximum benefit from these objectives, use these as soon as you begin reading the chapter. After you have completed reading and studying this chapter, you should be able to do the things listed below with ease, using only your memory.*

1. Define the two types of celibacy and discuss some of the reasons a person might become celibate.

2. Discuss erotic dreams and fantasy, making specific reference to the following:
   a. how common they are in men and women
   b. what nocturnal orgasm is, and when and in whom it occurs
   c. what research has demonstrated on the content of erotic fantasy
   d. functions that fantasies serve
   e. similarities and differences in the fantasy lives of men and women
   f. research that supports both the positive and negative aspects of sexual fantasy

3. Define masturbation, and discuss the following in regard to it:
   a. traditional and contemporary views of masturbation
   b. reasons why people masturbate
   c. research regarding ethnic differences in frequency of masturbation
   d. characteristics of people who tend to masturbate more than others
   e. various self-pleasuring techniques

4. Explain the significance of the Maltz hierarchy of sexual interactions and briefly describe the six levels of sexual interaction according to this model.

5. Explain some of the benefits of kissing and touching, and discuss areas of the body that are especially sensitive to stimulation.

6. Define cunnilingus and fellatio, discuss the origin of negative attitudes toward these sexual behaviors, and cite research concerning frequency of oral sex in recent years.

7. Describe some of the considerations in practicing anal stimulation and cite research concerning frequency of this sexual practice.

8. Describe variations in gay and lesbian sexual expression.

9. Define intromission and discuss considerations in using various coital positions.

10. Summarize how different racial, educational and religious backgrounds may affect a person's experience with oral sex.

11. Describe the history and process of Tantric sex.

12. Identify and discuss Mosher's sexual styles.

Concept Map

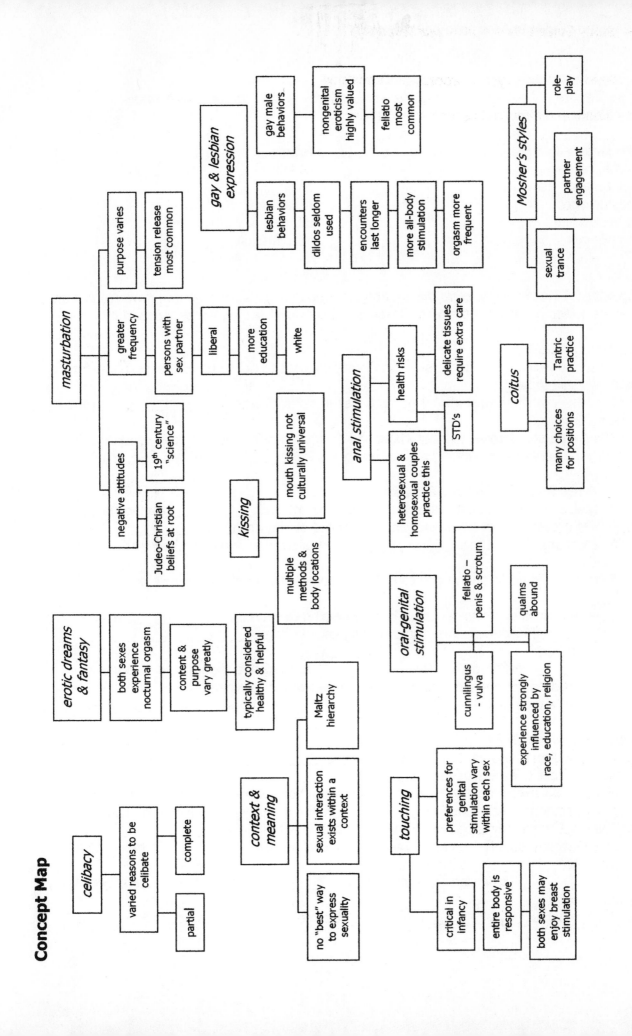

Key Terms . *Refer to the glossary or subject index in the back of your textbook for definitions and information.*

complete celibacy

partial celibacy

nocturnal orgasm

masturbation

autoeroticism

cunnilingus

fellatio

sodomy

anilingus

tribadism

interfemoral intercourse

intromission

Concept-Checks. *Complete this section by filling in each blank after you have studied the corresponding pages from the text. Answers are provided at the back of this chapter.*

Celibacy, pp. 234-235

1. When a physically mature person consciously chooses to not to engage in sexual behavior, a person is said to be _____.

2. If a person neither masturbates nor engages in sex with a partner, _____ celibacy is being practiced.

3. When a person chooses to masturbate and decides to refrain from sexual contact with a partner, the person is expressing their sexuality via _____ celibacy.

Erotic Dreams and Fantasy, pp. 235-239

1. Both women and men may experience erotic dreams and _____ during sleep.

2. A "wet dream" results from ejaculation produced during nocturnal _____.

3. A recent study found that _____ percent of women and men experience sexual fantasies.

4. Fantasies that occur during intercourse most commonly serve the purpose of _____ _____.

5. Other functions of sexual fantasies include helping to overcome _____, allowing for the expression of hidden desires, and providing escape from _____ _____ expectations.

6. _____ are more likely than _____ to fantasize about being forced to have sex, yet this does not imply that they would like this fantasy to come true.

7. Fantasies are typically thought to be a _____ part of our sexuality.

Masturbation, p. 239-244

1. Autoeroticism is another term used to describe _____, the stimulation of one's genitals in order to experience sexual pleasure.

2. Many of our negative views surrounding masturbation stem from Jewish and Christian religious traditions which hold that _____ is the primary purpose of sexual activity.

3. The most commonly cited reason for masturbating is to relieve _____ _____.

4. People who frequently engage in partnered sexual activity or who live with their sexual partner also _____ more often.

5. _____ Americans and those with _____ education levels are more likely to masturbate.

6. Few women use _____ insertion to obtain orgasm during masturbation.

Sexual Expression: The Importance of Context and Meaning, pp. 244-247

1. Since our sexuality is influenced by the quality of our intimate relationships as a whole, one writer believes that _____ is the way that partners have treated each other since their last sexual encounter.

2. The Maltz hierarchy consists of _____ positive levels of sexual interaction and _____ levels of increasingly destructive and abusive interactions.

Kissing and Touching, pp. 247-249

1. Many non-Western cultures such as Japan, China, the Chewa, and the Tonga have historically considered _____ in a negative light.

2. A classic study by Harlow and Harlow showed that when baby monkeys were deprived of their mother's touch they became _____ .

3. Many women report needing _____ and _____ rhythm and pressure of touch before and during orgasm.

4. Lubricants such as K-Y jelly, lotions without perfume or alcohol, or saliva can be used to lubricate the vulva in order to prevent _____ and provide greater pleasure.

5. Lubrication with lotion or _____ increases pleasure from manual stimulation for some men.

Oral-Genital Stimulation, pp. 249-251

1. Oral stimulation of the vulva is called _____ whereas oral stimulation of the penis and scrotum is referred to as _____.

2. Kinsey's studies found that _____ were less likely to orally stimulate their partners.

3. Uneasiness about oral sex is reflected in laws against _____, a poorly defined legal category of sexual behaviors other than coitus.

4. People may also disapprove of oral-genital stimulation because of the widespread, but scientifically unsupported, belief that this is a _____ act.

5. Since oral-genital sex may involve the exchange of bodily fluids, there is some risk of transmitting or contracting the _____ virus.

6. The National Health and Social Life Survey has demonstrated that the experience of oral sex is influenced by racial group, _____, religion, and socioeconomic _____.

Anal Stimulation, p. 252

1. About _____ percent of heterosexual couples regularly practice penile penetration of the anus.

2. The anus has a rich concentration of _____ endings that are capable of erotic response.

3. Gay and straight men, as well as women, can experience _____ from stimulation during anal penetration.

4. Anal intercourse carries greater risk of disease transmission for the _____ partner.

5. Other sex couples should never have vaginal intercourse following anal penetration because bacteria that are normally present in the anus can cause _____ _____.

6. "Rimming" or _____ is a sexual practice that carries a very high risk of transmitting hepatitis and other sexually transmitted diseases, even when safer sex measures are used.

Gay and Lesbian Sexual Expression, pp. 252-255

1. Kinsey's study found that lesbian women had a higher percentage of _____ than did heterosexual married women.

2. Hunt's 1974 study contradicts the widely held belief that _____ are used among lesbians.

3. Contrary to the popular saying "lesbian bed death", new research has revealed that sexual interactions among lesbians were associated with greater sexual _____ than heterosexual women..

4. _____ is the most common form of sexual expression among gay men.

5. Another study found that _____ percent of gay men liked hugging, kissing, snuggling and other similar interactions.

Coitus and Coital Positions, pp. 255-257

1. Positions such as woman above, sitting upright allow the _____ to receive manual stimulation.

2. The _____ position is an option during pregnancy, when pressure on the abdomen may be uncomfortable.

3. During _____ or entry of the penis into the vagina, mutual assistance may be desirable.

4. An important aspect of _____ sex consists of helping the male to learn to delay and control his orgasm so that sexual expression may become a vehicle for spiritual growth.

Crossword

<u>Across</u>
2. artificial penis moniker
3. sexual expression choice that excludes sexual contact
6. favorite form of gay male sexual expression
9. masturbation alias
10. one form of lesbian sex play

<u>Down</u>
1. Kellogg's masturbation stopper
3. penis-in-vagina intercourse synonym
4. site of cunnilingus
5. orgasm type that triggers a "wet dream"
7. legal term for "unnatural acts"
8. the Siriono abstain from this

Practice Test

This test will work best to guide your learning if you take it as part of a final review session before an exam.

1. Since he joined Alcoholics Anonymous last month, Frank has decided to refrain from having sexual contact, although he continues to masturbate. Frank appears to have chosen
   a. asceticism
   b. autoerotic exclusivity
   c. partial celibacy
   d. complete celibacy

2. Reasons for choosing celibacy include all of the following <u>except</u>
   a. Wanting to establish new relationships without the complications of sexual interaction
   b. Having the desire to avoid forming new relationships, so celibacy is used as an excuse
   c. The person is new to recovery from drug or alcohol dependency
   d. Waiting until one's standards for a sexual relationship have been met

3. The most common fantasy reported by men and women during masturbation is
   a. being forced to have sex
   b. sexual activities that could not be done in real life
   c. sex with more than one person
   d. intercourse with a loved one

4. Fantasies that occur during intercourse are <u>least</u> likely to serve the purpose of
   a. relieving boredom
   b. facilitating sexual arousal
   c. increasing a partner's attractiveness
   d. imaging forbidden activities

5. Which of the following statements about sexual fantasies among women and men is <u>true</u>?
   a. Men have fantasies during sexual activity with a partner more frequently than women
   b. Women are more likely to use romance in their sexual fantasies
   c. Women are more likely to have fantasies involving dominance
   d. Men are less likely to have fantasies involving multiple partners

6. Among college students, the most threatening fantasy a partner could have was about
   a. sex with a member of the same sex
   b. sex with a famous person or movie star
   c. sex with a mutual friend or classmate
   d. oral sex

7. Which of the following persons did <u>not</u> espouse negative views about masturbation?
   a. Dodson
   b. Tissot
   c. Graham
   d. Kellogg

8. Rates of masturbation are lowest among
    a. white women
    b. college educated, Asian men
    c. Hispanic women
    d. African American women

9. Which statement is <u>true</u> regarding masturbation among married and partnered persons?
    a. Masturbation is a sign that there is something wrong in the relationship
    b. Masturbation rates decrease sharply during the first year of togetherness
    c. Masturbation occurs more often among those who have partnered sex more frequently
    d. Masturbation occurs more often among couples who have partnered sex less frequently

10. Dave and Sam feel they can best express the profound love they feel for each other when they are sexually intimate, and they enjoy a sense of deep connection and spiritual ecstasy when they are together sexually. According to the Maltz Hierarchy, this couple is at
    a. Level +1, Positive Role Fulfillment
    b. Level +2, Making Love
    c. Level +3, Authentic Sexual Intimacy
    d. Level -1, Impersonal Interaction

11. _____ is to penis as _____ is to vulva.
    a. penilingus; cunnilingus
    b. fellatio; vulvalingus
    c. penilingus; vulvalingus;
    d. fellatio; cunnilingus

12. People feel ill-at-ease with oral-genital stimulation for all of the following reasons <u>except</u>
    a. Oral sex is considered a homosexual activity
    b. The "69" position has a higher risk of HIV transmission
    c. Genitals are thought to be dirty
    d. Sodomy is illegal in many states

13. Who is <u>most</u> likely to participate in oral-genital sex?
    a. a college educated African American woman
    b. a high school educated African American woman
    c. an Hispanic woman without a high school diploma
    d. an Asian-American homemaker without a high school diploma

14. Which statement is <u>true</u> regarding anal stimulation?
    a. 25% of adults have experienced anal intercourse at least once
    b. nearly ¾ of gay men consider this their most preferred sexual activity
    c. women cannot reach orgasm from anal intercourse
    d. 5% of heterosexual couples practice anal intercourse regularly

15. All of the following are characteristic of lesbian sexual expression <u>except</u>
    a. lesbian sexual relations last longer than those of heterosexual women
    b. lesbians are more likely to experience orgasm
    c. the use of dildos is common in lesbian sexual encounters
    d. nongenital sexual interaction is more common among lesbians than heterosexual women

16. Research shows that the most common form of sexual expression among gay men is
    a. interfemoral intercourse
    b. anal intercourse
    c. mutual masturbation
    d. fellatio

17. Which of the following coital positions would be most comfortable for a pregnant woman who wants to avoid pressure on her abdomen?
    a. woman on top, woman lying down
    b. rear-entry
    c. man above, face to face
    d. face to face, side lying

18. Mosher's styles of sexual expression include
    a. sexual trance, partner engagement, and role play
    b. sexual hypnosis, partner engagement, authentic enhancement
    c. sexual trance, romantic engagement, mutual role play
    d. sexual hypnosis, partner engagement, and role play

Answer Key – Chapter 9

<u>Concept Checks</u>

Celibacy
1. celibate
2. complete
3. partial

Erotic Dreams and Fantasy
1. fantasies
2. orgasm
3. 95
4. facilitating arousal
5. anxiety; gender role
6. women; men
7. healthy (or helpful)

Masturbation
1. masturbation
2. reproduction
3. sexual tension
4. masturbate
5. white; higher
6. vaginal

Sexual Expression: The Importance of Context and Meaning
1. foreplay
2. three; three

Kissing and Touching
1. kissing
2. maladjusted
3. steady; consistent
4. irritation
5. saliva

Oral-Genital Stimulation
1. cunnilingus; fellatio
2. women
3. sodomy
4. homosexual
5. HIV
6. education; status

Anal Stimulation
1. 10
2. nerve

3. orgasm
4. receptive
5. vaginal infections
6. anilingus

Gay and Lesbian Sexual Expression

1. orgasm
2. dildos
3. satisfaction
4. fellatio
5. 85

Coitus and Coital Positions

1. clitoris
2. rear-entry
3. intromission
4. Tantric

Crossword Puzzle

Across
 2. dildo
 3. celibacy
 6. fellatio
 9. autoeroticism
10. tribadism

Down
 1. cornflakes
 3. coitus
 4. vulva
 5. nocturnal
 7. sodomy
 8. kissing

Practice Test

1. c 2. b 3. d 4. a 5. b 6. c 7. a 8. c 9. c 10. c 11. d 12. b
13. a 14. a 15. c 16. d 17. b 18. a

Chapter 10 – Sexual Orientations

Introduction

The chapter begins with a discussion of the complexity of the concept of sexual orienation. Biological and psychosocial origins of sexual orientation are examined. Societal attitudes toward homosexuality are explored in both historical and contemporary frameworks. The diversity of lifestyles lived by gay men and lesbians are discussed, as is the process of coming out. Key events in the Gay Rights Movement are chronicled as the chapter comes to a close.

Learning Objectives. *In order to derive maximum benefit from these objectives, use these as soon as you begin reading the chapter. After you have completed reading and studying this chapter, you should be able to do the things listed below with ease, using only your memory.*

1. Define the following terms: homosexual, gay, lesbian, sexual orientation, and bisexual.

2. Describe Kinsey's continuum of sexual orientation and discuss how his estimates of the incidence of homosexuality in the general population compare to the findings in the National Health and Social Life Survey.

3. Discuss bisexuality and the problems in defining it, and compare it to other sexual orientations.

4. Briefly outline and describe how attitudes toward homosexuality have evolved over time, beginning with Judeo-Christian tradition in the seventh century B.C.

5. List and describe four current positions toward homosexuality represented in contemporary Christianity.

6. Discuss some cross-cultural perspectives on homosexuality, citing specific examples.

7. Define homophobia, discuss various ways in which it may be expressed, and explain how homophobic attitudes can change.

8. Define what a hate crime is, how hate crimes affect homosexuals, and legislative attempts to control hate crimes.

9. Making reference to relevant research, discuss the psychosocial and biological theories regarding how sexual orientation develops.

10. Discuss what research has revealed regarding the following:
    a. homosexual relationships
    b. homosexual family life

11. Define "coming out" and describe steps that may be involved in that process.

12. Discuss some of the significant events in the gay rights movement, beginning with the 1950s and continuing to the present time.

13. Discuss the goals of the gay rights movement.

14. Making reference to specific films and television programs, discuss how the portrayal of homosexuality has changed over the last decade.

15. Citing specific Native American, Hispanic, African-American and Asian-American examples, discuss the impact of being an individual who is both gay and a member of an ethnic minority group.

16. Discuss the effectiveness of various conversion therapies.

Concept Map

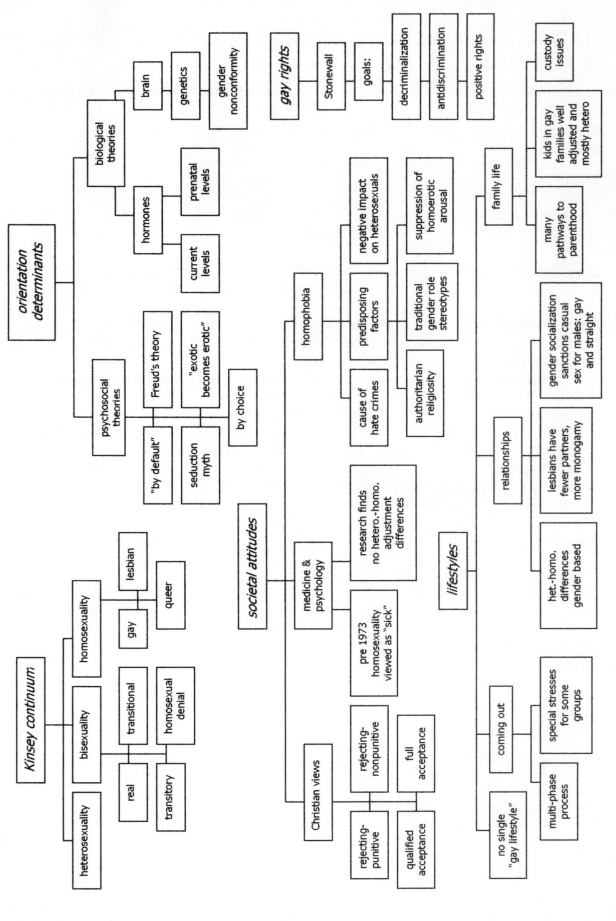

Kinsey continuum
- heterosexuality
- bisexuality
  - real
  - transitional
    - transitory
    - homosexual denial
- homosexuality
  - gay
  - lesbian
  - queer

orientation determinants
- psychosocial theories
  - Freud's theory
    - "by default"
    - seduction myth
  - "exotic becomes erotic"
  - by choice
- biological theories
  - hormones
    - current levels
    - prenatal levels
  - brain
  - genetics
  - gender nonconformity

gay rights
- Stonewall
- goals:
  - decriminalization
  - antidiscrimination
  - positive rights

societal attitudes
- medicine & psychology
  - pre 1973 homosexuality viewed as "sick"
  - research finds no hetero.-homo. adjustment differences
- Christian views
  - rejecting-punitive
  - rejecting-nonpunitive
  - qualified acceptance
  - full acceptance
- homophobia
  - cause of hate crimes
  - predisposing factors
    - authoritarian religiosity
    - traditional gender role stereotypes
  - negative impact on heterosexuals
    - suppression of homoerotic arousal

lifestyles
- coming out
  - no single "gay lifestyle"
  - multi-phase process
  - special stresses for some groups
- relationships
  - het.-homo. differences gender based
  - lesbians have fewer partners, more monogamy
  - gender socialization sanctions casual sex for males; gay and straight
- family life
  - many pathways to parenthood
  - kids in gay families well adjusted and mostly hetero
  - custody issues

Key Terms. *Refer to the glossary or subject index in the back of your textbook for definitions and information.*

homosexual	gender nonconformity
gay	gay affirmative therapy
lesbian	conversion therapy
queer	homophobia
sexual orientation	heterosexism
bisexuality	coming out
familial	passing
concordant	outing

Concept-Checks. *Complete this section by filling in each blank after you have studied the corresponding pages from the text. Answers are provided at the back of this chapter.*

A Continuum of Sexual Orientations, pp. 261-264
1. The authors remind us that sexual orientation is only _____ aspect of a person's life, not a label that describes all of a person's identity.
2. A person whose primary erotic, psychological, emotional and social orientation is to members of the same sex may refer to themselves as _____.
3. Nonheterosexual people born after 1970 sometimes call themselves _____, in part, to blur boundaries between subgroups of gay, lesbian, bisexual, and transgendered persons.
4. Attraction to both same and other-sex partners may be referred to as _____.
5. Kinsey used a _____ point continuum in his study of American sexual behaviors.
6. Estimates of the numbers of people with particular sexual orientations _____ depending on how the question is asked.
7. Types of bisexuality include bisexuality as a real orientation, as a _____ orientation, as a transitional orientation.

What Determines Sexual Orientation? 264-269
1. Explaining homosexual orientation as a sort of "consolation prize" for those who have had unsatisfactory heterosexual experiences reflects the _____ theory of sexual orientation.
2. Although studies show that many lesbians have had sex with _____, lesbians simply prefer to express their sexuality with other women.
3. Contrary to the seduction myth, research has shown that most homosexuals have their _____ sexual experiences with a same age peer.
4. Current research shows that sexual orientation most often develops _____ school age.
5. Research studies have found little support for the Freudian notion that unhealthy patterns in _____ life affect sexual orientation.
6. The idea that "the exotic becomes erotic" was proposed by _____.
7. Some studies have also suggested that _____ plays a role in determining sexual orientation, with this factor being a stronger influence on women than men.
8. Studies have shown that _____ hormones, rather than _____ levels of hormones may contribute to sexual orientation.

9. Another study has demonstrated that homosexuality is related to _____, a preference that develops prior to birth.

10. Genetic factors have been implicated as a determinant of sexual orientation because _____ twins show more similarity of orientation than _____ twins.

11. _____ _____ refers to the unwillingness to follow stereotypic masculine or feminine behaviors.

12. Homosexual adults in the United States and abroad are _____ likely to have experienced gender nonconformity in childhood.

13. At this point in time, research points to a _____ predisposition toward exclusive homosexuality.

14. The authors believe it is appropriate to think of sexual orientation as being influenced by an _____ of various psychological and biological factors, rather than thinking in terms of a single cause of orientation.

Societal Attitudes, pp. 269-277

1. The _____ orientation in contemporary Christianity views homosexuality as a sin.

2. The saying " condemn the sin, but love the sinner" reflects the _____ view of homosexuality.

3. Religious denominations that espouse a _____ _____ view include the Unitarian Universalist Association, the United Church of Christ, and Reconstructionist Jews.

4. The _____ of New Guinea require that adolescent males engage in same-sex sexual behavior until they marry.

5. Ford & Beach's 1951 study found that _____ of the 190 societies surveyed considered homosexuality acceptable under certain circumstances.

6. Prior to 1990, the Immigration and Naturalization Service considered _____ a reason to prohibit someone from entering the United States.

7. Same-sex couples may marry and adopt children with full legal support in the _____.

8. _____ _____ therapy views society's negative attitudes toward homosexuality as problematic, and therefore this therapy aims to homosexual clients cope with this negativity.

9. Some mental health professionals believe that sexual orientation can be changed, so they provide _____ therapy to their clients.

10. _____ may consist of irrational fears of homosexuality, fear that one may be homosexual, or self-hatred because one is homosexual.

11. The belief that only other-sex couples can be legally married is one example of _____, a variation of homophobia.

12. According to one study, _____ percent of lesbians and _____ percent of gay men have been victims of hate crimes.

13. Research studies have revealed that homophobia and hate crimes are related holding _____ gender role stereotypes and suppressing _____ feelings in oneself.

14. It appears that _____ adults are significantly more accepting of gay rights , as are students who take courses in _____ _____.

Lifestyles, pp. 277-286

1. Acknowledging, accepting, and openly expressing one's sexual orientation is commonly referred to as _____ _____.

2. The fact that some homosexual persons may have previously been married to other sex partners in order to avoid confronting their orientation shows that _____ is the initial step in coming out.

3. _____ is a difficult part of coming out because internalized homophobia must be surmounted.

4. Coming out is especially stressful for _____, who face harassment at school and experience often judgmental families.

5. The coming out stage of disclosure involves a decision about _____, or presenting a false image of being heterosexual.

6. When someone's sexual orientation is made known when they would otherwise keep this information to themselves, _____ has occurred.

7. Gay and lesbian people of color face "double jeopardy" because they must deal with prejudice toward _____ in their ethnic community and _____ from gay communities.

8. One noteworthy exception to the negative attitudes toward homosexuality held by many ethnic groups is found among _____ _____, whose families typically do not reject their homosexual members.

9. Anne Peplau's 1981 study revealed that _____ couples were more likely to follow traditional gender role expectations than _____ couples.

10. Peplau's study also found that most differences between couples had more to do with whether the partners were _____ or _____ than if they were homosexual or heterosexual.

11. Like heterosexual women, lesbians have had _____ sex partners than do straight or gay men.

12. Research studies have shown that most children of gay or lesbian parents develop a _____ orientation.

13. Lesbians become parents through a variety of means, such as being a biological mother from a prior heterosexual relationship, by _____ _____, and by adoption.

14. A homosexual father who is trying to get custody of children during divorce proceedings has the double disadvantage of being _____ and _____.

The Gay Rights Movement, pp. 286-289

1. The 1969 _____ _____ , a riot which ensued after police raided a gay bar, was pivotal in establishing the gay rights movement in the United States.

2. Goals of the gay rights movement include _____, antidiscrimination, and _____ rights.

3. Central to the goal of decriminalization is eradicating _____ laws.

4. In a survey of the general U.S. population, _____ percent said there was a lot of discrimination against homosexuals, whereas a separate survey found that _____ percent of gay Americans felt so.

5. A key issue in the pursuit of positive rights is the issue of legal gay _____.

Crossword

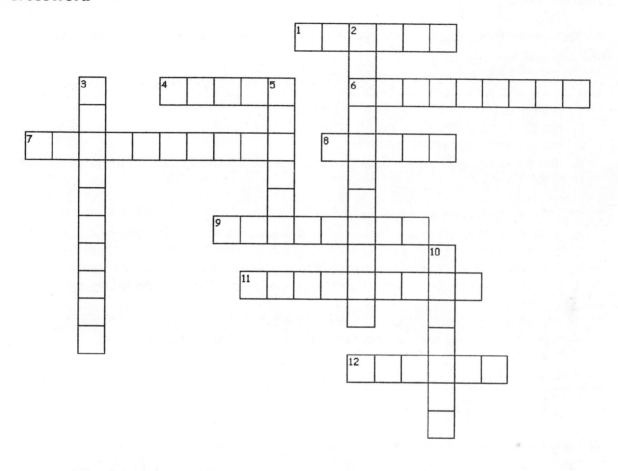

Across
1. teenage homosexual activity is required in this society
4. gay affirming organization for families and friends
6. gay rights movement catalyst
7. controversial therapy to change homosexual orientation
8. moniker preferred by some post-1970 born nonheterosexuals
9. fetal brain changing substance
11. twin type with higher concordance for homosexuality
12. disclosing someone's homosexual orientation without their consent

Down
2. threats to this male quality are a cause of hate crime
3. prebirth manual preference correlated with homosexuality
5. bending this in childhood is related to homosexual orientation
10. a closeted homosexual is forced to do this

Practice Test

This test will work best to guide your learning if you take it as part of a final review session before an exam.

1. A person with a homosexual orientation
   a. prefers to dress in the clothes of the other sex
   b. has the gender identity of the other sex
   c. has sex with a person of the same sex
   d. has a primary erotic, psychological, emotional, and social orientation toward members of the same sex

2. The Kinsey continuum is best described as
   a. a 10 point scale where 1 = exclusively heterosexual and 10 = exclusively homosexual
   b. a 7 point scale where 0 = exclusively heterosexual and 6 = exclusively homosexual
   c. a 6 point scale where 1 = exclusively homosexual and 6 = exclusively heterosexual
   d. a 6 point scale where 1= exclusively heterosexual and 6 = exclusively homosexual

3. The National Health and Social Life survey found that _____ percent of male and _____ percent of female respondents had sex with a same sex partner after age 18.
   a. 5; 4
   b. 6; 5.5
   c. 2.8; 1.4
   d. 2; 1

4. Sergio is a happily married, 36 year old father of three. When he visits his hometown in Mexico, Sergio occasionally has sex with men he meets at a gay bar, and in these encounters, Sergio is the insertive partner. Sergio's sexual orientation is most likely
   a. transitional biseuxal
   b. transitory bisexual
   c. homosexual
   d. homosexual denial

5. Megan's first teenage crush was on another woman, and she has fantasized about other women and men as long as she can remember. Megan's first kiss was with a woman, and her first sexual encounter was with a male. Megan is currently dating a woman after the breakup of a two year relationship with a man. Megan's sexual orientation most likely is
   a. lesbian
   b. transitory bisexuality
   c. homosexual denial
   d. bisexuality as a real orienation

6. What can be concluded from research examining Freud's theory of sexual orientation?
   a. gay men tended to come from families with a domineering mother and absent father
   b. lesbians were more likely than heterosexual women to have identified with their father
   c. no particular family life pattern is associated with developing a heterosexual or homosexual orientation
   d. penis envy is typically found among lesbians with poor father-daughter relationships

7. Research that compares hormone levels between heterosexuals and homosexuals has found that
   a. adult homosexual males have different levels of circulating estrogen than adult heterosexual males
   b. adult lesbians have more circulating testosterone than adult heterosexual women
   c. prenatal hormones have little influence on fetal brain development
   d. lesbians' finger length patterns are more like heterosexual males due to prenatal androgens

8. Which of the following statements about the psychosocial orignins of sexual orientation is true?
   a. gay men dated less frequently than heterosexuals during high school
   b. most homosexuals have their first sexual experience with a homosexual that is considerably older
   c. a majority of lesbians have had sexual experiences with men
   d. most gay and lesbian persons' childhood playmates were of the other sex

9. If a homosexual orientation has a genetic basis then
   a. identical twins should show a higher concordance rate than fraternal twins
   b. fraternal twins should show a higher concordance rate than identical twins
   c. other sex fraternal twins should show a higher concordance rate than same sex fraternal twins
   d. homosexuality should run in families

10. Gender nonconformity rates in childhood are higher for
   a. lesbians than heterosexual women
   b. gay men than heterosexual men
   c. lesbians and gay men than heterosexuals of both sexes
   d. homosexuals in all North, Central and South American countries except Guatemala and Brazil

11. Which statement best reflects current Christian views on homosexuality?
   a. Homosexuality is a sin
   b. Homosexuality is inherently unnatural
   c. Homosexuality cannot be changed except through religious conversion
   d. There is a great range of positions

12. All of the following countries have adopted national laws prohibiting discrimination against gays, lesbians, and bisexuals except
   a. Canada
   b. United States
   c. Israel
   d. South Africa

13. Which statement is true regarding homosexuality and mental health?
    a. Homosexual adults show significantly higher levels of psychological distress than heterosexual adults
    b. The American Psychiatric Association removed homosexuality from its list of mental disorders in 1973
    c. Hooker's research found that adjustment was better for lesbians than gay men
    d. Adjustment is better for gays and lesbians that are active in the gay community

14. Which of the following is the best example of homophobia?
    a. Brad refuses to talk to his lesbian sister because she has not paid back the money he loaned her
    b. Jeff asks his gay coworker about how his life partner is doing with his new job
    c. Kyle is afraid of hugging his best friend because he's afraid others will think he is gay
    d. Sara refuses to listen to the lesbian folk-rock duo *Indigo Girls* because she doesn't like folk-rock music

15. Research has revealed that hate crimes are related to
    a. holding traditional gender role stereotypes
    b. having conservative and authoritarian religious views
    c. denying homoerotic arousal in oneself
    d. all of the above are true

16. All of the following are ways that homophobia negatively impacts heterosexuals <u>except</u>
    a. heterosexual men may feel uneasy about having their nipples stimulated
    b. a woman may be reluctant to identify herself as a feminist
    c. a man is unwilling to wear soft and silky shirts, even though he likes how they feel
    d. all of the above are true

17. The coming out process consists of all of the following phases except
    a. self acceptance
    b. passing
    c. disclosure
    d. self acknowledgement

18. Which group listed below is likely to have the <u>least</u> negative attitude toward homosexuality?
    a. African Americans
    b. Hispanic Americans
    c. Native Americans
    d. Asian Americans

19. Which statement is true regarding lesbian sexual expression?
    a. Lesbians have fewer sex partners than gay men
    b. Lesbians are more likely to be monogamous
    c. Lesbians are more likely to wait to have sex until emotional intimacy is present
    d. All of the above are true

20. Current research shows that the children of gay and lesbian parents
    a. grow up to be heterosexual
    b. show more problem behaviors if the child is raised by gay parents than lesbian parents
    c. are more likely to have confused gender identity than children of heterosexuals
    d. have reduced self-esteem compared to children of heterosexuals

21. Goals of the gay rights movement include all of the following except
    a. decriminalization
    b. antidiscrimination
    c. government restitution
    d. positive rights

Answer Key – Chapter 10

<u>Concept Checks</u>

A Continuum of Sexual Orientations
1. one
2. homosexual
3. queer
4. bisexuality
5. seven
6. change
7. transitory

What Determines Sexual Orientation?
1. by default
2. men
3. first
4. before
5. family
6. Bem
7. choice
8. prenatal, circulating
9. handedness
10. identical, fraternal
11. Gender nonconformity
12. more
13. genetic
14. interaction

Societal Attitudes
1. rejecting-punitive
2. rejecting-nonpuntive
3. full acceptance
4. Sambia
5. two-thirds
6. homosexuality
7. Netherlands
8. Gay affirmative
9. conversion
10. Homophobia
11. heterosexism
12. 20, 25
13. traditional, homoerotic
14. young, human sexuality

Lifestyles
1. coming out
2. self-acknowledgement

3. Self-acceptance
4. teenagers
5. passing
6. outing
7. homosexuals, racism
8. Native Americans
9. heterosexual, homosexual
10. male, female (or vice versa)
11. fewer
12. homosexual
13. artificial insemination
14. male, gay

The Gay Rights Movement
1. Stonewall Incident
2. decriminalization, positive
3. sodomy
4. 33, 60
5. marriage

Crossword Puzzle

Across
1. Sambia
4. PLFAG
6. Stonewall
7. conversion
8. queer
9. hormones
11. identical
12. outing

Down
2. masculinity
3. handedness
5. gender
10. passing

Practice Test

1. d 2. b 3. a 4. b 5. d 6. c 7. d 8. c 9. a 10. c 11. d
12. b 13. b 14. c 15. d 16. d 17. b 18. c 19. d 20. a 21. c

Introduction

The social and historical context of contraceptive use are examined in this chapter that explores the advantages and disadvantages of current contraceptive methods. The benefits of sharing responsibility for contraception are stressed throughout the chapter. Suggestions are provided that will help you choose a fertility control method and use it safely and effectively. New developments that might result in a wider array of contraceptive choices are presented at the chapter's conclusion.

Learning Objectives. In order to derive maximum benefit from these objectives, use these as soon as you begin reading the chapter. After you have completed reading and studying this chapter, you should be able to do the things listed below with ease, using only your memory.

1. Explain when efforts to control conception first began and list various contraceptive methods that have been used throughout history.

2. From an historical and social perspective, briefly discuss each of the following:
    a. available methods of contraception throughout U.S. history
    b. obstacles to reliable contraceptive availability
    c. key people involved in promoting birth control
    d. key legislation related to contraceptive use

3. List some of the reasons why reliable contraception is a major worldwide concern today as well as what some of the objections are to contraceptive use.

4. Identify some of the ways in which couples can share responsibility for birth control.

5. List and describe several variables that influence the effectiveness of birth control.

6. Compare the effectiveness of various birth control methods.

7. For each of the following contraceptive methods, describe what it is and how it works, and list the advantages and disadvantages of each:
    a. "outercourse"
    b. oral contraceptives
    c. Norplant
    d. injectible contraceptives
    e. condoms
    f. diaphragms
    g. cervical caps
    h. vaginal spermicides
    i. intrauterine devices
    j. methods based on the menstrual cycle
    k. emergency contraception
    l. sterilization
    m. other methods such as nursing, withdrawal and douching

8. Discuss some of the future possibilities for contraceptive methods that may be available to men and women.

Concept Map

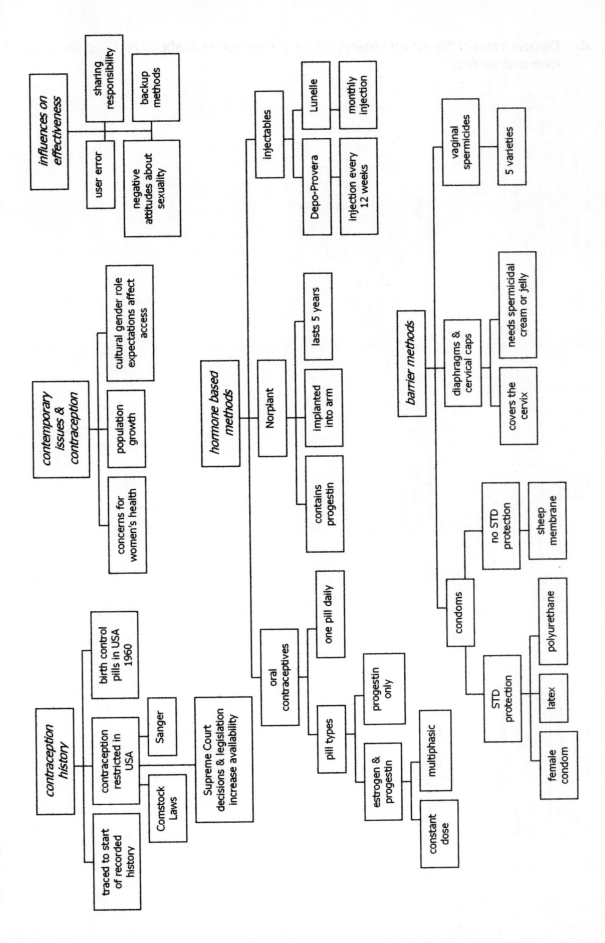

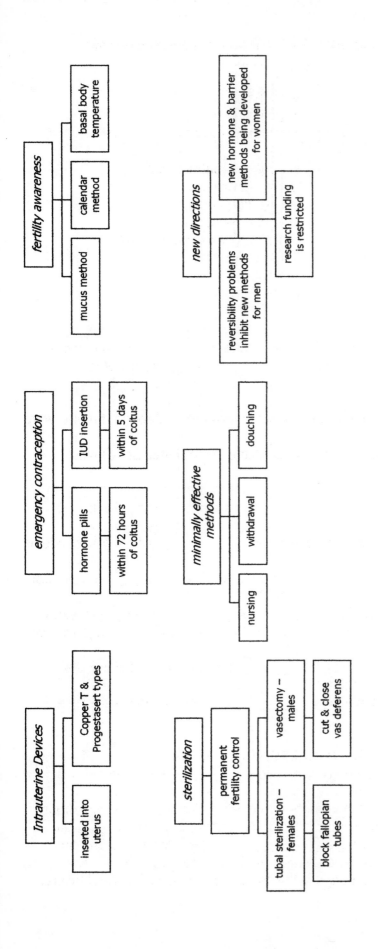

Key Terms . *Refer to the glossary or subject index in the back of your textbook for definitions and information.*

Comstock laws
failure rate
backup methods
outercourse
constant dose combination pill
multiphasic pills
progestin-only pills
ACHES
Norplant
Depo-Provera
Lunelle
condom
diaphragm

cervical cap
vaginal spermicide
intrauterine devices
PAINS
emergency contraception
fertility awareness
mucus method
calendar method
basal body temperature (BBT)
tubal sterilization
vasectomy
vasovasotomy

Concept-Checks. *Complete this section by filling in each blank after you have studied the corresponding pages from the text. Answers are provided at the back of this chapter.*

Historical and Social Perspectives, pp. 292-295
1. Laws that made it illegal to distribute information about contraception through the mail were called _____ _____.
2. The person most influential in making birth control available in the United States was

_____ _____.
3. Birth control pills could first be obtained in the United States in the year _____.
4. Two U. S. Supreme Court decisions that decriminalized the use of birth control were the 1965 _____ v. Connecticut ruling and Eisenstadt v. _____ ruling in 1972.
5. Research has revealed that rates of sexual activity do not _____ when free condoms are available in schools.
6. As many as 2/3 of insurance companies do not cover the cost of _____, yet the cost of Viagra to treat erectile dysfunction is covered in most plans.
7. In Japan birth control pills were not available until the year _____, largely because granting women control over their fertility runs counter to cultural norms which require women to be docile and compliant.
8. A recent survey of Catholic clergy found that _____ percent did not believe that contraceptive use by married couples was a sin.
9. Another study revealed that 88% of Catholic and _____ women used artificial contraceptive methods.

Sharing Responsibility and Choosing a Birth Control Method, pp. 295-301
1. Sharing the responsibility for contraception may reduce _____ and build

_____.
2. Ways that a partner can share in the responsibility for contraception include talking about _____ _____ before intercourse occurs for the first time; accompanying his partner for a medical _____ ; inserting a _____ or cervical cap, putting on _____ and sharing _____ for an exam and the birth control method.
3. _____ women up to 30 years old are most likely to experience birth control failure.

4. People who feel _____ about sex , who harbor _____ attitudes toward sexuality, and who take a _____ role in contraceptive decision making are more likely to use contraception ineffectively, if it is used at all.

5. The _____ rate refers to the number of women in 100 who become pregnant within a year, provided they are using the contraceptive correctly and consistently.

6. Some backup methods that can be used simultaneously with another method to increase effectiveness include _____, foam, or a(n) _____.

7. The number of infant murders _____ when birth control pills and abortion were legalized.

8. Forms of outercourse include kissing, touching, petting, mutual _____, oral and _____ sex.

9. Outercourse prevents pregnancy but may not prevent _____ _____ _____.

Hormone Based Contraceptives, pp. 301-306

1. Three basic types of oral contraceptives include _____ combination pill, _____ pills, and _____-only pills.

2. Combination and multiphasic pills primarily work by inhibiting _____.

3. Progestin-only pills alter the _____ mucus and change the lining of the _____.

4. Missing one of more birth control pills may cause _____ to occur.

5. Advantages of using oral contraceptives include maintaining spontaneity, being _____, reducing menstrual _____ and flow, as well as PMS symptoms.

6. Disadvantages of combination and multiphasic birth control pills include an increase or decrease in _____, decreased _____ motivation, decreased vaginal lubrication, and _____ with other medications.

7. Serious side effects of birth control pills may be summarized with the acronym ACHES, which stands for: _____ pain, _____ pain, **H**eadaches, _____ problems, and _____ leg pain.

8. Progestin-only pill users are more likely to experience the side effect of _____ menstrual bleeding than are users of the other pill types.

9. The contraceptive _____ consists of six thin, flexible capsules filled with progestin that are implanted into the upper arm

10. The capsules described above prevent against pregnancy 24 hours after insertion and work for _____ years.

11. Advantages of these capsules include: not remembering to take a _____ every day, not needing to use a _____ method to prevent pregnancy, and quick reversibility.

12. Disadvantages to the capsules include : high initial cost, no _____ protection, and menstrual _____.

13. Two contraceptives that may be injected are _____-_____ and _____.

14. Injectable contraceptives work by inhibiting _____ and changing the lining of the _____.

15. Injected contraceptives are advantageous because there is no need to take a _____ daily or to use a _____ method, and women can use these without anyone but their health care provider knowing.

16. Injectable contraceptives may be less desirable as they provide no protection against STD's, and may have the side effects of menstrual irregularity or _____ of menstruation.

Barrier Methods, pp. 306-316

1. The only barrier method that protects against STD's is the _____.

2. The _____ is a covering that fits over the erect penis.

3. Condoms are made of _____, _____ membrane, or polyurethane.

4. _____ _____ condoms may reduce loss of sensation, yet they allow the _____ virus to pass through.

5. Condoms should not be stored in _____ places, such as a glove compartment in a car or a wallet carried in one's pocket.

6. In order for condoms to be effective they must be used _____ the penis has any contact with the vulva.

7. If a condom is the unlubricated type it may break more easily, so lubricants such as _____, K-Y jelly, or some vaginal secretion need to be put on the outside of the condom and vulva to reduce the chance of breakage.

8. The condom must be held at the _____ of the penis before withdrawing from the vagina or else the condom may come off, spilling semen inside the vagina or on the labia.

9. Condoms may be a desirable form of birth control because latex and polyurethane ones provide protection against STD's; they are available without a _____; and they may prolong the duration of _____ before ejaculation.

10. Condoms may be less desirable because they may interrupt _____, can _____ penile sensitivity, and may have pinhole sized leaks or slip off.

11. The female condom fits the contours of the vagina and fits over some of the _____, providing more protection against STD's than male condoms.

12. Female condom users find them advantageous because sex is less _____.

13. Diaphragms are a soft, round latex dome which covers the _____.

14. Diaphragms are used with _____ _____ or _____.

15. Spermicide is placed in the _____ of the diaphragm and around the _____.

16. A diaphragm can be inserted up to _____ hours before intercourse, though some sources suggest two hours for maximum protection.

17. In order to kill all the sperm that may reside in the vagina, a diaphragm must be left inside for at least _____ hours after intercourse.

18. Diaphragm users and their partners may experience the advantages of becoming more knowledgeable about a woman's _____ and may reduce the risk of cell changes that lead to _____.

19. Some diaphragm users are less satisfied because of the high _____ rate, its failure to prevent _____, and that cream or jelly is _____.

20. The _____ _____ is similar to the diaphragm but can be left in place for a longer period of time.

21. Like the diaphragm, the cervical cap must be filled with _____.

22. The absence of _____ _____ is the major advantage of the cervical cap.

23. Cervical caps have a high _____ rate, rendering them less desirable.

24. Types of vaginal spermicides include _____, suppositories, the _____, creams or _____, and VCF – vaginal contraceptive film.

25. For highly effective birth control protection, spermicides may be used together with a _____.

26. Vaginal spermicides have the advantages of no dangerous side effects; they can be purchased _____ the _____; and they are _____.

27. Vaginal spermicides may irritate _____ tissues in some users, and may taste _____.

Intrauterine Devices, pp. 316-317

1. IUD's are inserted into the _____ through the cervical os.

2. Both types of IUD work by preventing _____.

3. A woman may safely use an IUD if she is in a stable, monogamous relationship, if she is at least _____ years old, has at least one _____ or completed _____, and has ready access to medical facilities.

4. IUD users and their partners must check to see if the _____ is the same length as when the IUD was first inserted.

5. Many users like their IUD because sexual activity remains _____ and the IUD may be used when a woman is _____.

6. IUD users and their partners must be watch for PAINS, the acronym that summarizes the serious problems associated with IUD use: **P**eriod late/no period; _____ pain, _____ temperature, fever, or chills; **N**asty or foul _____, and **S**potting, bleeding, heavy periods, or clots.

Emergency Contraception, pp. 317-318

1. Insertion of a(n) _____ and _____ pills are methods used for emergency contraception.

2. Emergency contraception involving hormones must be used within _____ hours after unprotected intercourse.

3. In order to access emergency contraception methods a _____ must be obtained, except in Washington state.

4. Copper IUDs used for emergency contraception have a failure rate of less than _____ percent, rendering it the most effective form of emergency contraception.

Fertility Awareness Methods, pp. 318-321

1. Fertility awareness methods are also known as _____ family planning.

2. The _____ method, the calendar method, and _____ body temperature are the three fertility awareness methods.

3. The mucus method involves monitoring changes in the _____ mucus produced throughout the menstrual cycle.

4. The calendar method requires that a woman keep a chart of the length of her menstrual cycles for _____ year(s) when she is not using oral contraceptives.

5. The basal body temperature method demands that a woman take her temperature upon waking in the morning, in order to detect a(n) _____ in temperature prior to ovulation, and a(n) _____ after ovulation.

6. Fertility awareness methods' major advantage is the _____ of side effects and very low cost.

7. Fertility awareness methods' effectiveness can be hampered because unrestful sleep, colds, and low grade infections may slightly alter basal body _____, and vaginal infections, semen, or spermicides may make it difficult to interpret _____ _____.

Sterilization, pp. 321-324

1. Sterilization is the most effective birth control method except _____.

2. Sterilization is the most popular method of birth control in the _____ _____.

3. The various methods of tubal sterilization work by severing , cauterizing, or tying the _____ _____, thereby preventing sperm from reaching an egg.

4. One recent study has revealed that sterilization does not have harmful effects on a woman's _____ satisfaction.

5. Male sterilization has _____ complications than female sterilization and is _____ expensive.

6. A vasectomy involves removing a section of each _____ _____ and closing it.

7. Vasectomy prevents the _____ produced in the testes from reaching the semen manufactured by internal pelvic organs.

8. The amount of _____ remains almost the same after vasectomy since sperm make up less than 5% of the ejaculate.

9. Surgical reconnection of the vas deferens is called _____ , and has a current effectiveness rate of only 50%.

10. Research has shown that most men report that vasectomy does not affect _____ functioning.

Less-Than-Effective Methods, p.324

1. Breast feeding is not an effective method of birth control because 80% of women may _____ before menstruation resumes.

2. Two other methods with high failure rates include _____ and _____.

New Directions in Contraception, pp. 324-325

1. A substance that reduces the number and motility of sperm is being studied, and this is administered using a _____.

2. Research shows that a majority of men would take a male contraceptive _____.

3. Like Norplant, other contraceptive _____ are being studied for women.

4. Other developments for women include variations on the diaphragm and cervical cap, spermicides that stop _____ transmission, and a new IUD.

Matching

Match each characteristic with the birth control method that fits. An answer may be used more than once. There may be more than one answer for each blank.

a. constant-dose combination pill
b. multiphasic pill
c. progestin-only pill
d. Norplant
e. Depo-Provera
f. Lunelle
g. diaphragm
h. cervical cap
i. male condom

j. female condom
k. spermicidal foam, jelly, suppositories
l. vaginal contraceptive film (VCF)
m. contraceptive sponge
n. IUD
o. fertility awareness methods
p. tubal sterilization
q. vasectomy

_____ 1. can be purchased over-the-counter

_____ 2. users will get ACHES if serious side effects are present

_____ 3. no serious medical side effects

_____ 4. high failure rate among women who have been pregnant

_____ 5. failure rate of less than 5% in typical use

_____ 6. provides the bonus of STD protection

_____ 7. don't have to remember to use it or take it

_____ 8. contains progestin

_____ 9. may produce menstrual irregularities

_____ 10. requires practice or training to use correctly

_____ 11. no reapplication needed for repeated acts of intercourse

_____ 12. difficult to reverse

_____ 13. serious side effects bring PAINS

_____ 14. may produce mood changes

_____ 15. can be used if allergic to foam or jelly

_____ 16. inhibits ovulation

_____ 17. contains estrogen

Crossword

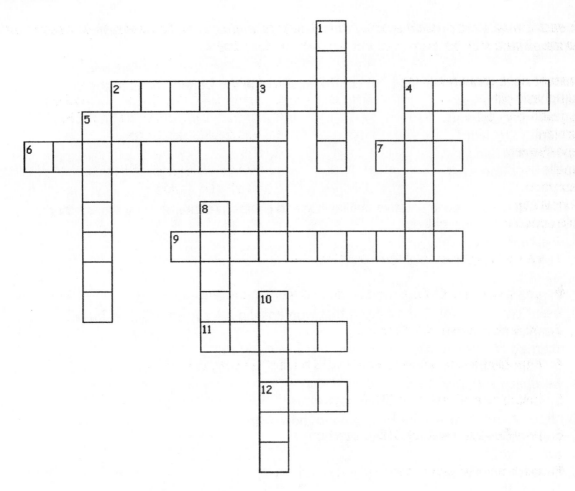

Across

2. Norplant's key ingredient
4. poor _____ may alter basal body temperature
6. birth control pills inhibit this process
7. condoms must not be stored in this type of place
9. type of condom that is least likely to break
11. vasectomy keeps this out of semen
12. spermicidal "matchbook"

Down

1. emotion that leads to ineffective contraceptive use
3. Comstock law violator and *Woman Rebel* author
4. Seinfeld's Elaine stashed this contraceptive
5. estrogen containing injectable contraceptive
8. careful monitoring of this may reveal the fertile period
10. a diaphragm covers this

Practice Test

This test will work best to guide your learning if you take it as part of a final review session before an exam.

1. Who is credited with making birth control available in the United States in the late 19th and early 20th centuries?
    a. Anthony Comstock
    b. Gloria Steinem
    c. Margaret Sanger
    d. Eleanor Roosevelt

2. Factors that affect contraceptive availability and choice in contemporary times include
    a. gender role expectations.
    b. insurance coverage.
    c. religious mandates.
    d. all of the above.

3. A recent cross cultural study showed that women who have fewer children have
    a. happier marriages.
    b. married at an early age.
    c. more education.
    d. European ancestry.

4. Contraceptive failure is more likely among those who
    a. feel guilty about their sexuality.
    b. are under 30.
    c. have lower incomes.
    d. two of the above are true.
    e. all of the above are true.

5. Outercourse is a form of sexual sharing that includes all of the following except
    a. oral sex.
    b. anal sex.
    c. coitus.
    d. mutual masturbation.
    e. petting.

6. Of the following birth control methods, _____ is least effective when used correctly and consistently?
    a. male condoms
    b. sponge , with a woman who has never been pregnant
    c. spermicides
    d. Lunelle

7. The most common reversible birth control method among women in the United States is/are
    a. Depo-Provera.
    b. Norplant.
    c. oral contraceptives.
    d. spermicide.
    e. condoms.

8. Multiphasic and constant-dose combination pills prevent pregnancy by releasing
    a. gonadotropic releasing hormones (GnRH).
    b. LH and FSH.
    c. prostaglandins.
    d. estrogen and progestin.

9. In order to maximize the effectiveness of oral contraceptives users should
    a. take the pill at the same time each day.
    b. take multiphasic pills.
    c. take constant dose pills.
    d. miss a pill occasionally in order to give the body a "rest".

10. Users of birth control pills may experience all of the following except
    a. reduced menstrual flow.
    b. relief from endometriosis.
    c. increased risk of ovarian cancer.
    d. decreased PMS symptoms.
    e. reduced menstrual cramps.

11. All of the following medications reduce the effectiveness of oral contraceptives except
    a. ibuprofen.
    b. antihistamines.
    c. ampicillin.
    d. tetracycline.

12. Norplant works by releasing _____ into the bloodstream.
    a. relaxin
    b. estrogen
    c. progestin
    d. inhibin
    e. oxytocin

13. Which of the following statements about Norplant is true?
    a. Norplant is inserted below the skin of the shoulder blades.
    b. Norplant lasts for a period of three years.
    c. Norplant costs about the same as five years of birth control pills.
    d. Menstrual irregularities are rare.

14. The failure rate of the injectable contraceptive Depo-Provera is
    a. considerably higher than birth control pills when they are used correctly and consistently.
    b. considerably lower than birth control pills when they are used correctly and consistently.
    c. about the same as birth control pills when they are used correctly and consistently.
    d. decreased if the user experiences side effects.

15. Hormone based contraceptives
    a. have minimal side effects.
    b. contain progestin and estrogen.
    c. can be safely used by women who smoke.
    d. fail to provide protection against STD's.
    e. are less effective in women who have had children.

16. There is less chance of a condom breaking if it is
    a. made of polyurethane.
    b. lubricated.
    c. made of sheep membrane.
    d. ribbed.

17. Which type of condom does not provide protection against STD's?
    a. latex
    b. polyurethane
    c. sheep membrane
    d. plain-end

18. In order to correctly use condoms to prevent pregnancy
    a. the condom must be used before the penis has contact with the vulva
    b. water-based lubricants should be used.
    c. the condom must be held at the base of the penis as it is withdrawn from the vagina.
    d. none of the above are true.
    e. all of the above are true

19. When a diaphragm is used contraceptive cream or jelly is
    a. spread around inside of the rim.
    b. squeezed into the cup.
    c. spread around the outside of the rim.
    d. spread around inside of the rim and squeezed into the cup.
    e. spread on the outside of the cup.

20. A diaphragm must be left in place for at least _____ hours after intercourse.
    a. two
    b. three
    c. five
    d. six

21. Which disadvantage do the diaphragm and cervical cap have in common?
    a. increased risk of cervical cell changes
    b. headaches
    c. high failure rate
    d. repeated applications of spermicide are needed with additional acts of intercourse

22. The various types of vaginal spermicides include
    a. foam, suppositories, ointment, jelly, and film.
    b. foam, suppositories, cream, jelly, sponge, and film.
    c. foam, cream, jelly, sponge, lotion, and film.
    d. cream, jelly, suppositories, sponge, spray, and film.

23. Which of the following is not considered an advantage of vaginal spermicides?
    a. The sponge is effective for repeated acts of intercourse.
    b. They do not require a visit to the doctor's office.
    c. There are no known dangerous side effects.
    d. Long term use is associated with reduced vaginal lubrication.
    e. Vaginal contraceptive film can be used by people allergic to other spermicides.

24. While a woman is using an IUD she or her partner must
    a. refrain from the woman-on-top intercourse position, to prevent dislodging the IUD.
    b. avoid using tampons during menstruation.
    c. check the length of the string after menstruation.
    d. abstain from the "doggie" intercourse position, to avoid perforating the uterus.

25. Some women find an IUD a highly desirable form of contraception because
    a. it is highly effective.
    b. it does not interrupt spontaneity.
    c. a woman doesn't have to remember to use it.
    d. all of the above are true.
    e. two of the above are true

26. Which of the following represent methods of emergency contraception?
    a. GnRH antagonists
    b. copper IUDs
    c. hormone pills
    d. copper IUDs and hormone pills
    e. misoprostol

27. Fertility awareness methods include
    a. mucus, calendar, and basal body temperature methods.
    b. rhythm, calendar, and basal body temperature methods.
    c. ovulation, mucus, and calendar methods.
    d. ovu-quick, calendar, and rhythm methods.

28. Tubal sterilization involves
     a. removing the fallopian tubes.
     b. inserting gel into the fallopian tubes.
     c. severing, cauterizing, typing, or placing a clip on the fallopian tubes.
     d. removing a woman's ovaries and her fallopian tubes.

29. A vasectomy involves
     a. removing one or more testicles.
     b. placing a clip on the epididymis.
     c. permanently closing the ejaculatory duct.
     d. cutting and closing each vas deferens.

30. A vasectomy is as effective as _____ and has _____ complications than tubal sterilization.
     a. tubal sterilization; fewer
     b. tubal sterilization; more
     c. oral contraceptives; fewer
     d. oral contraceptives; more

31. All of the following are reasons why withdrawal is ineffective <u>except</u>
     a. If ejaculation does not occur "blue balls" may result
     b. Preejaculatory secretions may contain sperm
     c. It is difficult for a man to know when to withdraw
     d. If sperm settle on the labia they can swim into the vagina

Answer Key -- Chapter 11

Concept Checks

Historical and Social Perspectives
1. Comstock Laws
2. Margaret Sanger
3. 1960
4. Griswold; Baird
5. increase
6. contraceptives
7. 1999
8. 44
9. Protestant

Sharing Responsibility and Choosing a Birth Control Method
1. stress; trust
2. birth control; exam; diaphragm; condoms; expenses
3. Unmarried
4. guilty; negative; passive
5. failure
6. condoms; diaphragm
7. decreased
8. masturbation; anal
9. sexually transmitted diseases

Hormone Based Contraceptives
1. constant-dose; multiphasic; progestin
2. ovulation
3. cervical; uterus
4. ovulation
5. reversible; cramps
6. depression; sexual; interactions
7. Abdominal; Chest; Eye; Severe
8. irregular
9. Norplant
10. five
11. pill; barrier
12. STD; irregularity
13. Depo Provera; Lunelle
14. ovulation; uterus
15. pill; barrier
16. lack

Barrier Methods
1. condom
2. condom
3. latex; sheep

4. Sheep membrane; AIDS
5. hot
6. before
7. saliva
8. base
9. prescription; coitus
10. spontaneity; decrease
11. vulva
12. messy
13. cervix
14. spermicidal cream; jelly
15. dome; rim
16. six
17. six
18. body; cancer
19. failure; STD's; messy
20. cervical cap
21. spermicide
22. side effects
23. failure
24. foam; sponge; jelly
25. condom
26. over; counter; small
27. genital; badly

Intrauterine Devices
1. uterus
2. fertilization
3. 25; child; childbearing
4. string
5. uninterrupted; nursing
6. Abdominal; Increased; discharge

Emergency Contraception
1. IUD; hormone
2. 72
3. prescription
4. one

Fertility Awareness Methods
1. natural
2. mucus; basal
3. cervical
4. one
5. drop; increase
6. lack
7. temperature; cervical mucus

Sterilization
1. abstinence
2. United States
3. fallopian tubes
4. sexual
5. fewer; less
6. vas deferens
7. sperm
8. semen
9. vasovasotomy
10. sexual

Less-Than-Effective Methods
1. ovulate
2. withdrawal; douching

New Directions in Contraception
1. vaccine
2. pill
3. implants
4. STD

Matching

1. i, j, k, l, m
2. a, b, c
3. g, h, i, j, k, l, m, o
4. h, m
5. a, b, c, d, e, f, n, p, q
6. i, j
7. d, e, n, p, q
8. a, b, c, d, e, n (Progestasert IUD)
9. c, d, e, f
10. g, h, o
11. m
12. p, q
13. n
14. a, b
15. l
16. a, b, c, d, e, f
17. a, b, f

Crossword Puzzle

Across
2. progestin
4. sleep
6. ovulation

7. hot
9. lubricated
11. sperm
12. VCF

Down
1. guilt
3. Sanger
4. sponge
5. Lunelle
8. mucus
10. cervix

Practice Test

1. c 2. d 3. c 4. e 5. c 6. b 7. c 8. d 9. a 10. c 11. a 12. c
13. c 14. c 15. d 16. b 17. c 18. a 19. d 20. d 21. c 22. b 23. d
24. c 25. d 26. d 27. a 28. c 29. d 30. a 31. a

Introduction

The decision you make about whether or not you will be a parent profoundly alters your life course. To assist you with this process, or to help you better understand the decision you have already made about parenting, the advantages and disadvantages of remaining child-free or becoming parents are explored. The physical and psychological aspects of conception, pregnancy, childbirth, and postpartum adjustment are addressed. Opportunities to experience parenthood for infertile couples are examined, as wells as the psychological impact of coping with infertility. Historical, sociological, and political lenses are brought to bear upon the modern-day controversy of elective abortion.

Learning Objectives. *In order to derive maximum benefit from these objectives, use these as soon as you begin reading the chapter. After you have completed reading and studying this chapter, you should be able to do the things listed below with ease, using only your memory.*

1. Discuss each of the following in relationship to becoming a parent:
    a. advantages and disadvantages of becoming a parent
    b. how common remaining childless is
    c. how women who voluntarily remain childless feel about the decision
    d. how common adoption is
    e. why people choose to adopt children

2. List several factors that will increase the possibility of conception.

3. Cite statistics that indicate how common infertility is, how successful treatment is, and then describe some of the factors that contribute to both female and male infertility.

4. Explain how problems with fertility may affect a couple's emotional and sexual relationship.

5. List and describe options for conception available to couples with infertility problems.

6. Identify the initial signs of pregnancy a woman may experience and how these may be confirmed.

7. Discuss the incidence of and issues, including the emotional experience, involved in spontaneous abortion (miscarriage).

8. Cite statistics that indicate how common elective abortion is among women from various age groups and discuss the characteristics that women who seek elective abortions have in common.

9. Describe surgical and medical procedures that may be used in having an abortion.

10. Discuss research data related to the following:
    a. effects of first-trimester abortion on subsequent fertility
    b. effects of having two or more abortions
    c. number of women that have abortions who have had a previous abortion
    d. what factors can contribute to repeat abortions

     e. percentage of women who have abortions as a result of contraceptive failure

     f. how often late abortions occur

11. Describe how a woman's partner might share the responsibility of an unwanted pregnancy.

12. Make reference to research that addresses the emotional effects of legal abortion on both women and men.

13. Explain why some women may risk an unwanted pregnancy by not using contraceptives reliably.

14. Outline and elaborate upon some of the reasons why elective abortion is such a controversial social and political issue.

15. Compare the beliefs of individuals who hold strong pro-choice values with those individuals who are anti-abortion.

16. Discuss some of the following aspects of a healthy pregnancy:
     a. fetal development
     b. prenatal care
     c. detection of birth defects
     d. pregnancy after age 35

17. Compare the different emotional and physical reactions to pregnancy from both a female and male perspective.

18. Discuss how sexual interaction may be affected during pregnancy.

19. List and describe the three stages in the process of childbirth.

20. Outline and briefly explain some contemporary philosophies regarding childbirth.

21. List and briefly describe three birthplace alternatives and under what circumstances each is appropriate.

22. Discuss the advantages and disadvantages of various medical procedures used during childbirth, making reference to appropriate research studies that support each position.

23. Describe the physical and psychological adjustments that family members experience during the postpartum period.

24. Explain the physiological changes that accompany nursing and list the advantages and disadvantages of it.

25. Describe some of the considerations a couple may need to make in resuming sexual interaction after childbirth.

26. Discuss current techniques that are being used to predetermine the sex of a child, and the impact this has had in various countries in which there is a strong preference for having sons.

27. Discuss new reproductive technologies, including those available for post menopausal women, and some of the controversies surrounding these technologies.

28. Discuss prenatal care guidelines for pregnant women.

Concept Map

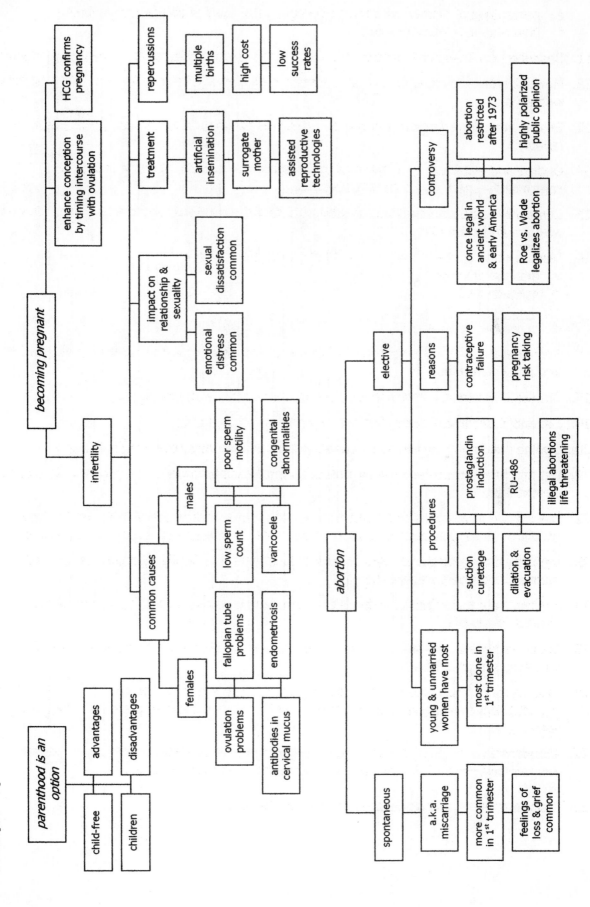

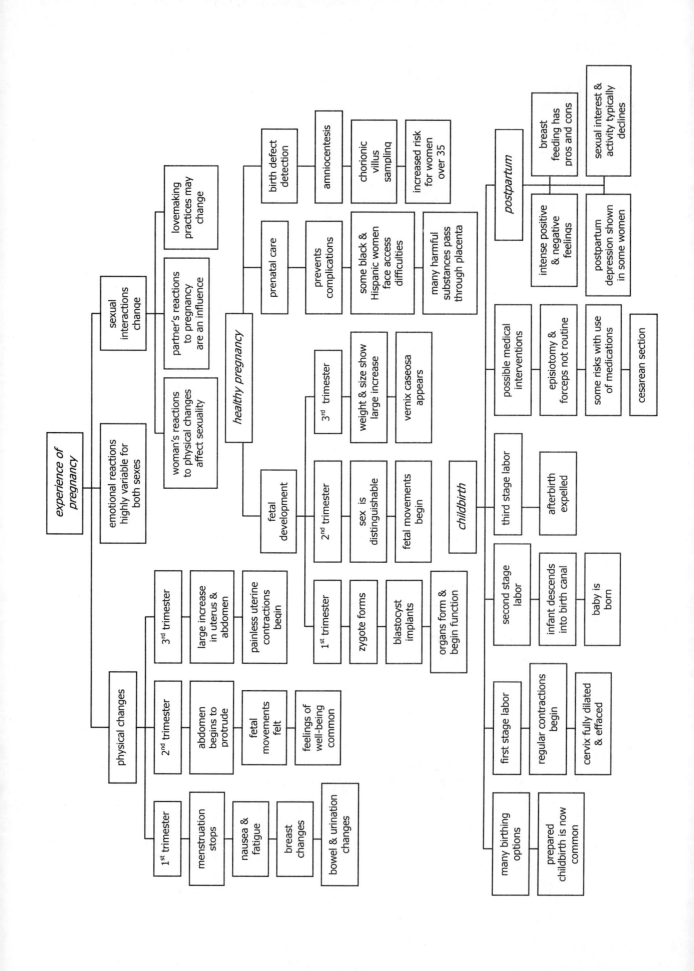

Key Terms. *Refer to the glossary or subject index in the back of your textbook for definitions and information.*

varicocele
intracytoplasmic sperm injection (ICSI)
artificial insemination
surrogate mother
assisted reproductive technology (ART)
in vitro fertilization (IVF)
zygote intrafallopian transfer (ZIFT)
gamete intrafallopian transfer (GIFT)
human chorionic gonadotropin (HCG)
spontaneous abortion
miscarriage
elective abortion
suction curettage
dilation and evacuation (D & E)
prostaglandins
quickening
viability
colostrum
zygote
blastocyst
vernix caseosa

placenta
fetal alcohol syndrome (FAS)
amniocentesis
amniotic fluid
chorionic villus sampling (CVS)
Lamaze
prepared childbirth
placenta previa
toxemia
first-stage labor
effacement
dilation
second-stage labor
third-stage labor
afterbirth
episiotomy
forceps
cesarean section
postpartum period
postpartum depression (PPD)
lochia

Concept-Checks. *Complete this section by filling in each blank after you have studied the corresponding pages from the text. Answers are provided at the back of this chapter.*

Parenthood as an Option, pp. 329-330
1. Child free marriages often have more time and energy for _____ and _____.
2. Marriages without children are typically less _____ and _____ satisfying than marriages with children, especially in the years following the birth of the first child.
3. Parenting may bring the advantages of a sense of _____, build _____, and provide tremendous personal growth.

Becoming Pregnant, pp. 330-338
1. Within three months, _____ percent of couples become pregnant.
2. If a couple does not conceive after _____ months, a physician should be consulted.
3. Conception is most likely to occur during a six day period _____ ovulation.
4. Nearly 50% of infertility cases involve _____ factors.
5. Failure to _____ at regular intervals is a common cause of female infertility.
6. If a woman is ovulating normally, a _____ test may reveal if sperm are viable in the cervical mucus.
7. Scar tissue from past infections or STDs can block _____ _____, and is a major cause of female infertility.
8. The majority of male infertility results from abnormalities in sperm _____ or _____.

9. Common causes of male infertility include mumps, STD caused infections, cigarette smoking; using _____ , cocaine, or alcohol; exposure to environmental _____, and enlarged veins called a _____.

10. Sperm may be retrieved from the testes and used during _____ _____ _____, where sperm is directly placed into an egg.

11. Both women and men may experience _____ distress when coping with infertility.

12. Studies of infertile couples have revealed that most experience some _____ or dysfunction with their sexual relationship.

13. In historical and contemporary times methods of sex selection have included _____ _____ after X and Y sperm have been separated; infanticide, and _____ _____, which is largely done with female fetuses.

14. During artificial insemination _____ are mechanically placed into a woman's vagina, cervix, or _____.

15. Assisted reproductive technologies (ART) for infertile couples may involve _____ _____ _____ (IVF) where mature eggs are harvested and fertilized in a laboratory dish.

16. Variations of IVF include _____ intrafallopian transfer (ZIFT), where the egg is fertilized in the laboratory and placed into the fallopian tube and _____ intrafallopian transfer (GIFT) where egg and sperm are placed into the fallopian tube so that fertilization may occur in its normal location.

17. Problems associated with assisted reproductive technologies include _____ success rates, _____ births, and high financial cost.

18. In addition to missing a menstrual period, other indications that a woman is pregnant are _____ tenderness, nausea, vomiting, _____, or a change in appetite.

19. Blood and urine tests for pregnancy look for the presence of _____ _____ _____ (HCG), which is detectable one month after conception.

Spontaneous and Elective Abortion, pp. 338-347

1. Another name for a spontaneous abortion is a(n) _____, where the fetus is spontaneously expelled from the uterus due to genetic, hormonal, or medical problems.

2. Loved ones can help those coping with miscarriage by openly acknowledging the loss, _____ and refraining from giving advice.

3. When a pregnancy is terminated using medical procedures it is called a(n) _____ abortion.

4. Most women who have abortions are under age _____.

5. Catholic women are _____ likely to have an abortion as other women, and 18% of abortions are obtained by _____ Christians.

6. _____ _____ is a procedure in which the cervix is dilated and the uterine contents removed using a vacuum aspirator.

7. Suction curettage may be done from seven to _____ weeks after the last menstrual period (LMP).

8. About _____ out of six abortions are performed at or before 12 weeks, the first trimester.

9. D and E stands for _____ and _____ and may be done from 13 to 21 weeks after the last menstrual period.

10. Some second-trimester pregnancies are terminated using _____, substances which begin uterine contractions.

11. Medical abortions can be done up to _____ weeks of pregnancy.

12. Mifepristone or RU-486 works by blocking the action of the hormone _____, causing the lining of the uterus to break down, preventing the fertilized egg from attaching to the wall of the uterus.

13. The second drug taken in a medical abortion is _____ , which causes the uterus to contract and expel its contents.

14. _____ doctor visits are typically required in a medical abortion using RU-486.

15. About _____ percent of abortions occur after 20 weeks of pregnancy.

16. Research has indicated that having _____ abortion(s) has little impact on a woman's ability to conceive or carry a pregnancy.

17. Studies show that _____ is a common feeling once the abortion is completed, and that abortion does not cause lasting psychological _____.

18. Feeling _____ , using alcohol or drugs, or "getting away with it" has been shown to increase contraceptive risk taking.

19. Nearly _____ percent of women were using contraception during the month in which they became pregnant.

20. The Supreme Court Roe vs. Wade decision in the year_____ made it legal for a woman to terminate a pregnancy before the fetus was viable.

21. Leading medical groups such as the American Medical Association _____ mandatory parental consent requirements for abortion.

22. The 1991 Rust vs. Sullivan decision _____ federally funded health clinics from discussing abortion with patients.

23. Opinion polls currently show that 55 to _____ percent of Americans believe abortion should be legal.

24. Research studies of abortion attitudes show that people who _____ of abortion are more likely to support civil liberties and women's rights, and to see intimacy as the primary purpose of sex whereas those who _____ of abortion are more likely to frown upon nonmarital sex, hold traditional attitudes toward women's roles, and to view procreation as the primary purpose of sex.

The Experience of Pregnancy, pp. 347-350

1. Studies of women's emotional responses to pregnancy show that women experience a _____ range of feelings.

2. During the first three months of pregnancy breasts may increase in size, the nipples and areola become _____ , fatigue and urination increase, and the abdomen shows _____ increase in size.

3. _____ and _____ typically abate during the middle three months of pregnancy, and some women experience increased feelings of _____.

4. Fetal movements or quickening are typically experienced during the _____ or _____ month of pregnancy.

5. During the last three months of pregnancy the uterus increases in size and begins to _____.

6. Expectant fathers frequently respond to the pregnancy with feelings of _____.

7. Most research to date shows a _____ in sexual activity during pregnancy.

8. Women who have higher levels of sexual interest and interaction during pregnancy have more _____ attitudes about sexuality prior to pregnancy.

9. Even though there are some overall trends in women's experience of pregnancy, reactions to pregnancy and sexuality are highly _____.

10. In pregnancies with no risk factors, _____ activity and _____ may be experienced until labor begins.

A Healthy Pregnancy, pp. 351-355

1. After fertilization the _____ develops into a multicelled _____ which implants into the wall of the uterus about one week after conception.
2. At the end of the _____ month internal organs begin limited function.
3. During the _____ trimester the sex of the fetus can be seen and fine downy hair appears over the body.
4. During the last trimester a protective, waxy substance called _____ caseosa covers the fetus' skin, and the fetus may double its weight.
5. Good prenatal care should focus upon nutrition, general health, adequate _____, routine health care, _____, and _____ education.
6. Women who are most likely to have difficulty accessing prenatal care are _____ black or Hispanic women who are under _____, have not graduated from high school, and are uninsured.
7. Black women are _____ times more likely to die from childbirth than white women, primarily due to inadequate prenatal care.
8. The _____ is attached to the uterine wall and to the fetus by the _____ cord.
9. The placenta acts as a conduit for nutrients, _____, and waste products and may prevent *some* germs and drugs from being passed to the fetus.
10. Children of mothers who smoke during pregnancy are more likely to have _____ birth weight, increased chance of cleft palate, lower developmental scores, and more _____ diseases than children born to nonsmoking mothers.
11. Alcohol can cross the placenta and result in _____ _____ syndrome, a leading cause of birth defects and developmental disabilities in newborns.
12. Rates of fetal alcohol syndrome are _____ times higher among Native Americans than the general population of the United States.
13. Given our limited knowledge about drugs and other substances ingested by pregnant women, it is recommended that _____ medications be used during pregnancy unless absolutely necessary and under the close medical supervision.
14. Procedures used to detect fetal abnormalities include _____, where a sample of amniotic fluid is taken and _____ _____ _____ .
15. As a pregnant woman's age rises the risk of birth defects due to abnormal chromosomes _____.

Childbirth, pp. 355-360

1. A full term of pregnancy lasts _____ weeks.
2. Prepared childbirth is based upon the _____ and Dick-Read philosophies which stress using breathing techniques, education, muscle relaxation, and social support to reduce pain.
3. Research has shown that women with trained birth attendants had _____ cesarean births, less pain medication, _____ length of labor and greater satisfaction with their birth experience.
4. Prior to first stage labor the cervix usually begins the process of _____, where it becomes thinned and flattened.

5. Characteristics of first stage labor typically include a bloody "show", rupturing of the amniotic sac, regular _____ and dilation of the cervix to a maximum of _____ centimeters.

6. First stage labor may also be divided into three substages, these being early; active, and _____.

7. The key event of _____ stage labor is the descent of the baby into the vagina and the subsequent birth of the infant(s).

8. The afterbirth is expelled during the _____ stage of labor.

9. Although it is currently presumed that the risks to the infant are small, some medications can slow or stop labor, _____ the mother's blood pressure, and _____ the urge to push during second stage labor.

10. An _____ is the name for an incision in the perineum that is believed to relieve pressure on the infant's head and reduce vaginal tearing.

11. Research has shown that episiotomy performed during uncomplicated labor presents _____ risks than benefits.

12. Some babies are delivered with a _____ section in which an incision is made through the abdominal wall and _____.

13. Studies have indicated that most women who have had a cesarean section _____ have vaginal births in the future.

14. Currently _____ percent of births are done via cesarean section.

Postpartum, pp. 360-362

1. Postpartum depression affects about _____ percent of mothers.

2. Symptoms of postpartum depression include depression, insomnia, _____, panic attacks and _____, making this condition different than "baby blues".

3. Right after birth a yellow liquid called _____ is produced by the breasts.

4. Lactation or milk production begins one to _____ days after birth.

5. Breast milk contains _____ and other immunity producing substances.

6. Nursing stimulates _____ contractions and may temporarily inhibit _____.

7. Breast feeding temporarily reduces production of the hormone _____, which may reduce sexual desire and vaginal lubrication and cause discomfort from intercourse.

8. Women who are most likely to breast feed and resume sexual activity are women with _____ attitudes toward sexuality.

9. One sign that a women is physically ready to have vaginal intercourse is when the flow of _____ stops, a reddish uterine discharge.

10. In addition to physical readiness to have intercourse, _____ readiness is another important dimension couples may consider.

Crossword

Across
2. life sustaining organ that connects mother and fetus
3. fetus "swims" in this fluid
5. pregnancy complication resulting from high blood pressure
7. common post-abortion feeling
8. yellowish breast milk predecessor
9. birth type that is common with ART
11. fetuses of this sex are a selective abortion target

12. longest stage of labor
Down
1. abortion type associated with miscarriage
4. blastocyst implants on this wall
6. thinning & flattening of the cervix prior to childbirth
10. morning jolt associated with low birth weight

Practice Test

This test will work best to guide your learning if you take it as part of a final review session before an exam.

1. Having childless marriage is associated with all of the following <u>except</u>
   a. less marital satisfaction.
   b. greater spontaneity in work and leisure.
   c. more financial resources.
   d. less stress.

2. Choosing to have children may bring all of the following <u>except</u>
   a. a sense of accomplishment.
   b. saving a troubled marriage.
   c. discovering untapped dimensions in oneself.
   d. increased personal growth.

3. Conception is most likely to occur
   a. during the three days after ovulation.
   b. during the five day period after ovulation.
   c. during the six day period ending with ovulation.
   d. during the three day period ending with ovulation.

4. Male factors account for _____ percent of infertility.
   a. 14
   b. 28
   c. 31
   d. 50

5. Which of the following is NOT a cause of low sperm count and motility?
   a. childhood measles
   b. a varicocele
   c. smoking
   d. marijuana use

6. Ovulation may be adversely affected by
   a. poor nutrition.
   b. smoking.
   c. emotional stress.
   d. below normal levels of body fat.
   e. all of the above.

7. Problems with fallopian tubes are frequently caused by
   a. tubes that are too thin.
   b. tubes that are scarred from past STDs.
   c. being on birth control pills for many years.
   d. using an IUD.

8. Which of the following statements best reflects responses to infertility?
   a. Intercourse becomes more pleasurable because it on a schedule.
   b. Performance anxiety is typically lower.
   c. Partners often feel grief, anxiety, and depression.
   d. Couples feel a sense of connection with others discussing child rearing.

9. Artificial insemination involves introducing sperm into the
   a. vagina.
   b. cervix.
   c. uterus.
   d. all of the above.

10. Which technique involves placing a fertilized egg into a woman's fallopian tubes?
    a. IVF (in vitro fertilization)
    b. GIFT (gamete intrafallopian transfer)
    c. ZIFT (zygote intrafallopian transfer)
    d. ICSI (intra cytoplasmic sperm injection)

11. Success rates for assisted reproductive technologies are no higher than
    a. 28%.
    b. 33%.
    c. 51%.
    d. 64%.

12. Pregnancy tests are designed to detect _____ which is present in the blood or urine of pregnant women.
    a. estrogen
    b. progesterone
    c. lutenizing hormone
    d. human chorionic gonadotropin

13. Which of the following statements about spontaneous abortion (miscarriage) is <u>true</u>?
    a. Early miscarriages may appear as a heavier than normal menstrual period.
    b. One miscarriage increases the risk that subsequent pregnancies will be unsuccessful.
    c. Miscarriages are most commonly experienced during the second trimester.
    d. Miscarriages are seldom perceived as a loss.

14. Which of the following women is <u>most</u> likely to have an elective abortion?
    a. Sallie, a 39 year old married woman with two children
    b. Beth, a 27 year old affluent lawyer
    c. Shawn, an 18 year old single college student
    d. Barbara, a 30 year old Catholic living in a rural area

15. Most elective abortions are performed
    a. before 8 weeks.
    b. before 12 weeks.
    c. between 13-16 weeks.
    d. between 14-26 weeks.

16. A medical abortion using RU486 can be done
    a. before 7 weeks.
    b. between 6-9 weeks.
    c. any time prior to the 13th week.
    d. only on women who have already given birth to one child.

17. All of the following are methods of elective abortion except
    a. prostaglandin induction.
    b. suction curettage.
    c. dilation and evacuation.
    d. laminaria evacuation.

18. Which of the following women is most likely to engage in contraceptive risk taking leading to unwanted pregnancy?
    a. Tanika, who has a low degree of guilt about sex.
    b. Mai, who frequently gets drunk with her boyfriend before having intercourse.
    c. Marisol, who has a strong sense of self-esteem.
    d. Sarah, who does not care if her partner thinks she is "that kind of girl".

19. Which Supreme Court decision made abortion legal as long as it was done before the fetus was viable?
    a. Rust vs. Sullivan
    b. Planned Parenthood vs. Casey
    c. Roe vs. Wade
    d. Griswold vs. Connecticut

20. Studies of attitudes toward elective abortion have shown that those
    a. opposed to abortion are more likely to oppose government spending.
    b. opposed to abortion tend to have smaller families.
    c. who approve of abortion have larger families.
    d. who approve of abortion are more likely to be politically conservative.

21. Early pregnancy is characterized by all of the following except
    a. increased fatigue.
    b. decreased urination.
    c. increased breast size.
    d. nausea.

22. Fetal movements may first be noticed
    a. during the third month.
    b. during the last three months.
    c. at the sixth month.
    d. during the fourth or fifth month.

23. Research involving expectant fathers has shown that
    a. fathers' involvement during pregnancy does not predict positive interaction between fathers and newborns.
    b. few fathers feel frightened about the upcoming birth.
    c. few fathers fear loosing their wife's affection to the baby.
    d. fathers who shared their feelings with their partner had their relationships deepen.

24. In pregnancies with no risk factors sexual activity and orgasm can continue until
    a. Braxton-Hicks contractions begin.
    b. colostrum secretions are noted.
    c. as desired until the beginning of labor.
    d. until the start of the 3rd trimester.

25. When a sperm and egg are united the developing organism is called a(n)
    a. gamete.
    b. zygote.
    c. blastocyst.
    d. embryo.

26. The waxy, protective coating called *vernix caseosa* appears during the
    a. first trimester.
    b. fourth month of pregnancy.
    c. six month of pregnancy.
    d. third trimester.

27. Nutrients, oxygen, and waste products pass between the fetus and mother using the
    a. chorionic villus
    b. amniotic sac
    c. placenta
    d. intestinal transfuser

28. Infants of mothers who smoke are more likely to
    a. be born with cleft lip or palate
    b. have lower birth weight
    c. have lower developmental scores
    d. all of the above
    e. two of the above

29. Which of the following statements is false regarding pregnancy after age 35?
    a. One of every three women has her first baby after 35.
    b. Birth defects due to abnormal chromosomes are more common.
    c. A woman's ability to conceive may diminish.
    d. Women 35 and over feel less anxiety during pregnancy than women in their mid 20's.

30. Which is the correct sequence of events in childbirth?
    a. bloody show, expulsion of the afterbirth, infant descends into birth canal
    b. pushing, expulsion of the afterbirth, bloody show
    c. effacement, dilation, expulsion of the afterbirth, infant is born
    d. full dilation of the cervix, infant descends into birth canal, expulsion of the afterbirth

31. Which stage of labor is the longest?
    a. first
    b. second
    c. third
    d. delivering the placenta

32. The baby is born during the _____ stage of labor.
    a. first
    b. second
    c. third
    d. transition

33. Routine, normal births without complications do not include
    a. use of forceps.
    b. episiotomy.
    c. medications.
    d. two of the above.
    e. all of the above.

34. What do Lamaze and Dick-Read have in common?
    a. They are both medical doctors.
    b. They are both certified nurse-midwives.
    c. They developed methods of prepared childbirth.
    d. They were both advocates of water births.

35. The postpartum period
    a. is a time of intensified emotional highs and lows.
    b. lasts during the year following the baby's birth.
    c. is characterized by the routine presence of postpartum depression.
    d. is shorter for women who have had a cesarean birth.

36. Advantages of breast-feeding include all of the following except
    a. providing the infant with antibodies.
    b. speeding the return of the uterus to pregnant size.
    c. close physical contact with the baby.
    d. reduced levels of estrogen.

37. Which of the following is <u>true</u> regarding sexual interaction after pregnancy?
    a. Intercourse may begin when lochia appears.
    b. A majority of mothers continue to experience sexual problems as long as six months after birth.
    c. Decreased sexual interest is common in women only.
    d. Most women discussed sexual concerns with their health care provider.

Answer Key – Chapter 12

<u>Concept Checks</u>

Parenthood as an Option
1. companionship; intimacy
2. stressful; more
3. accomplishment; self-esteem

Becoming Pregnant
1. sixty
2. six
3. before
4. male
5. ovulate
6. postcoital
7. fallopian tubes
8. count; motility
9. marijuana; toxins; varicocele
10. intracytoplasmic sperm injection
11. emotional
12. dissatisfaction
13. artificial insemination; selective abortion
14. sperm; uterus
15. in vitro fertilization
16. zygote; gamete
17. low; multiple
18. breast; fatigue
19. human chorionic gonadotropin

Spontaneous and Elective Abortion
1. miscarriage
2. listening
3. elective
4. 25
5. as; conservative
6. Suction curettage
7. 13
8. five
9. dilation; evacuation
10. prostaglandins
11. seven
12. progesterone
13. misoprostol
14. Three
15. one
16. one
17. relief; distress

18. guilty
19. 58
20. 1973
21. oppose
22. prohibits
23. 65
24. approve; disapprove

The Experience of Pregnancy
1. wide
2. darker; little
3. Nausea; fatigue; well-being
4. fourth; fifth
5. contract
6. ambivalence
7. decline
8. positive
9. individual
10. sexual; orgasm

A Healthy Pregnancy
1. zygote; blastocyst
2. third
3. second
4. vernix
5. rest; exercise; childbirth
6. unmarried; 20
7. four
8. placenta; umbilical
9. oxygen
10. low; respiratory
11. fetal alcohol
12. nine
13. no
14. amniocentesis; chorionic villus sampling
15. increases

Childbirth
1. 40
2. Lamaze
3. fewer; shorter
4. effacement
5. contractions; ten
6. transition
7. second
8. third
9. lower; eliminate
10. episiotomy

11. more
12. cesarean; uterus
13. can
14. 21

Postpartum
1. 15
2. anxiety; hopelessness
3. colostrum
4. three
5. antibodies
6. uterine; ovulation
7. estrogen
8. positive
9. lochia
10. psychological

Crossword Puzzle

Across
2. placenta
3. amniotic
5. toxemia
7. relief
8. colostrum
9. multiple
11. female
12. first

Down
1. spontaneous
4. uterus
6. effacement
10. caffeine

Practice Test

1. a 2. b 3. c 4. d 5. a 6. e 7. b 8. c 9. d 10. c 11. a 12. d 13. a
14. c 15. b 16. a 17. d 18. b 19. c 20. a 21. b 22. d 23. d 24. c 25. b
26. d 27. c 28. d 29. a 30. d 31. a 32. b 33. d 34. c 35. a 36. d 37. b

Chapter 13 – Sexuality During Childhood and Adolescence

Introduction

The changing nature of our sexuality as we grow from infancy through adolescence is profiled in this chapter. The role of common experiences such as self-pleasuring and childhood sex play in shaping sexuality are explored. The often misunderstood experience of adolescence is demystified as the authors trace the psychosocial impact of puberty and the sexual double standard. Forms of sexual expression, their frequency and onset, developing sexual identity, and sexual risk-taking are frankly discussed. The phenomenon of adolescent pregnancy and its origins and consequences are discussed in a cross cultural perspective, and strategies for reducing teenage pregnancy are offered. Suggestions for helping parents provide good sex education for their children are outlined, and research examining the effectiveness of current school-based sex education programs is analyzed.

Learning Objectives. In order to derive maximum benefit from these objectives, use these as soon as you begin reading the chapter. After you have completed reading and studying this chapter, you should be able to do the things listed below with ease, using only your memory.

1. Discuss examples that demonstrate how infants of both sexes are born with the capacity for sexual pleasure and response.

2. Discuss common features of sexual development that occur during childhood and cite research that supports these various phases.

3. Define adolescence, and explain how childhood and adolescent sexuality in Western society compares to that of other cultures.

4. Define puberty and explain what happens during this period of development for males and females.

5. Describe the changes that occur in adolescent friendships during puberty.

6. Discuss the double standard as it affects adolescent social and sexual behavior, and make specific reference to what research suggests regarding the current status of the sexual double standard among adolescents.

7. Describe the incidence and frequency of masturbation among male and female adolescents.

8. Define petting and discuss how common it is among adolescent females and males.

9. Explain how likely ongoing sexual relationships are among adolescents.

10. Discuss why the term "premarital sex" may be misleading and then summarize what the research reveals regarding the following:
    a. incidence of intercourse among adolescents and reasons for engaging in this behavior
    b. percentage of men and women who abstain from adolescent intercourse
    c. the effect of AIDS education on teenage sexual behavior

11. Discuss how common same-sex contact may be during adolescence and explain how this may reflect a transitory, experimental phase of sexual development or how it may be indicative of a homosexual orientation.

12. Summarize available research and statistical data regarding various aspects of adolescent pregnancy, including strategies for how to reduce it.

13. Discuss how an adolescent mother's decision to keep her child may affect her education, financial status, and the life of her child.

14. Explain how prevalent contraceptive use is among adolescents and what factors affect contraceptive use on a regular basis.

15. Summarize the result of comparative studies of adolescent pregnancy and discuss factors that may contribute to the difference in pregnancy rates

16. Summarize the authors' list of four suggestions for reducing the teenage pregnancy rate.

17. Making reference to relevant research, describe some general guidelines that the authors suggest in talking to children about sex.

18. Discuss the nature of sex education programs in schools, and what the research says regarding the effects of sex education on behavior.

19. Discuss the benefits of raising children in an androgynous manner.

20. Describe differences in the onset of puberty and menarche between African-American and white girls.

21. Discuss American ethnic diversity in adolescent coitus among African-American, Hispanic and white adolescents.

22. Discuss normative sexual behavior in young children and maternal correlates of sexual behavior.

Concept Map

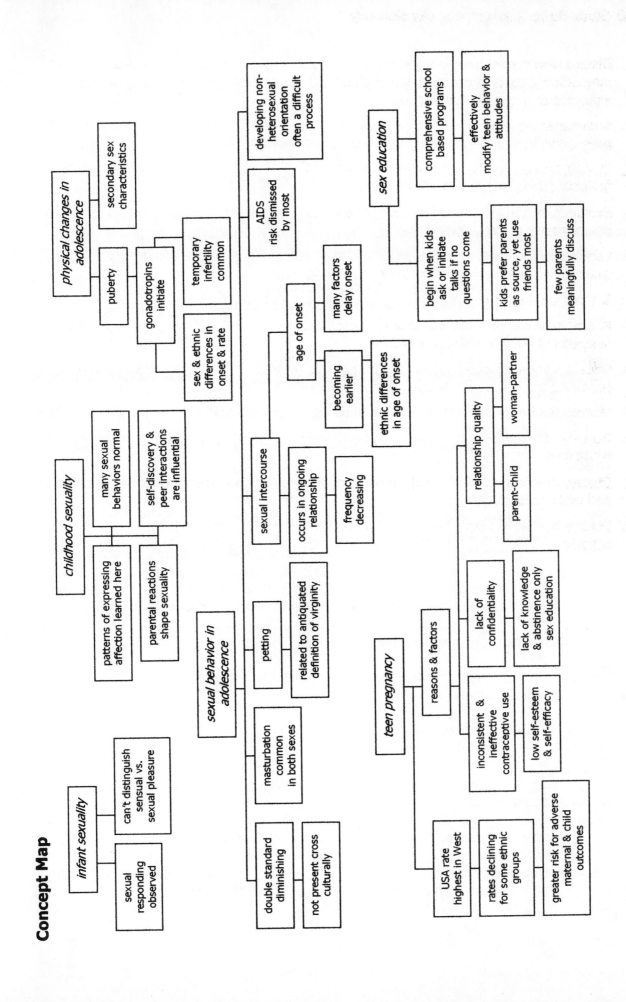

Key Terms. *Refer to the glossary or subject index in the back of your textbook for definitions and information.*

puberty   menarche
gonadotropins   petting
secondary sex characteristics   personal fable

Concept-Checks. *Complete this section by filling in each blank after you have studied the corresponding pages from the text. Answers are provided at the back of this chapter.*

Sexual Behavior During Infancy and Childhood, pp. 366-372
1. Infants have been observed to show signs of sexual response such as vaginal _____ penile _____, and _____.
2. Our comfort with giving and receiving _____ is probably related to childhood experiences, especially those with parents and others important to us.
3. A study of 49 societies found that societies with _____ levels of violence were those where children received little physical affection.
4. The rhythmic movements common to adult _____ usually do not occur until a child is two and a half or three years of age.
5. Several studies have shown that _____ of females and _____ of males have masturbated before adolescence.
6. Playing "doctor" and _____ were two of the most common forms of sexual behavior among children reported in Friedrich and colleagues' interview study of mothers.
7. Friedrich and colleagues also noted that as children grow older, they become more _____ about sexual expression.
8. Mothers with higher levels of _____ and a more "relaxed" attitude toward sexuality reported higher levels of sexual behavior in their children in the Friedrich study.
9. Parents and other caregivers can convey acceptance of self-pleasuring by refraining from acting _____ to the self-touch that is a typical and normal part of childhood development.
10. Numerous studies have revealed that a majority of children have engaged in some form of _____ play.
11. Sex play with children of the same sex is not necessarily indicative of a _____ or bisexual orientation in adulthood.

The Physical Changes of Adolescence, pp. 372-375
1. The period of rapid physical changes that occur during early adolescence is called _____.
2. The pituitary gland releases powerful hormones called _____ that promote activity in the ovaries and testes.
3. Facial hair, deepened voice, and breast development are considered _____ _____ characteristics, or outward signs of sexual maturity.
4. Early signs of puberty are _____ budding and growth of pubic hair.
5. The growth spurt typically occurs two years _____ in females than males.
6. Initial menstrual periods in teenage girls are irregular and often occur without _____.

7. Many girls begin menstruation at _____ or _____, though there is much variation that is considered normal.

8. One study has revealed that a sizable number of girls show some secondary sex characteristics before age _____, suggesting that the timing of sex education many need to be changed.

9. Although boys may experience orgasm prior to puberty, _____ is not possible until testosterone levels have risen.

10. Sperm initially appear in the ejaculate around age _____.

11. Facial and armpit hair typically occur _____ pubic hair has developed.

Sexual Behavior During Adolescence, pp. 375-385

1. Some newer research has shown that the sexual double standard may be _____.

2. Two proposed explanations for the sexual double standard are _____ _____ theory and _____ psychology.

3. The notion that women are penalized for behaving in sexually permissive ways and that men are rewarded for similar behavior is referred to as _____ _____ theory.

4. Evolutionary psychology asserts that because men are fertile year round, it is advantageous for them to have sex with _____ female(s) in order to increase the chances of having surviving offspring.

5. Research on the sexual double standard is still inconclusive, as one study showed that men and women viewed partners with _____ levels of sexual experience as undesirable partners, whereas other studies showed that respondents believed it was more acceptable for a _____ to have more sexual partners.

6. The sexual double standard encourages sexual conquest for _____, and those who do not conform to the standard may be called derogatory names.

7. Young women are taught that it is necessary to look sexy to attract males, yet these women often experience _____ about engaging in seductive behavior.

8. Of the two sexes _____ tend to masturbate less frequently than _____.

9. In addition to relieving sexual tension, masturbation provides a way to learn about one's _____ and one's preferences.

10. Noncoital forms of sexual sharing such as kissing, manual, or oral-genital stimulation are sometimes referred to as _____.

11. The frequency of oral-genital sex among teenagers has _____ substantially in recent years, with _____ being more commonly reported than _____.

12. The authors take issue with our culture's narrow definition of _____, as teens of differing sexual orientations experience many forms of sexual intimacy without engaging in coitus.

13. Today's adolescents are _____ likely to experience partnered sex within the context of a continuing relationship than teens in Alfred Kinsey's era.

14. The authors point out that the term "premarital sex" may be a misnomer, as studies have revealed that couples engage in a wide range of sexual activity, sometimes leading to orgasm, without experiencing _____.

15. A recent study by the Centers for Disease Control shows that the overall proportion of teens who have had sexual intercourse _____ somewhat from 1991 to 1999.

16. The age of first coitus seems to be _____ in both sexes, a finding that occurs among a variety of ethnic groups.

17. Several recent studies show that _____ American teens are more likely have had sexual intercourse than other ethnic groups.

18. The finding described above is most likely related to economic status rather than ethnicity alone, because teens from less affluent segments of society are _____ likely to engage in sexual activity than teens from more affluent classes.

19. Curiosity and affection for their partner were the most frequently cited reasons by _____ for having first intercourse, whereas for _____ the reasons were reversed.

20. A handful of new studies suggest that strong religious beliefs , regular religious attendance, and _____ _____ with friends may delay the experience of first coitus for teens.

21. Other studies point to the role of _____ grades, _____ quality parent-child relationships and communication as factors that delay coitus.

22. Since one-fifth of AIDS cases occurs between 20-29 year olds, it is assumed that these persons were infected when they were _____, since AIDS has a ten year incubation period.

23. Most teenagers know the basic facts about AIDS, yet many do not believe they are _____ _____ for AIDS, therefore they fail to change their behavior to avoid infection.

24. The concept of the _____ fable has been used to help understand why many teens feel they will not suffer the consequences of high-risk sexual behavior.

25. Many teens taking oral contraceptives who are at risk for HIV do not use _____ or spermicide regularly to protect against STD's because they believe being protected against unwanted pregnancy is enough.

26. For many gay, lesbian, bisexual, or questioning teens, coming to terms with their sexuality can be a _____ and sometimes painful process.

27. Studies have revealed that gay, lesbian or bisexual teens are subjected to higher rates of physical and verbal _____ than their heterosexual peers, and are often emotionally or physically abandoned by their _____.

28. In an effort to create a more positive and welcoming atmosphere for non-heterosexual students, many _____ _____ alliances (GSAs) have emerged on high school campuses.

Adolescent Pregnancy, pp.385-390

1. The _____ _____ has the highest rate of teen pregnancy in the Western world.

2. Teenage pregnancy rates have _____ since 1991.

3. More effective _____ use, rather than increases in abstinence, is the primary reason for the trend noted above.

4. The trend noted in number 2 above was not found among _____ Americans.

5. The adolescent pregnancy rate in the United States is four times higher than many Western European nations, even though rates of sexual activity are _____.

6. Prenatal and infant mortality rates among adolescent women are _____ than among older pregnant women.

7. The children of teenage mothers and fathers are at _____ risk of having physical , emotional, and cognitive problems, and deficits in school performance than children of adult mothers and fathers.

8. A _____ of teenagers do not use consistently or effectively use contraceptives, even though they are readily available.

9. Lack of knowledge about contraception and the prevalence of _____ -_____ sex education program in schools combine to make effective and consistent use of contraception unlikely among teenagers.

10. Additional factors that also help explain nonuse of birth control among teens include having _____ religious beliefs, being under age _____, having a partner more than three years older, experiencing coitus at a(n) _____ age, and having infrequent coitus.

11. Adolescents who are more likely to use birth control correctly and consistently are those in stable, long-term relationships with good communication patterns; those having _____ who discussed contraception; those having a strong sense of _____ - _____ , the belief that one can competently perform an action; and being knowledgeable about birth control.

12. In countries with comparable rates of sexual activity among teens, but lower teen birth rates than the United States, sexuality is viewed as _____ and healthy, in contrast to prevailing views in the U.S.

Sex Education, pp. 390-394

1. Research has shown that most children begin asking, "Where do babies come from" around age _____.

2. The authors suggest that caregivers and parents avoid _____ a child who may often expect a short, straightforward answer.

3. When children want to know more, they will typically _____, provided that a caregiver has been responsive to their questions.

4. The authors maintain that there is _____ evidence to support the notion that children will rush out to experiment if parents admit that sex is enjoyable.

5. If children do not ask questions about sexuality, the authors suggest that parents initiate _____.

6. The authors' experience with their students suggest that _____ women students knew little about menstruation before their period began; likewise _____ men knew about the likelihood of ejaculation from masturbation or a nocturnal orgasm.

7. Studies show that most children and teens prefer that _____ be the primary source of sexuality information.

8. Studies also show that less than _____ percent of parents have participated in meaningful conversation about sexuality with their children.

9. Among parents _____ are more likely to take an active role in providing sexuality education to their children.

10. Many studies have revealed that _____ are the main resource for information about sexuality.

11. The overwhelming majority of studies show that teenagers who have had frequent, positive, and open discussions about sexuality with their parents engage in _____ frequent sexual activity, and they do so at a _____ date.

12. Even though studies show that most parents want school-based sexuality education for their children, _____ schools provide comprehensive sex-education courses.

13. Comprehensive, high-quality studies of abstinence-only sex education programs have provided _____ evidence that such programs delay the onset of sexual activity and intercourse.

Crossword

Across
4. partner in most teen same-sex sexual contact
5. a critical ratio of body fat is need to trigger this
6. deprivation of _____ comfort impairs formation of intimate relationships
7. the only country that surpasses USA teen pregnancy rate
8. misleading type of sex that excludes noncoital and homosexual experiences
9. this didn't "kill the cat"; instead it's a common reason for adolescent coitus
10. girls are often taller than boys during this period

Down
1. boys most likely self-pleasuring teacher
2. this fable, not Aesop's, promotes risk taking in adolescence
3. form of sexual expression that creates "technical" virgins
4. increases the probability of adolescent coitus more than ethnicity
6. type of sex education that reduces teen pregnancy

Practice Test

This test will work best to guide your learning if you take it as part of a final review session before an exam.

1. Which of the following statements best reflects current understanding about infant sexuality?
   a. Vaginal lubrication, penile erection, and masturbation have been observed.
   b. Infant males have displayed erections, but infant girls have yet to develop the capacity for vaginal lubrication.
   c. Infant females have shown vaginal lubrication and what appears to be orgasm, but infant boys do not develop erectile function until puberty
   d. Sexuality remains latent until puberty, as Freud theorized

2. During childhood
   a. self-pleasuring is primarily observed in sexually abused children.
   b. ethnicity strongly predicts the types of sexual behaviors observed in children.
   c. responses to the child's expressions of affection help shape the way sexuality is expressed later in life.
   d. most girls learn about masturbation from childhood friends.

3. Masturbation is practiced more frequently by _____ children than _____ children.
   a. African-American male; White male
   b. Hispanic-American male; African-American male
   c. female; male
   d. male; female

4. According to the authors, which of the following is the best response for a parent to give to their child who was discovered masturbating?
   a. "Stop doing that"!
   b. Ignore the behavior, in order to discourage excess masturbation in the future.
   c. "I bet that feels good".
   d. Cast a stern look at the child and announce that you're taking away a privilege.

5. Friedrich and colleagues' interview study of mothers identified _____ as behaviors that occurred most frequently among children.
   a. talking about sex acts, self-stimulation, exhibitionism
   b. touches breasts, self-stimulation, exhibitionism
   c. self-stimulation, touches others' sex parts, tries to have coitus
   d. exhibitionism, self-stimulation, rubbing against another person

6. Which statement most accurately summarizes research on childhood sex play?
   a. The majority of children experience sex play, and same-sex play in and of itself is not necessarily indicative of a homosexual orientation.
   b. The majority of children experience sex play, and same-sex play is associated with a homosexual orientation in adulthood.
   c. The majority of children do <u>not</u> experience sex play, and same-sex play in and of itself is not necessarily indicative of a homosexual orientation.
   d. The majority of children do <u>not</u> experience sex play, and same-sex play is associated with a homosexual orientation in adulthood.

7. Which of the following best represents a secondary sex characteristic?
   a. external genitalia
   b. gonads
   c. underarm hair
   d. increase in height

8. A growing body of research data suggests that menarche is triggered by
   a. secretion of prostaglandins.
   b. the presence of a minimum percentage of body fat.
   c. reaching a threshold of breast development.
   d. a decline in the excretion of growth hormone from the pituitary gland.

9. The seminal vesicles and prostate gland must function with sufficient testosterone before _____ can occur.
   a. orgasm
   b. erection
   c. ejaculation
   d. epididymal aptosis

10. Which statement below best illustrates the effect of the sexual double standard on adolescents?
    a. Steve brags to his male friends about the kind of sex he and his girlfriend have; Emily tells her friends little about sex with Steve, fearing they'll think she's a slut.
    b. Jose is proud of being a virgin and doesn't care what his friends think about it; Lora is determined to have intercourse so she'll feel like a real woman.
    c. Carmen wishes that her boyfriend would wear the earring she bought for him; Dave is worried that his classmates will think he's a sissy since he seldom dates.
    d. Sierra feels proud of her body and enjoys wearing sexy clothes; Kyle loves to "catch" a girl and then drop her as soon as she falls for him.

11. Current research shows that the sexual double standard
    a. shows no signs of eroding.
    b. has decreased, especially among men.
    c. has decreased, especially among women.
    d. decreased during the early 90's, and is beginning to increase.

12. Which society openly encourages children to masturbate and have homosexual contacts during childhood?
    a. The Truk
    b. The Ashanti
    c. The Kwoma
    d. The Marquesans

13. Petting is an important form of sexual expression among teenagers for all of the following reasons except
    a. Petting is less emotionally involving than other forms of sexual expression.
    b. A set of sexual behaviors can be learned that do not carry the risk of pregnancy.
    c. Within the boundaries of an intimate relationship, teens can learn about their own sexual responses.
    d. Sexual intimacy may be experienced while technically remaining a virgin.

14. Teenagers are most likely to be sexually intimate with
    a. casual acquaintances.
    b. someone for whom they feel affection.
    c. a somewhat older adult.
    d. strangers that have been met for the first time.

15. Recent studies have revealed that the age of first adolescent coitus
    a. is occurring earlier.
    b. was at its lowest in the 70's.
    c. has begun to rise.
    d. is dropping, but only for Hispanic Americans.

16. Ethnic differences in the age of first intercourse are best explained by
    a. differences between rural and urban youth.
    b. economic status.
    c. religious beliefs among ethnic groups.
    d. differing sexual mores among ethnic groups.

17. According to the National Health and Social Life Survey the most common reason reported for first intercourse was
    a. "It was my wedding night" – reported by women
    b. curiosity/readiness for sex – reported by men
    c. affection for partner – reported by men
    d. curiosity/readiness for sex – reported by women

18. Who is most likely to delay the onset of adolescent intercourse?
    a. Tyrone, who gets good grades in school
    b. Shoshanna, whose friends share the same spiritual beliefs
    c. Trinh, who feels she can talk openly with her parents
    d. two of the above are true
    e. all of the above are true

19. Which of the following decreases a teenager's risk for contracting HIV infection?
    a. the personal fable
    b. using alcohol or other drugs
    c. delaying first intercourse until after age 15
    d. believing that condoms are a hassle because you or your partner uses birth control pills

20. All of the following are reasons why sexual contact with a member of the same sex during adolescence does not reflect sexual orientation later in life except
    a. Many heterosexual persons have had early homosexual experiences.
    b. Same sex contact may be experimental.
    c. Same sex contact with peers does not predict adult sexual orientation, but same sex contact with adults does.
    d. Persons with a homosexual orientation may not act on those feelings until they are adults.

21. Which country has the highest rate of teenage pregnancy?
    a. the Netherlands
    b. Sweden
    c. England
    d. the United States

22. Teen birth rates have begun to decline for all ethnic groups except
    a. Hispanic Americans.
    b. African Americans.
    c. White Americans.
    d. Native Americans.

23. Of the one million teenage pregnancies in the United States each year, how many result in a live birth?
    a. 17 percent
    b. 50 percent
    c. 66 percent
    d. 73 percent

24. Which of the following is true regarding the consequences of teenage pregnancy?
    a. Teenage mothers have a lower prenatal mortality rate than older women.
    b. Pregnant teenagers may be legally prevented from attending public school.
    c. Teenage mothers provide parenting that is of lower quality than adult mothers.
    d. Children of teenage mothers are no more likely than other children to have problems with school performance.

25. Of the persons below, who is most likely to correctly and consistently use contraception?
    a. Adam, who had first intercourse at age 12
    b. Alex, who has frequently talked with his mother about birth control
    c. Brianna, whose boyfriend is six years older than her
    d. Betse, who has intercourse infrequently

26. Research has revealed that _____ adolescents use effective contraception consistently after they have been sexually active for a long period of time.
    a. a minority of
    b. two-thirds of
    c. 71% of
    d. most female

27. The authors suggest all of the following to reduce adolescent pregnancy except
    a. establishing compulsory sex education at all grade levels.
    b. stressing that males must share responsibility for birth control as well as females.
    c. implementing abstinence-only sex education programs on a wider basis.
    d. removing restrictions on advertising nonprescription contraceptives.

28. One strategy the authors suggest for providing sex education with one's own children is
    a. Wait to have "the talk" until puberty is imminent.
    b. Integrate information about sex into everyday conversations, where appropriate.
    c. Avoid expressing the idea that sex is pleasurable.
    d. Be sure to provide detailed responses every chance you get, even though the child may not want a thorough reply

29. Numerous research studies have demonstrated that comprehensive sex education programs
    a. increase the frequency of sexual intercourse.
    b. lead teens to have intercourse at an earlier age.
    c. increase the number of a teen's sexual partners.
    d. none of the above are true.
    e. all of the above are true.

30. Studies have revealed that teenagers get most of their sexuality information from _____ yet they would prefer to get such information from _____.
    a. television; friends
    b. friends; parents
    c. parents; friends
    d. friends; magazines

Answer Key -- Chapter 13

Concept Checks

Sexual Behavior During Infancy and Childhood
1. lubrication; erection; orgasm
2. affection
3. high
4. masturbation
5. one-third; two-thirds
6. self-stimulation
7. private
8. education
9. negatively
10. sex
11. homosexual

The Physical Changes of Adolescence
1. puberty
2. gonadotropins
3. secondary sex
4. breast
5. earlier
6. ovulation
7. twelve; thirteen
8. eight
9. ejaculation
10. 14
11. after

Sexual Behavior During Adolescence
1. diminishing
2. social learning; evolutionary
3. social learning
4. multiple
5. high; man
6. males
7. ambivalence
8. women; men
9. body
10. petting
11. risen; cunnilingus; fellatio
12. virginity
13. more
14. coitus
15. decreased
16. earlier
17. African

18. more
19. men; women
20. spiritual interconnectedness
21. good; high
22. teenagers
23. at risk
24. personal
25. condoms
26. difficult
27. assault; families
28. gay straight

Adolescent Pregnancy
1. United States
2. declined
3. contraceptive
4. Hispanic
5. similar
6. higher
7. greater
8. majority
9. abstinence-only
10. conservative; 17; early
11. parents; self efficacy
12. natural

Sex Education
1. four
2. overloading
3. ask
4. little
5. conversations
6. most; few
7. parents
8. 20
9. mothers
10. friends
11. less; later
12. few
13. no

Crossword Puzzle

Across
4. peer
5. menarche
6. contact

7. Russia
8. premarital
9. curiosity
10. puberty

Down
1. friends
2. personal
3. petting
4. poverty
6. comprehensive

Practice Test

1. a 2. c 3. d 4. c 5. d 6. a 7. c 8. b 9. c 10. a 11. c 12. d
13. a 14. b 15. a 16. b 17. b 18. e 19. c 20. c 21. d 22. a 23. b
24. c 25. b 26. a 27. c 28.

Introduction

Adulthood brings the possibility of experiencing several different lifestyles. The variations of intimate and sexual relationships within single living, cohabitation, marriage, extramarital relationships, divorce, and older adulthood are examined. The psychological adjustments that typically occur in these lifestyles and developmental transitions are also explored.

Learning Objectives. *In order to derive maximum benefit from these objectives, use these as soon as you begin reading the chapter. After you have completed reading and studying this chapter, you should be able to do the things listed below with ease, using only your memory.*

1. Discuss single living, making specific reference to the following:
   a. what factors account for the increasing number of single people and what forms being single takes
   b. sexual activity among single people as opposed to married people

2. Discuss cohabitation, making specific reference to the following:
   a. social attitudes toward it over time
   b. how prevalent it is in our society
   c. advantages and disadvantages of cohabitation
   d. how cohabitation may affect a subsequent marital relationship
   e. domestic partners

3. Discuss the institution of marriage, making specific reference to the following:
   a. statistically how common it is and what marital trends indicate
   b. the functions it serves
   c. the various forms it takes
   d. changing expectations and marital patterns
   e. factors that contribute to marital satisfaction as well as factors that are indicative of marital discord
   f. sexual behavior patterns within marriage

4. Describe consensual and nonconsensual extramarital relationships, noting the motivations for, the prevalence and the effects of.

5. Discuss divorce, making specific reference to the following:
   a. what divorce statistics reveal
   b. factors that account for high and low divorce rates
   c. how covenant marriage is attempting to lower divorce rates
   d. adjustments a person must make as the result of a divorce
   e. sexual behavior of divorced people

6. Discuss some of the reasons why aging in our society is associated with sexlessness.

7. Explain how the double standard relates to male and female sexual expression throughout the aging process.

8. Discuss three factors that affect sexual activity in later years.

9. Describe the nature of sexual expression and relationships in the later years for both heterosexual and homosexual individuals.

10. Explain why people tend to become more androgynous when they age and how that may be expressed.

11. Discuss widowhood, making specific reference to the following:
    a. Describe how the ratio of widows to widowers has changed since the turn of the century.
    b. Compare and contrast the adjustments of widowhood to those of divorce.

12. Discuss how attitudes toward extramarital sex vary cross-culturally.

13. Distinguish between miscegenation and interracial marriage. Discuss how incidence of interracial marriage has changed over time and how this may affect census categories.

14. Discuss some of the controversial issues related to extramarital affairs in cyberspace.

Concept Map

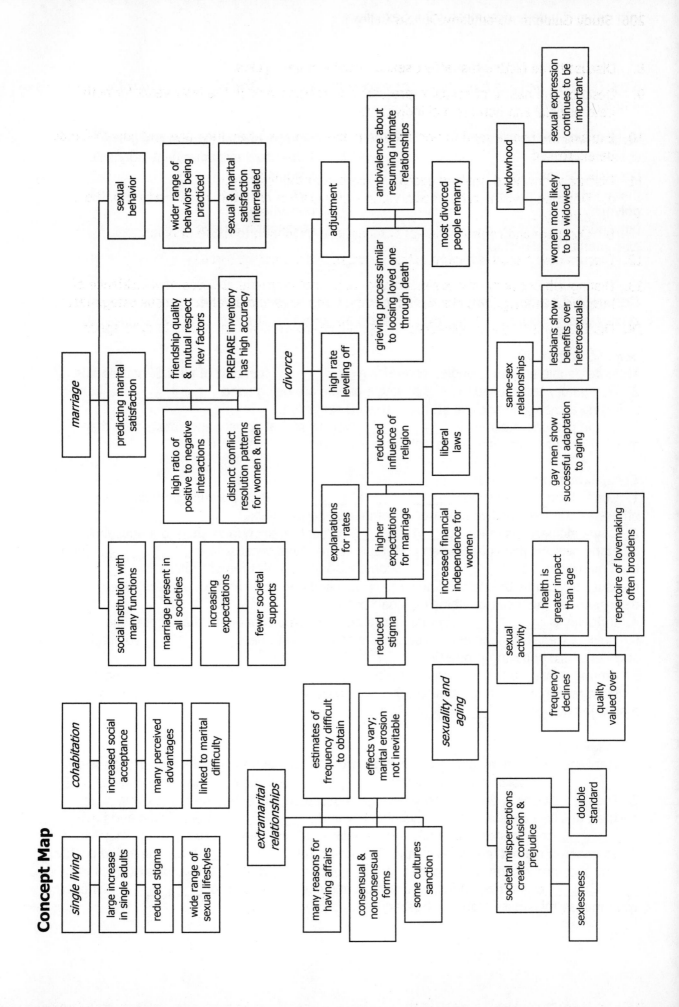

Key Terms. *Refer to the glossary or subject index in the back of your textbook for definitions and information.*

serial monogamy
cohabitation
domestic partnership
miscegenation
polygyny
polyandry
extramarital relationship

nonconsensual extramarital sex
consensual extramarital relationships
swinging
open marriage
polyamory
covenant marriage

Concept-Checks. *Complete this section by filling in each blank after you have studied the corresponding pages from the text. Answers are provided at the back of this chapter.*

Single Living, p. 398
1. More people are living single, comprising _____ percent of all U.S. households.
2. Derogatory terms used to refer to single people are being used _____ frequently, reflecting a change in societal attitudes toward single life.
3. Single persons experience _____ levels of sexual activity and satisfaction than married persons, according to recent research studies.

Cohabitation, pp. 399-400
1. Cohabitation is also called _____ _____, incorporating both same-sex and other-sex couples who live together in committed partnerships.
2. Domestic partners made up _____ percent of all couples sharing a household.
3. Many persons find cohabitation preferable to marriage because it is _____ informal than marriage; there is _____ stigma associated with breakup; there is _____ pressure to assume the demanding roles of husband and wife; and couples are together out of desire, not as the result of a binding legal contract.
4. Infidelity is _____ common among those who cohabitate than those who marry.
5. Unlike Swedish cohabitators, Americans who cohabitate have _____ vulnerabilities, such as difficulty buying property.
6. Among newly married persons, more than _____ lived together before marriage.
7. Most research has shown that couples who cohabitate have _____ difficulty in their marriage and _____ risk of divorce.

Marriage, pp. 400-407
1. Marriage serves many purposes, such as providing stable family units, imparting social _____, establishing an economic _____, and defining inheritance rights.
2. Feeling that one is prepared for marriage is based on more than finding a compatible partner, because people who are educationally and _____ accomplished and have _____ from friends and family are more likely to feel they are ready to get married.
3. In general, married people are typically happier and _____ than unmarried people.
4. The Western version of marriage is not practiced worldwide, as some cultures encourage _____, or marriage between one man and several women; or _____, where a woman may take more than one husband.

5. The cultural institution of marriage is undergoing change in the United States, as there is a wide _____ between actual marriage practices and our ideals of marriage.

6. People's expectations of marriage are _____ while society's support for marriage is _____.

7. Contemporary couples typically expect that marriage will guarantee _____ and tend to marry for _____, unlike marriage in earlier times.

8. Extended families and small communities have become _____ prevalent, thereby eroding societal support for marriage, placing more stress on marriage to meet human needs.

9. Interracial marriage is still not widely accepted, as communities of color often chastise those who marry whites, calling them "_____-_____" or "whitewashed".

10. Survey studies have shown that _____ percent of white Americans do not approve of black-white marriages.

11. Research by Gottman and his associates has demonstrated that a ratio of _____ positive interactions to one negative interaction was found among couples with longer, happier marriages.

12. Other factors that predict whether couples will divorce include facial expressions of disgust; _____ heart rate levels; defensiveness; verbal expression of _____ by wives; and _____ by husbands.

13. In order to have a long and happy marriage, maintaining the proper ratio of positive to negative interactions is more important than having a particular _____ of marriage, or how much a couple fights.

14. Gottman identified three styles of marriage, these being volatile, _____, and _____ _____.

15. Newlyweds who create happy and stable marriages are those where _____ begin discussions about marital problems in a calm, diplomatic manner and where _____ accept their partner's influence.

16. One study has shown that a premarital inventory called _____ predicted with 80% accuracy which couples would divorce after three years.

17. Couples who choose to participate in premarital counseling have _____ risk factors for marital difficulty than couples who avoid premarital counseling.

18. A very recent study of married couples found that _____ in initiating sexual interaction and _____ of sexual interaction increased marital and sexual satisfaction.

19. Women are most likely to regularly experience orgasm when they are _____, according to a recent study.

20. Other research shows that the quality of _____ with their spouse was an important part of marital satisfaction, and that happiness occurred when couples liked and _____ one another.

Extramarital Relationships, pp.407-412

1. Terms such as "cheating", "adultery" and "infidelity" refer to _____ extramarital sex.

2. The National Health and Social Life Survey identified several characteristics that increased the probability of having extramarital sex: being under 30; having more _____ sexual attitudes; higher interest in _____; living in a large city; having _____ ties to the spouse's family and interests; and not being involved in a religious community.

3. This same survey has yielded the most reliable estimates of extramarital affairs, where _____ percent of husbands and _____ percent of wives having had an affair at some point during their marriage.

4. Emotions commonly experienced by the betrayed spouse include feelings of inadequacy, intense _____, resentment, shame and _____.
5. Among those participating in extramarital affairs, loss of self-respect, severe _____, stress, damage to _____ , loss of love, and the complications of STDs are frequent consequences.
6. _____ refers to a form of consensual extramarital sex, with the husband and wife participating at the same time, and in the same location.
7. Multiple loving, consensual relationships are now referred to as _____, or open marriage.
8. Those practicing polyamory see themselves as different than swingers, because polyamorists stress _____ commitment as the basis for extramarital relationships.
9. Save a handful of exceptions, _____ across cultures are given more permission for extramarital partners than _____.
10. Cultures with more permissive attitudes toward extramarital relationships include the _____ of Australia's west Arnhem land; the Polynesian _____; and the _____ of central Tanzania.
11. "Honor killings" where women are murdered for real or perceived adultery are often reported as _____ or accidental death.

Divorce, pp. 412-416
1. Current estimates reveal that _____ of all marriages end in divorce.
2. The recent tapering off of the divorce rate is believed to be due to an increased in the number of _____ couples.
3. Nearly _____ percent of adults marry at some point in their lifetime.
4. Divorce statistics do not present a complete picture of the status of marriage in our culture, as a significant percentage of divorces involves people who have had more than one _____ or _____.
5. Louisiana and a handful of other states have offered the choice of _____ marriage, where a couple receives premarital counseling and additional counseling if problems arise later in the marriage.
6. Reasons for the rising divorce rate include the liberalization of divorce laws, reduced social _____, increased _____ for marriage and sexual fulfillment, and a reduced influence of organized _____.
7. Research has revealed a correlation between age and divorce, with _____ couples being more likely to divorce.
8. Couples with _____education are also less likely to divorce.
9. Many divorced people experience a loss and grieving process that is _____ to when a loved one dies.
10. People who are newly divorced often experience _____ about establishing intimate or sexual relationships.
11. Most divorced persons eventually remarry, yet second marriages are _____ likely to end in divorce.

Sexuality and Aging, pp. 416-424
1. Our society believes aging goes hand-in-hand with sexlessness because sexuality is associated with _____, and because American society emphasizes _____.
2. Perceiving an older woman as someone who has "let herself go" whereas an older man is viewed as 'distinguished" reflects the _____ standard of aging.

3. Feelings of well-being are related to sexual performance for _____, while feeling attractive to the other sex is more important for _____.

4. Studies reveal that about _____ of women and men over 60 are sexually active.

5. A close correlation has been found between levels of sexual activity in _____ and sexual activity in the older adult years.

6. In order to maintain sexual activity in older adulthood, it is important to keep good health and to maintain _____ sexual expression.

7. Studies have shown that _____ elderly people approved of masturbation than actually engaged in it.

8. Our sexuality changes as we age, as genital sex with a partner becomes less frequent, whereas noncoital activities such as kissing and caressing may _____.

9. Nearly half of older women and _____ percent of older men gave oral stimulation to their partners.

10. Both Kinsey's study and a more recent study show that _____ socioeconomic classes were more likely to cease being sexually active when intercourse was not feasible.

11. In general, older adult sexual relationships seem to emphasize _____ over _____.

12. In some respects gay men and lesbians may be _____ prepared than heterosexuals for coping with the financial, relationship adjustments, and losses that come with aging.

13. Studies have revealed that older gay men _____ or _____ similar groups in the general population on measures of life satisfaction.

14. Older lesbians are _____ likely to be left alone through death of a partner than heterosexual women, and lesbians have a _____ pool of potentially eligible partners from which to choose.

15. In a biological sense the sexes become more androgynous as they age, because _____ differences tend to diminish.

16. Psychosocial gender differences blur with aging, as one study has shown that _____ are more likely to have increased power in a relationship as it reaches it later stages.

17. In older men _____ and fantasy become more important than orgasm in sexual behavior; for women an _____ interest in genital sex is often experienced.

18. In most other-sex couples it is the _____ who dies first, a trend that has become stronger over the last 100 years.

19. For older adults who live in _____ homes, the circumstances that allow for sexual expression are often restricted.

20. Widowed persons face a different adjustment process than divorced persons, as widowed persons typically do not have the sense of having _____ at marriage, and _____ may be more intense.

Crossword

Across
2. anthropologist Fisher's itch that predicts divorce
5. primary socialization partner reported by older adult gay males
8. emotion commonly experienced by the "cheating" spouse
9. NHSLS predictor of extramarital relationships
10. the double standard means older males prefer this type of mate
11. found in satisfying and longer lasting marriages
Down
1. accepting this from a wife promotes a happy marriage
3. gender-blending style that may develop in old age
4. aging is associated with being this, much to older adults' dismay
6. one woman with many husbands
7. stronger influence on older adult sexuality than age
12. comarital sex

Practice Test

This test will work best to guide your learning if you take it as part of a final review session before an exam.

1. Which of the following statements is <u>true</u> regarding single living?
   a. The number of adults who choose not to marry at all has remained relatively the same since 1970.
   b. Single people have higher levels of sexual activity than married persons.
   c. Larger numbers of couples living together outside of marriage has helped increase the number of single adults.
   d. Choosing to be celibate is the most common reason reported for living single.

2. Given research on cohabitation, what will most likely happen to Susheela and Raj, who have been living together for the past 14 months?
   a. If they marry, they have a lower risk of divorce than couples who did not cohabitate.
   b. If they marry, they have the same risk of divorce as couples who did not cohabitate.
   c. If they marry, they have a greater risk of divorce than couples who did not cohabitate.
   d. Research has shown there is no relationship between cohabitation and divorce, so nothing about this couple can be predicted.

3. People choose to cohabitate for all of the following reasons <u>except</u>
   a. They do not wish to feel the pressure of assuming marital roles.
   b. They wish to reduce the chance that their partner will engage in infidelity.
   c. They do not wish to have the binding legal contract associated with marriage.
   d. They wish to avoid the stigma associated with divorce.

4. Marriage has served all of the following functions <u>except</u>
   a. defining inheritance rights.
   b. providing a structured economic partnership.
   c. regulating sexual behavior.
   d. providing a place to ensure happiness.

5. Gottman and colleague's study of marital interaction patterns demonstrated that all of the following predict marital discord with the exception of
   a. high levels of heart rate
   b. defensive behaviors
   c. stonewalling
   d. husbands' verbal expressions of contempt

6. A ratio of _____ positive to _____ negative interaction(s) was found in couples with satisfying marriages.
   a. 5:1
   b. 3:2
   c. 4:1
   d. 6:2

7. Studies with the PREPARE premarital inventory show _____ percent accuracy in predicting which couples would divorce.
   a. 55
   b. 62
   c. 80
   d. 90

8. Compared with Kinsey's study, newer studies of sexual activity during marriage show
   a. a wider array of sexual activities among couples.
   b. couples spending more time having coitus.
   c. a reduction in cunnilingus.
   d. more frequent masturbation.

9. Recent studies by Gottman and Wallerstein & Blakeslee identified _____ as important influences on marital satisfaction.
   a. low frequency of arguments and expression of anger
   b. quality of friendship and respect
   c. the validating and conflict-avoiding marital styles
   d. a predictable routine and feelings of security

10. According to a recent study using the NHSLS sample, those most likely to engage in extramarital sex are people who
    a. are over 50.
    b. have a desire for revenge.
    c. have more permissive sexual attitudes.
    d. are more thrilled by secrecy than others.

11. Which statement regarding extramarital affairs in cyberspace is true?
    a. If the online lover is never met in person, no harm is done to the relationship.
    b. If sex with the online lover never occurs, many therapists believe there is no infidelity.
    c. A person is considered faithful if they have only engaged in masturbation while communicating with the on-line lover.
    d. Extramarital affairs in cyberspace have similar consequences for a relationship as traditional infidelity.

12. What can be concluded about the effect of extramarital sex on marriage?
    a. Discovering infidelity can prompt a couple to solve problems that improve the marriage.
    b. Infidelity inevitably leads to divorce.
    c. If the participating partner feels guilty, there is hope of saving the marriage.
    d. The betrayed spouse should suppress feelings of jealousy and anger in order for counseling to be effective.

13. Which cultural group has the least restrictive norms regarding extramarital sexuality?
    a. Jordanians
    b. The Truk
    c. aborigines of Australia's Arnhem Land
    d. the Irish of Ines Beag

14. Of the persons described below, who is <u>most</u> likely to divorce?
    a. Rick, who gets married at age 32.
    b. Kristina, who gets married at age 19.
    c. Thich, who has a bachelor's degree.
    d. Letitica, who has a bachelor's degree.

15. Which of the following was <u>not</u> mentioned as a possible explanation for high divorce rates?
    a. liberalization of divorce laws
    b. increased economic independence of women
    c. the demise of covenant marriage
    d. changing expectations for marital fulfillment

16. All of the following are reactions commonly experienced by people adjusting to divorce <u>except</u>
    a. shock.
    b. loneliness.
    c. unwavering interest in establishing intimacy or sexual relationships.
    d. a sense of relief and acceptance several months to a year later.

17. An older woman's sense of well being is most strongly influenced by
    a. her sexual performance.
    b. feeling she is attractive to the other sex.
    c. the type of hormone replacement therapy she receives.
    d. frequency of sexual activity.

18. Who is most likely to maintain sexual activity in their later years?
    a. Susan, who had frequent sexual activity during early adulthood and middle age.
    b. Stan, who belongs to an organized religion.
    c. Nina, who seldom masturbated in earlier adulthood.
    d. Nestor, who has diabetes and heart disease.

19. Which of the following is <u>true</u> regarding sexual expression in older adulthood?
    a. Older women masturbate as frequently as older men.
    b. Men do not experience an age-related decline in frequency of masturbation.
    c. Lower income adults are somewhat more likely to explore noncoital forms of lovemaking.
    d. Greater opportunities often exist for relaxed and prolonged lovemaking.

20. Older lesbians may have which of the following advantages over heterosexual women?
    a. Lesbians experience fewer of the physical effects of aging.
    b. She is less likely to be living without her life partner than a heterosexual woman.
    c. If her life partner dies, a lesbian has numerous cultural rituals and supports to assist with the grieving process.
    d. The stigma associated with a non-heterosexual orientation declines with age.

21. A man who becomes more androgynous in his later years is likely to experience
    a. greater emotional expression and interest in non-genital forms of sex.
    b. greater declines in sexual performance than non-androgynous males.
    c. a somewhat more fragmented sense of self.
    d. an greater interest in achieving orgasm than was present in earlier adulthood.

Answer Key – Chapter 14

<u>Concept Checks</u>

Single Living
1. 25
2. less
3. lower

Cohabitation
1. domestic partnership
2. seven
3. more; less; less
4. more
5. legal
6. half
7. more; greater

Marriage
1. norms; partnership
2. financially; support
3. healthier
4. polygyny; polyandry
5. discrepancy
6. increasing; decreasing
7. happiness; love
8. less
9. race traitor
10. 30
11. five
12. high; contempt; stonewalling
13. style
14. validating; conflict avoiding
15. wives; husbands
16. PREPARE
17. fewer
18. mutuality; frequency
19. married
20. friendship; respected

Extramarital Relationships
1. nonconsensual
2. permissive; sex; weak
3. 25; 15
4. anger; jealousy
5. guilt; reputation
6. swinging
7. polyamory

8. emotional
9. men; women
10. aborigines; Marquesans; Turu
11. suicides

Divorce

1. half
2. cohabitating
3. 96
4. marriage; divorce
5. covenant
6. stigma; expectations; religion
7. younger
8. more
9. similar
10. ambivalence
11. more

Sexuality and Aging

1. procreation; youth
2. double
3. men; women
4. half
5. youth
6. regular
7. more
8. increase
9. 56
10. lower
11. quality; quantity
12. more
13. match; exceed
14. less; larger
15. hormonal
16. women
17. ambience; increased
18. man
19. nursing
20. failed; grief

Crossword Puzzle

Across
2. fouryear
3. peer
8. guilt
9. age

10. younger
11. respect

Down
 1. influence
 3. androgyny
 4. sexless
 6. polyandry
 7. health
12. swinging

Practice Test

1. c 2. c 3. b 4. d 5. d 6. a 7. c 8. a 9. b 10. c 11. d 12. a
13. c 14. b 15. c 16. c 17. b 18. a 19. d 20. b 21. a

Introduction

Sexual problems are relatively common experiences that can hinder optimal sexual functioning. Organic, cultural, individual, and relationship-based factors that can lead to a variety of sexual problems are described. Some of the more commonly experienced desire, excitement, and orgasm phase difficulties are discussed, as are potential causes of painful intercourse in women and men.

Learning Objectives. *In order to derive maximum benefit from these objectives, use these as soon as you begin reading the chapter. After you have completed reading and studying this chapter, you should be able to do the things listed below with ease, using only your memory.*

1. Discuss how common various sexual problems are among men and women, making reference to the National Health and Social Life Survey.

2. Discuss some of the physiological factors that may contribute to sexual problems, making specific reference to the effects of some abused and/or illicit drugs.

3. Explain how chronic illness may affect sexual function and expression, making specific reference to each of the following:
    a. diabetes
    b. arthritis
    c. cancer
    d. multiple sclerosis
    e. cerebrovascular accidents (CVA)

4. Explain how major disabilities may affect sexual function and expression, making specific reference to each of the following:
    a. spinal cord injury
    b. cerebral palsy
    c. blindness and deafness

5. Discuss how each of the following may affect sexual desire, arousal and orgasm:
    a. psychiatric medications
    b. antihypertensive medications
    c. miscellaneous medications

6. Describe how various cultural influences may contribute to sexual problems, making specific reference to each of the following:
    a. negative childhood learning
    b. the sexual double standard
    c. a narrow definition of sexuality
    d. performance anxiety

7. Describe how various individual factors may contribute to sexual problems, making specific reference to each of the following:
    a. sexual knowledge and attributes
    b. self-concept

8. Describe how various relationship factors may contribute to sexual difficulties, making specific reference to each of the following:
   a. unresolved relationship problems
   b. ineffective communication
   c. fears about pregnancy or sexually transmitted diseases
   d. sexual orientation

9. Distinguish between generalized and situational sexual problems.

10. Describe each of the following desire phase difficulties and some of the factors that may contribute to or be associated with each:
    a. hypoactive sexual desire
    b. dissatisfaction with frequency of sexual activity
    c. sexual aversion disorder

11. Define each of the following excitement phase difficulties and discuss some of the factors that might contribute to or be associated with each:
    a. female sexual arousal disorder
    b. male erectile dysfunction

12. Define each of the following orgasm phase difficulties and discuss some of the factors that might contribute to or be associated with each:
    a. female orgasmic disorder
    b. male orgasmic disorder
    c. premature ejaculation
    d. faking orgasms

13. Define dyspareunia, and discuss some of the reasons why men and women may experience it.

14. Define vaginismus, and explain how common it is and under what circumstances it may occur

Concept Map

Origins of Sexual Difficulties

- **Organic Factors**
  - chronic illness
  - disabilities
  - medications & recreational drugs

- **Cultural Factors**
  - negative childhood learning
  - narrow definition of sexuality
  - sexual double standard
  - performance anxiety

- **Individual Factors**
  - sexual knowledge & attitudes
  - emotional difficulties
  - self-concept
  - sexual abuse & assault

- **Relationship Factors**
  - unresolved relationship problems
  - fears of pregnancy & STDs
  - ineffective communication
  - sexual orientation

Desire Phase Difficulties

- hypoactive sexual desire disorder (HSD)
  - reflects lack of interest in sexual activity
  - more common in women
- dissatisfaction with frequency of activity
  - unresolved relationship problems & abusive relationships key factors
- sexual aversion disorder

Excitement Phase Difficulties

- female sexual arousal disorder
  - reflects inability to lubricate & swell
- male erectile dysfunction
  - is inability to attain or keep erection
  - more common with increasing age
  - results from a combination of factors

Orgasm Phase Difficulties

- female orgasmic disorder
  - a.k.a. anorgasmia
  - involves absence of orgasm
  - common, yet decreasing
  - lack of clitoral stimulation & cultural perceptions key factors
- male orgasmic disorder
  - is inability to ejaculate during intercourse
- premature ejaculation
  - found in almost 1 in 3 men
  - physiological basis currently unknown
  - faking orgasms

Dyspareunia

- is painful intercourse
- occurs in women & men
- in many cases, physical conditions at root
- vaginismus is one form

Key Terms. *Refer to the glossary or subject index in the back of your textbook for definitions and information.*

diabetes
arthritis
cancer
multiple sclerosis (MS)
cerebrovascular accidents (CVA)
spinal cord injury (SCI)
sensory amplification
cerebral palsy (CP)
self-concept
hypoactive sexual desire disorder (HSD)
sexual aversion disorder
female sexual arousal disorder

erectile dysfunction (ED)
impotence
anorgasmia
male orgasmic disorder
premature ejaculation (PE)
faking orgasms
dyspareunia
Peyronie's disease
vulvar vestibulitis syndrome
endometriosis
vaginismus

Concept-Checks. *Complete this section by filling in each blank after you have studied the corresponding pages from the text. Answers are provided at the back of this chapter.*

Origins of Sexual Difficulties, pp. 427-440
<u>Organic Factors</u>
1. It is often difficult to isolate specific causes of sexual difficulties, because there are many _____ and experiences that may be important, and the experiences that affected one person may not influence another.
2. Factors that influence sexual difficulties can be grouped into categories, these being _____ factors, cultural factors, individual factors, and _____ factors.
3. More research has been conducted on organic factors that affect _____ sexuality than _____ sexuality.
4. Chronic illnesses, surgeries, disabilities, medications, smoking and _____ drugs can contribute to sexual difficulties.
5. Cigarette smoking decreases the frequency and duration of _____ in men.
6. Alcohol abuse changes hormone production, thereby reducing the size of _____ in males.
7. Marijuana reduces _____ levels in men and diminishes sexual desire.
8. Diabetes can cause nerve and _____ system damage, leading to _____ problems in men.
9. Women with diabetes may experience problems with sexual desire, _____, and orgasm.
10. Arthritis causes chronic inflammation of the joints, producing _____, destruction of the joint, reduced _____, and disfigurement in some cases.
11. Arthritis does not directly affect sexual response, yet _____ image problems, depression, chronic pain and _____, and medications may dampen a person's interest in sex.
12. Pain or joint destruction in the hands may make _____ or manual stimulation of a partner difficult, and arthritis in the hips, knees, shoulders, arms and hands may prompt a couple to consider other _____ positions.
13. Cancer and its treatment may reduce sexual _____ and response, and produce a _____ body image.

14. Cancers of the _____ organs present special issues and concerns for sexual functioning.

15. Side effects of cancer treatment that may affect sexual arousal and response include pain, _____, fatigue, _____ loss, skin changes, and body alterations resulting from surgeries.

16. Multiple sclerosis is a neurological disease that affects the _____ and _____ cord where the myelin sheath that covers nerve cells is damaged.

17. Persons with MS may experience reduction in sexual interest, reduced genital _____, difficulty achieving _____, hypersensitivity to genital stimulation, and vaginal _____.

18. Cerebrovascular accidents or strokes result when _____ tissue is destroyed by hemorrhage or a blockage in the veins or arteries that supply blood.

19. Stroke survivors commonly experience _____ sexual desire and arousal.

20. People who have had a stroke may experience _____ mobility, altered or lost sensation, difficulty with communication and thinking, as well as _____.

21. Spinal cord injury (SCI) does not directly impair psychological arousal or sexual desire, however SCI may affect physiological arousal and _____, depending on factors unique to that individual's injury.

22. Many men with SCI are able to produce _____, yet they may be unable to _____ or experience orgasm.

23. An individual with a spinal cord injury may be able to intensify stimulation in a part of the body that retains some sensation and achieve mental orgasm using a process known as _____ _____.

24. Cerebral palsy (CP) results from damage to the brain that occurs during _____ or early childhood, resulting in problems with _____ control, and in some cases, changes in intellectual functioning.

25. Genital sensation is _____ by CP, yet involuntary movements or deformity of the hands and arms may make _____ difficult, and problems with the legs and hips may make certain _____ positions difficult.

26. Women who have CP may experience involuntary contractions of the muscles surrounding the _____, making intercourse difficult.

27. In and of themselves, the sensory deficits of _____ and _____ do not impair sexual arousal and response.

28. Good communication is especially important for couples affected by illness or disability; if an able-bodied partner is present, it is _____ they will know what the disabled or ill partner can or cannot do.

29. Expanding one's concept of sexual activity beyond _____ arousal and intercourse may enhance sexual expression for able-bodied and disabled persons.

30. Medications that may adversely affect sexual functioning include _____ medications and _____ medications used to treat high blood pressure, antihistamines and gastrointestinal medications, and motion sickness medications.

Cultural Influences

1. Researchers and therapists have noted that many people with sexual difficulties have a religious background that associates sex with _____.

2.   Many of us may not have been directly told that sex was shameful, yet if our early experiences with genital self-pleasuring were punished, _____ may arise, setting the stage for conflict about our sexuality.

3. Other cultural lessons about sexuality and human relationships are learned from our _____.

4. When a man is encouraged to "score" in order to lay claim to being masculine, and a woman is encouraged to be sexually cautious in order to preserve her reputation, the sexual _____ _____ is operating.

5. Acting in accordance with gender role expectations requires that men suppress _____ characteristics such as tenderness and receptivity, and that each sexual interaction be considered a _____, thereby creating feelings of frustration, inadequacy, and resentment in both partners.

6. Same-sex couples tend to have a more _____ sexual repertoire, due to an absence of a script describing how sex "should be".

7. Our society's tendency to equate sex with _____ leads to inadequate stimulation for women, and heavy expectations on intercourse.

8. According to Bernie Zilbergeld, a narrow definition of sexuality results in _____ "robbing ourselves of pleasure and of fully experiencing the stimulation necessary for an enjoyable sexual response".

9. _____ anxiety can reduce pleasurable sensations and natural arousal as sex becomes work.

Individual Factors

1. Increases in _____-_____ may contribute to women having fewer sexual problems as they get older.

2. Negative sexual attitudes promote poor sexual _____ and reduced feelings of desire.

3. Studies have found that higher self-esteem and self-_____ are related to greater sexual satisfaction and lack of sexual _____.

4. Other studies have indicated that even when boys and girls have the same percentage of body fat, _____ report greater dissatisfaction with their bodies than _____.

5. Another study found that _____ percent of women reported body image self-consciousness during lovemaking with a male partner.

6. Mass media helps shape our culture's view of what constitutes an attractive female, as in the early 1980's the average model weight 8% less than the average American female, whereas the average model now weighs _____ less than the average woman.

7. Men's perceptions of their bodies are becoming more negative, as one study showed that most men preferred a body with _____ pounds more muscle than their own.

8. Toys that transmit the male body ideal to young boys are also changing, as G.I. Joe's biceps measurement has increased from 12 to _____ inches.

9. Emotional difficulties such as _____ with life and _____ often show in our lives as diminished sexual interest.

10. Schnarch's work suggests that people who experience _____ as threatening often have sexual problems.

11. Experiencing sexual abuse may profoundly affect our sexuality, and the National Health and Social Life Survey indicates that _____ percent of men and _____ percent of women were abused before adolescence; such individuals are more likely to report difficulties with sexuality.

12. The effect of a sexual assault can be long-lasting, as _____ percent of rape survivors reported having sexual problems for more than three years after the attack.

<u>Relationship Factors</u>
1. _____ relationship problems and _____ communication skills can contribute to sexual problems.
2. Trouble with communicating to a partner the desire for direct clitoral stimulation is common in women who do not experience _____.
3. Heterosexual relationships may also be adversely affected by fear of _____, making it difficult to enjoy sex.
4. In an effort to cope in a society uncomfortable with homosexuality, many homosexual persons force themselves to be sexually intimate with other-sex partners, setting the stage for a lack of sexual _____.

Desire Phase Difficulties, pp. 441-443
1. Hypoactive sexual desire disorder (HSD) affects more _____ than _____, and is the most frequently experienced problem with sexual functioning.
2. Persons who neither masturbate nor experience sexual fantasy or sexual activity would have the rare condition of _____ , lifelong HSD.
3. Low levels of sexual desire are often associated with relationship problems, and one study showed that the woman's partner did not behave _____ except when intercourse would follow; that communication was unsatisfactory; and that the couple did not maintain love, _____ and emotional closeness.
4. Lack of sexual desire is also a problem in gay men and lesbians who have not fully accepted their _____ _____.
5. Other desire phase difficulties include dissatisfaction with the _____ of sexual activity, and _____ _____ disorder, an irrational fear and disgust with sexual activity.

Excitement Phase Difficulties, pp. 443-444
1. Female sexual arousal disorder reflects a persistent inability to maintain a lubrication-swelling response may be influenced by low _____ levels which tend to occur during perimenopause, _____, and breast feeding.
2. Male Erectile Dysfunction (ED) is sometimes mistakenly referred to as _____, a derogatory term that literally means without _____.
3. Erectile dysfunction is classified into two types, _____ where the man has previously had erections but is unable to do so now, and _____ where maintained penetration has never been experienced.
4. The frequency of erectile dysfunction increases with _____, as diabetes, coronary heart disease, and high blood pressure become more common.
5. Nearly _____ percent of ED cases are due to the side effects of medication, with the majority of cases being due to a combination of psychological, physical, and cultural factors.

Orgasm Phase Difficulties, pp. 444-447
1. Female orgasmic disorder is referred to as _____ by sex educators and therapists, but also as _____, a disparaging term.

2. A woman with _____ anorgasmia experiences orgasm rarely or in some encounters, but not others, whereas as women with _____ lifelong anorgasmia has never experienced orgasm by any means.

3. Anorgasmia is quite common, as _____ percent of women were 18 or older when they first experienced orgasm, and as many as _____ percent of adult women have never experienced orgasm.

4. Most sex therapists would agree that a woman who enjoys intercourse and experiences orgasm in some way other than from coitus does not have a _____.

5. Most men with male orgasmic disorder are able to reach orgasm through masturbation, manual or oral stimulation, but not from _____.

6. In general, about _____ percent of men experience premature ejaculation (PE).

7. It is not known at this time if PE has a _____ basis.

8. Faking orgasm is quite common, as one study showed that _____ percent of heterosexual females had done so, and _____ percent of gay or bisexual males had done so.

9. Faking orgasms may create _____ _____ at a time when many persons would like to be close and connected.

Dyspareunia, pp. 447-449

1. When intercourse becomes painful for men or women, _____ is said to occur.

2. Common sources of painful intercourse for men include inadequate hygiene among the uncircumcised, problems and infections of the reproductive tract, undiagnosed STD's, and _____ disease, resulting in pain and curvature of the penis.

3. As many as _____ percent of women experience painful intercourse at some point in their lives.

4. Discomfort at the vaginal entrance or vaginal walls is often caused by inadequate arousal and _____.

5. Vaginal infections and using _____ foam, cream, condoms or _____ may irritate the vagina, causing dyspareunia.

6. Other conditions associated with dyspareunia include _____ _____ syndrome, or discomfort in the clitoral glans caused by smegma accumulation.

7. If pain is experienced deep in the pelvis, it may result from jarring of the pelvic organs or stretching of ligaments during intercourse, or _____, the growth of uterine wall tissue outside the uterus.

8. Physical trauma from sexual assault and _____ , which results in infection of the uterus, may also cause dyspareunia.

9. In general dyspareunia is typically caused by a combination of physical and _____ factors.

10. Involuntary contractions of the muscles of the outer third of the vagina is called _____.

11. Vaginismus is relatively infrequent, affecting about _____ percent of women.

Crossword

Crossword

Across
6. HSD means one's sexual _____ is reduced
7. drug that increased awareness of erectile dysfunction
8. sexual double standard inhibits expression of this quality in men
10. gender for whom body image issues loom large
12. medical shorthand for stroke

Down
1. originator of myth that clitoral orgasms are inferior
2. when sex is restricted to this, problems may ensue
3. may produce negative body image via hair loss and skin changes
4. emotion that is a big part of sexual aversion disorder
5. orgasm inhibiting sniffable "snow"
9. equating sex with this often induces conflict about erotic pleasure
11. a vicious circle may begin when this is faked

Practice Test

This test will work best to guide your learning if you take it as part of a final review session before an exam.

1. Which of the following "recreational" drugs may impair erectile functioning?
    a. alcohol
    b. tobacco
    c. marijuana
    d. LSD

2. Diabetes may adversely affect sexual expression by
    a. promoting erectile dysfunction.
    b. reducing vaginal lubrication.
    c. increasing the risk of Peyronie's disease.
    d. a and b.
    e. all of the above.

3. Which of the following would most likely occur in someone with arthritis?
    a. reduced genital sensation
    b. involuntary spasms of the outer third of the vagina
    c. difficulty with certain intercourse positions
    d. erectile dysfunction

4. A cerebrovascular accident or _____ may result in _____.
    a. stroke; depression
    b. heart attack; impaired communication
    c. epilepsy; limited mobility
    d. aneurysm; altered sensation

5. Multiple sclerosis (MS) alters sexuality because of damage to the
    a. prostate gland.
    b. vulva.
    c. brain and spinal cord.
    d. musculoskeletal system.

6. Spinal cord injury does not adversely affect
    a. sexual arousal.
    b. orgasm.
    c. sensation.
    d. sexual desire.

7. Many men with spinal cord injury are able to have erections, yet most are unable to
    a. ejaculate.
    b. stop having retrograde ejaculation.
    c. utilize sensory amplification.
    d. utilize sensate focus exercises.

8. One study demonstrated that about 50% of women with spinal cord injury who experienced _____ before their injury could do so after their injury.
   a. vaginal intercourse
   b. orgasm
   c. the sex flush
   d. the G-spot reflex

9. All of the following medications may have undesirable effects on sexual functioning except
   a. antidepressants.
   b. tranquilizers.
   c. ginko biloba.
   d. antihistamines.

10. Which of the following would NOT be considered a cultural factor that contributes to difficulties in sexual functioning?
    a. negative childhood learning
    b. emotional difficulties
    c. narrow definition of sexuality
    d. sexual double standard
    e. performance anxiety

11. Which of the following is true regarding the impact of body image on sexuality?
    a. Newer studies suggest that men's desire for a body with a more muscular appearance has decreased.
    b. A woman may avoid positions that allow her lover to look at body parts she thinks are too fat.
    c. Women's concerns about body image do not tend to surface until adolescence.
    d. Self- consciousness during lovemaking was reported primarily by older women and men.

12. Emotional difficulties that can negatively affect sexuality include all of the following except
    a. depression.
    b. extreme work stress.
    c. fear of intimacy.
    d. satyriasis.

13. Which of the following is the best example of an unresolved relationship difficulty that affects sexuality?
    a. Steve, who expresses his resentment toward his partner by showing disinterest in sex.
    b. Soraya, who believes that intercourse is the only acceptable form of sexual activity.
    c. Cau, whose fear of contracting AIDS results in erectile dysfunction.
    d. Carol, who will not have intercourse with her husband since she was raped while walking home from the bus stop.

14. Gina won't tell her boyfriend that she needs clitoral stimulation to reach orgasm because she believes that if her boyfriend really loved her, he would know what to do. Gina is showing the impact of which relationship factor on sexuality?
    a. fear of pregnancy
    b. unresolved relationship problems
    c. emotional difficulties
    d. ineffective communication

15. Hypoactive sexual desire disorder (HSD) is more common among
    a. gays or lesbians that have not fully accepted their sexual orientation.
    b. women.
    c. people with unresolved relationship problems.
    d. all of the above.

16. Someone who has generalized, lifelong HSD
    a. masturbates, but does not have sex with a partner.
    b. engages in sexual fantasy, but will not masturbate or have sex with a partner.
    c. had sexual experiences earlier in prior relationship, but has low desire in the current relationship.
    d. does not engage in fantasy, masturbation, or other sexual activity.

17. For the last 8 months, Miguel has been unable to have an erection of sufficient quality to penetrate his partner. During this time Miguel and his partner have been enjoying sensual massage, kissing, caressing, and don't mind if he cannot have an erection. What can be concluded about this couple?
    a. Miguel has erectile problems stemming from diabetes.
    b. Miguel has dyspareunia.
    c. The couple does not have a problem, as they are content with the situation.
    d. The couple has unresolved relationship difficulties and should seek sex therapy.

18. A woman with situational anorgasmia
    a. may have orgasm during masturbation, but not when her partner orally stimulates her
    b. does not experience lubrication.
    c. experiences lubrication, but does not experience psychological arousal
    d. is at greater risk of developing HSD

19. What would most sex therapists conclude about a woman who enjoys sex, but does not experience orgasm during intercourse without clitoral stimulation?
    a. She is emotionally immature.
    b. She is showing a normal and common pattern.
    c. She has lifelong anorgasmia.
    d. She is showing early signs of sexual aversion disorder.

20. A man can have ejaculate when he masturbates, yet when he has vaginal intercourse, he is unable to ejaculate. He most likely would be diagnosed with
    a. priapism.
    b. phismosis.
    c. male orgasmic disorder.
    d. retrograde ejaculation.

21. In surveys of the authors' sexuality classes, over _____ percent of male students reported that premature ejaculation was sometimes a problem.
    a. 82
    b. 75
    c. 61
    d. 29

22. Dyspareunia refers to
    a. painful intercourse.
    b. involuntary contractions of the vaginal muscles.
    c. involuntary contractions of the scrotal muscles.
    d. accumulations of smegma under the clitoral or penile glans.

23. Which of the following is not a possible cause of dyspareunia?
    a. untreated infections of the reproductive tract
    b. Peyronie's disease
    c. oral contraceptive use
    d. endometriosis

24. Vaginismus may be related to
    a. religious taboos about sex.
    b. use of high absorbency tampons.
    c. past sexual assault.
    d. a and c.
    e. all of the above.

Answer Key – Chapter 15

Concept Checks

Origins of Sexual Difficulties

Organic Factors
1. influences
2. organic; relationship
3. male; female
4. recreational
5. erection
6. testes
7. testosterone
8. circulatory; erectile
9. lubrication
10. pain; mobility
11. body; fatigue
12. masturbation; intercourse
13. arousal; negative
14. reproductive
15. nausea; hair
16. brain; spinal
17. sensation; orgasm; dryness
18. brain
19. decreased
20. limited; depression
21. response
22. erections; ejaculate
23. sensory amplification
24. birth; muscular
25. unaffected; masturbation; intercourse
26. vagina
27. blindness; deafness
28. unlikely
29. genital
30. psychiatric; antihypertensive

Cultural Influences
1. sin
2. guilt
3. family
4. double standard
5. feminine; performance
6. varied
7. coitus
8. men
9. Performance

Individual Factors
1. self-knowledge
2. attitudes
3. confidence; problems
4. girls; boys
5. 35
6. 23
7. 30
8. 16½
9. unhappiness; depression
10. intimacy
11. 12; 17
12. 60

Relationship Factors
1. Unresolved; ineffective
2. orgasm
3. pregnancy
4. desire

Desire Phase Difficulties
1. women; men
2. generalized
3. affectionately; romance
4. sexual orientation
5. frequency; sexual aversion

Excitement Phase Difficulties
1. estrogen; menopause
2. impotence; power
3. acquired; lifelong
4. age
5. 25

Orgasm Phase Difficulties
1. anorgasmia; frigidity
2. situational; generalized
3. 62; 10
4. problem
5. coitus
6. 29
7. physiological
8. 60; 27
9. emotional distance

Dyspareunia
1. dyspareunia
2. Peyronie's
3. 60
4. lubrication
5. contraceptive; diaphragms
6. vulvar vestibulitis
7. endometriosis
8. gonorrhea
9. psychological
10. vaginismus
11. 2

Crossword Puzzle
Across
6. appetite
7. Viagra
8. tenderness
10. women
12. CVA

Down
1. Freud
2. coitus
3. cancer
4. fear
5. cocaine
9. sin
11. orgasm

Practice Test
1. b 2. d 3. c 4. a 5. c 6. d 7. a 8. b 9. c 10. b 11. c 12. d 13. a
14. d 15. d 16. d 17. c 18. a 19. b 20. c 21. b 22. a 23. c 24. d

Introduction

The often misunderstood process of sex therapy is clarified in this chapter. In addition to describing basic sex therapy approaches and techniques, the authors discuss numerous strategies that individuals and couples can use to enhance sexual expression and increase satisfaction. Guidelines for finding a qualified sex therapist are also provided.

Learning Objectives. *In order to derive maximum benefit from these objectives, use these as soon as you begin reading the chapter. After you have completed reading and studying this chapter, you should be able to do the things listed below with ease, using only your memory.*

1. Discuss each of the following and how they can improve body awareness and enhance a relationship with a partner:
   a. self-awareness
   b. communication
   c. sensate focus
   d. masturbation with a partner present

2. Explain some of the procedures involved for women who are learning to become orgasmic, both alone and with a partner.

3. Describe what treatment procedures are available for dealing with vaginismus and under what conditions vaginismus may be difficult to treat.

4. Outline at least six specific strategies used to cope with premature ejaculation.

5. Describe various treatment alternatives that are available for men who experience erectile difficulties and how successful they typically are.

6. Outline some of the strategies used to treat men who experience ejaculatory disorder.

7. Discuss some of the dynamics and specific treatment strategies involved in dealing with people who experience hypoactive sexual desire.

8. List and describe the four levels of treatment involved in the PLISSIT model of sex therapy.

9. Discuss the following in regard to seeking help for sexual difficulties:
   a. how sessions with a therapist might be structured
   b. the differences among psychosexual therapy, systems therapy and eye movement desensitization and reprocessing (EMOR)
   c. criteria to consider in selecting a therapist

10. Citing specific examples, explain how modern sex therapy may clash with the values of other cultures.

Concept Map

sexual enhancement & therapy basics

self-awareness
- body exploration
- genital self-exam
- emotions & needs

communication
- intimacy is learned ability

sensate focus
- nondemand touching
- active & passive roles
- masturbation with partner present

suggestions for women

becoming orgasmic
- self-awareness exercises
- effective self-stimulation

orgasm with partner
- sexological exam
- assertiveness & feedback
- nondemand genital touch

orgasm during intercourse
- wait for her readiness
- bridge maneuver
- use positions that provide direct clitoral stimulation

vaginismus
- relaxation & self-awareness exercises
- progressive insertion of fingers & dilators
- partner participation later in treatment

suggestions for men

lasting longer
- ejaculate more often
- talk with partner
- change coital positions
- consider activities besides intercourse
- stop-start technique
- squeeze technique

erectile dysfunction, no organic basis
- reduce anxiety
- sensate focus
- use behavioral focused therapy

erectile dysfunction, organic basis
- medications
- injections
- penile implants
- vacuum suction devices

orgasmic disorder
- resolve resentment
- behavioral approach & sensate focus

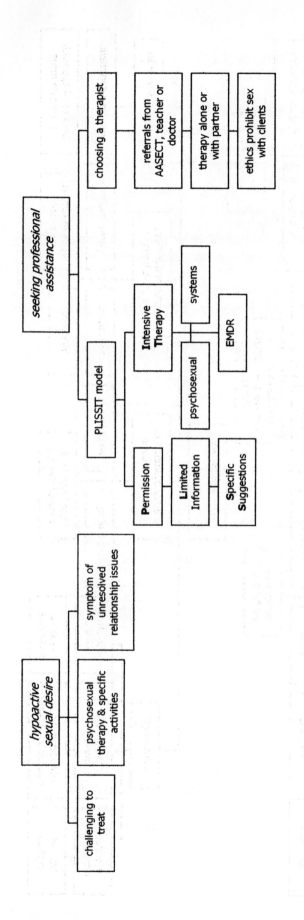

Key Terms. *Refer to the glossary or subject index in the back of your textbook for definitions and information.*

sensate focus
sexological exam
bridge maneuver
stop-start technique
squeeze technique

PLISSIT model
psychosexual therapy
systems therapy
postmodern sex therapy
EMDR

Concept-Checks. *Complete this section by filling in each blank after you have studied the corresponding pages from the text. Answers are provided at the back of this chapter.*

Basics of Sexual Enhancement and Sex Therapy, pp. 452-456
1. Awareness of our bodies, our feelings and needs may be promoted by visually examining the body, exploring with touch, and by using _____ exercises.
2. In addition to treating specific sexual problems, sex therapy may help a couple improve _____ skills.
3. Examples of some cultural groups whose values may disagree with sex therapy include Muslims; _____, who consider it shameful to discuss sex; and _____ _____, who do not condone masturbation.
4. Masters and Johnson developed a series of touching exercises called _____ _____.
5. The goal of the touching exercises described above is to reduce _____ that may be caused by a goal or performance orientation toward sex, and to increase _____, pleasure and closeness.
6. When doing Masters and Johnson's touching exercises, the person receiving the touch should remain _____ except to inform the toucher that something is uncomfortable.
7. In early sensate focus exercises, couples are instructed to avoid touching the _____ and the _____ .
8. In subsequent sessions with sensate touch, partners are asked to _____ roles.
9. Couples may also choose to _____ in the presence of a partner, as this may allow the partners to know what kind of touch is appealing.

Specific Suggestions for Women, pp. 456-460
1. Therapy programs for women who would like to become orgasmic are based on progressive _____ - _____ exercises that are done at home between therapy sessions.
2. Learning effective _____-_____ is the cornerstone of treatment for women who have never experienced orgasm.
3. For women with a partner, it is often suggested that she become orgasmic first by _____.
4. In order to enrich her sexual experience, a woman is encouraged to develop sexual _____ by doing what is arousing to her and communicating this to her partner.
5. _____ in the presence of a partner is an important step toward building a more satisfying sexuality.
6. Another exercise that may help a woman become orgasmic involves having a partner provide _____ manual-genital pleasuring.

7. A couple may wish to consider waiting until the woman feels "_____" to begin intercourse, instead of beginning when she is lubricated.

8. Adopting a more active role in intercourse by _____ and controlling pelvic movements, manually stimulating the _____ , or using a vibrator may provide the increased stimulation that many women need if they are to be orgasmic during intercourse.

9. Exploring coital positions or using Kaplan's _____ maneuver may allow a woman to experience orgasm in some cases.

10. A treatment program for vaginismus typically begins with a _____ exam where a health care provider demonstrates the spasmodic response of the vagina.

11. The woman also performs _____ and self-awareness exercises at home, and therapy eventually includes insertion of a _____ , and progressively larger dilators into the vagina, while maintaining a state of relaxation to prevent vaginal spasms.

12. Therapy for vaginismus may also include the integration of a _____ into the exercises, with the goal of eventually experiencing penis-vagina intercourse, where both partners are comfortable.

Specific Suggestions for Men, pp. 460-467

1. Having more frequent orgasms may promote ejaculatory control, so the authors suggest that men _____ more frequently.

2. Discovering the varieties of sexual expression that are possible after a man has had an initial _____ may allow a couple to resume intercourse when a man's _____ has returned.

3. Coital positions with high degrees of muscle tension affect speed of orgasm, and the _____-_____ position is associated with a more rapid orgasm.

4. The _____-_____ position allows a man to lie on his back, thereby reducing the muscle tension that promotes rapid ejaculation.

5. It also helps if a man tries to relax and avoid _____ pelvic movements if he and his partner wish to delay ejaculation.

6. Since a couple will need to communicate with each other in order to regulate movements, it is essential that a man feel comfortable asking his partner for _____.

7. Couples are also encouraged to consider ways of lovemaking other than _____, as orgasm can come from many methods

8. James Semans, a urologist, is credited with formulating the _____-_____ technique used to delay ejaculation.

9. Another treatment for premature ejaculation is the _____ technique, where a partner applies strong pressure to specific areas of the _____.

10. Techniques to improve ejaculatory control can be practiced during _____ masturbation sessions, as well as with a partner.

11. Masters and Johnson reported that the stop-start technique has a _____ percent success rate, making it one of the most effective sex therapies.

12. For those erectile difficulties that are not organically caused, _____ is a major obstacle to overcome in establishing a satisfactory erectile response.

13. Treatment for erectile dysfunction begins with _____ _____exercises.

14. Couples receiving treatment for erectile dysfunction are reminded that the exercises are not intended to produce an _____, but rather, to enjoy the sensations in a manner that is not goal oriented.

15. While doing the exercises to treat erectile dysfunction, the couple is restricted from having _____ and ejaculation.

16. During treatment it is hoped that the couple will learn that erections can be
_____ and _____, thereby abating the fear that an erection will never return.
17. Some men who experience erectile dysfunction as the result of physical problems may
adjust to the absence of an erection by exploring other ways of sexual _____.
18. Viagra works by improving _____ flow to the penis, yet in order for an erection to
occur, _____ stimulation is required.
19. Common side effects of Viagra include _____, headaches, and _____
congestion.
20. Research has not been conducted on the effects of Viagra for enhancement or
_____ purposes.
21. Some men with may also develop an erection from medications that are _____ into
the cavernous bodies of the penis.
22. Mechanical devices that may produce an erection include devices that suction _____ into
the penis, vacuum devices, and a penile support sleeve called _____.
23. In order to develop an erection, some men find that a surgically implanted penile
_____ works best for them.
24. Treatment for male _____ disorder is based upon a behavioral approach and
psychotherapy aimed at reducing resentment and improving communication skills.

Treating Hypoactive Sexual Desire, p. 467
1. Many therapists consider desire problems the _____ difficult to treat, and as a result,
therapy is often more intense than for other problems.
2. Treating HSD involves helping the client to understand their motivations for suppressing
sexual _____, and reasons for declining opportunities for sexual intimacy.
3. A therapist may also work with the couple to ameliorate unresolved _____ problems.
4. Many aspects of treating HSD are _____ to specific suggestions for resolving other
sexual problems.

Seeking Professional Assistance, pp. 467-470
1. Only _____ to_____ percent of people with a sexual problem seek
professional help.
2. The PLISSIT model of sex therapy stands for Permission, Limited _____,
_____ Suggestions, and Intensive Therapy.
3. In _____ therapy the therapist provides interpretation and reflection to help clients
gain awareness and understanding of feelings and thoughts that contribute to sexual problems.
4. Instead of focusing on issues within an individual, _____ therapy focuses on the
relationship, and the functions that sexual problems serve in that relationship.
5. Some therapists use a new therapy called _____ that uses eye movements to
stimulate information and emotional processing in the brain.
6. Professional associations in psychology, social work, psychiatry, and counseling all have
codes of ethics that prohibit _____ _____ between therapists and their clients.
7. In addition to asking your sexuality teacher or health care provider for referrals, the
American Association of _____ _____, Counselors, and _____ (AASECT)
can provide referrals for properly qualified therapists in your area.

Crossword

Across
2. perplexing terminus of erectile dysfunction treatment
4. imbalance of this sort found with hypoactive sexual desire
7. emotion that is focus of erectile dysfunction treatment
11. communication skill helpful to anorgasmic women
12. Tiefer's largest sex organ and site of sensate focus

Down
1. "wonder" drug that may force couples to face their problems
3. type of touch present in sensate focus
5. masturbation can be done with this person present
6. _____ orgasm often assumed to be the end of lovemaking
8. this type of tension promotes rapid ejaculation
9. exam that's part of vaginismus treatment
10. urologist inventor of the stop-start technique

Practice Test

This test will work best to guide your learning if you take it as part of a final review session before an exam.

1. All of the following are parts of basic sex therapy <u>except</u>
   a. masturbation exercises.
   b. the squeeze technique.
   c. sensate focus.
   d. genital self-exam.

2. Which cultural group would be least likely to discuss sexual matters with a therapist?
   a. Orthodox Jews
   b. Wiccans
   c. Asians
   d. Native Americans

3. Which of the following is <u>false</u> regarding sensate focus exercises?
   a. Early sessions focus on bringing the partners to orgasm.
   b. Partners switch roles.
   c. The toucher explores for their own pleasure, not their partner's.
   d. The recipient of touch remains quiet, except when touch is uncomfortable.

4. For a woman who has never experienced orgasm what would be most helpful?
   a. the bridge maneuver
   b. the man-on-top coital position
   c. Viagra
   d. masturbation

5. Couples who wish to increase the possibility of a woman's orgasm during intercourse would be advised to do all of the following <u>except</u>
   a. begin intercourse when she feels ready, instead of when she is adequately lubricated.
   b. use the bridge maneuver.
   c. avoid use of water-soluble lubricants like K-Y Jelly.
   d. use an intercourse position that allows for direct clitoral stimulation.

6. The bridge maneuver is best described as
   a. a variation of sensate focus exercises.
   b. manual stimulation of the clitoris during intercourse until climax is near, followed by active pelvic movements.
   c. the rear-entry or "doggie" intercourse position, where the woman keeps her back flat like a table top.
   d. using a vibrator to approach climax during masturbation, then switching to manual stimulation of the clitoris.

7. Which of the following would <u>not</u> be included in a treatment program for vaginismus?
   a. using SS-cream
   b. relaxation exercises
   c. manual stimulation
   d. insertion of fingers or dilators

8. All of the following techniques may delay ejaculation <u>except</u>
   a. having more frequent orgasms.
   b. continuing sexual activity after a first ejaculation.
   c. using energetic pelvic movements.
   d. using the woman-above position during intercourse.

9. The stop-start technique involves
   a. communicating the level of stimulation one is experiencing to the partner.
   b. applying the technique using oral or manual stimulation first.
   c. stopping stimulation until pre-ejaculatory sensations are reduced.
   d. all of the above.
   e. two of the above.

10. Of the following statements, which is <u>true</u> regarding the squeeze technique?
    a. Urologist James Semans developed the technique.
    b. Pressure is applied to the frenulum and glans of the penis to delay ejaculation.
    c. The base of the penis is grasped firmly and given three quick squeezes.
    d. The squeeze technique is used to treat retrograde ejaculation.

11. A treatment program to deal with erectile dysfunction would include
    a. sensate focus exercises.
    b. viewing erotic films.
    c. using manual or genital stimulation to first cause an erection, then beginning penetration immediately to prevent loss of an erection.
    d. using the EROS treatment device to produce an erection.

12. Which of the following statements is <u>true</u> about Viagra?
    a. It allows erections to continue after ejaculation.
    b. It promotes blood flow to the penis.
    c. Flushing and headaches are common side effects.
    d. b and c are true
    e. all of the above are true

13. Erections may be produced by all of the following methods <u>except</u>
    a. penile implants.
    b. vacuum suction.
    c. injections.
    d. gossypol.

14. A major goal of treatment approaches for erectile dysfunction that does not have an organic basis is
    a. getting the client stabilized on a proper dose of Viagra.
    b. encouraging a man to attempt intercourse as often as possible.
    c. reducing anxiety.
    d. using EMDR to increase arousal.

15. Treatment of male orgasmic disorder involves
    a. asking the couple to express affection at times other than intercourse.
    b. using antidepressants to increase orgasmic response.
    c. using anti-anxiety agents to promote relaxation.
    d. using behavioral approaches and psychotherapy to reduce resentment.

16. Hypoactive sexual desire
    a. can often be treated through therapy that is less intensive than that used for other problems.
    b. is often a symptom of unresolved relationship problems.
    c. is uncomplicated to treat.
    d. is most often caused by hormonal imbalances.

17. The acronym PLISSIT refers to a model of sex therapy that emphasizes
    a. Playfulness, Love, Integration, Specific Suggestions, Information, and Therapy.
    b. Permission, Love, Information, Specific Suggestions, Integration, and Therapy.
    c. Passion, Limited Information, Specific Suggestions, Integration Therapy.
    d. Permission, Limited Information, Specific Suggestions, Intensive Therapy.

18. Leila and Irene are seeing a sex therapist that is helping them gain awareness of unconscious feelings regarding their early relationships with their parents. This couple is experiencing _____ therapy.
    a. postmodern
    b. systems
    c. psychosexual
    d. EMDR

19. All of the following may happening in sex therapy except
    a. a medical history will be taken.
    b. screening for major psychological problems.
    c. sexual relations with the therapist may occur.
    d. homework assignments may be given.

Answer Key – Chapter 16

<u>Concept Checks</u>

Basics of Sexual Enhancement and Therapy
1. masturbation
2. communication
3. Asians; Orthodox Jews
4. sensate focus
5. anxiety; intimacy
6. quiet
7. breasts; genitals
8. switch
9. masturbate

Specific Suggestions for Women
1. self-stimulation
2. self-stimulation
3. masturbation
4. assertiveness
5. Masturbating
6. nondemanding
7. readiness
8. initiating; clitoris
9. bridge
10. pelvic
11. relaxation; finger
12. partner

Specific Suggestions for Men
1. ejaculate
2. ejaculation; erection
3. man-above
4. woman-above
5. energetic
6. help
7. intercourse
8. stop-start
9. squeeze; penis
10. solo
11. 98
12. anxiety
13. sensate focus
14. erection
15. intercourse
16. stopped; resumed
17. sharing
18. blood; physical

19. flushing; nasal
20. recreational
21. injected
22. blood; Rejoyn
23. implant (or prosthesis)
24. orgasmic

Treating Hypoactive Sexual Desire
1. most
2. feelings
3. relationship
4. similar

Seeking Professional Assistance
1. 10; 20
2. Information; Specific
3. psychosexual
4. systems
5. EMDR
6. sexual relations
7. Sex Educators; Therapists

Crossword Puzzle

Across
2. coitus
4. power
7. anxiety
11. assertiveness
12. skin

Down
1. Viagra
3. nondemand
5. partner
6. male
8. muscle
9. pelvic
10. Semans

Practice Test

1. b   2. c   3. a   4. d   5. c   6. b   7. a   8. c   9. d   10. b   11. a
12. e   13. d   14. c   15. d   16. b   17. d   18. c   19. c

Introduction

Being informed about the realities of sexually transmitted diseases can help facilitate the good decision making that is part of sexual health and well-being. Your likelihood of contracting an STD, their symptoms, consequences, and treatments are candidly discussed, as are prevention strategies you can adopt to keep your sexual expression joyful.

Learning Objectives. *In order to derive maximum benefit from these objectives, use these as soon as you begin reading the chapter. After you have completed reading and studying this chapter, you should be able to do the things listed below with ease, using only your memory.*

1. Cite statistics that indicate in what age groups sexually transmitted diseases will most commonly occur.

2. Discuss some of the factors that give rise to the incidence of sexually transmitted diseases.

3. Describe the cause, incidence and transmission, symptoms and complications and treatment alternatives for the following bacterial infections: chlamydia infection; gonorrhea; nongonococcal urethritis; syphilis; chancroid.

4. Describe the cause, incidence and transmission, symptoms and complications and treatment alternatives for the following viral infections: herpes; genital warts; viral hepatitis.

5. Describe the cause, incidence and transmission, symptoms and complications and treatment alternatives for the following vaginal infections: bacterial vaginosis; candidiasis; trichomoniasis.

6. Describe the cause, incidence and transmission, symptoms and complications and treatment alternatives for the following ectoparasitic infections: pubic lice; scabies.

7. Describe each of the following in reference to acquired immunodeficiency syndrome (AIDS):
    a. what causes it and how it is diagnosed
    b. when it was first recognized in the U.S. and around the world
    c. some of the serious diseases to which AIDS patients are vulnerable
    d. incidence and transmission in the U.S. and worldwide
    e. symptoms and complications
    f. HIV antibody tests
    g. development of AIDS
    h. treatment
    i. prevention
    j. HIV/AIDS issues and the law
    k. the development of vaccines for AIDS
    l. new drug treatments for AIDS, particularly the HAART regime

8. Outline and describe strategies that can help reduce the likelihood of contracting a sexually transmitted disease.

9. Describe developing research on vaginal microbicides.

10. Describe cross-cultural difficulties in AIDS prevention and treatment citing differences between China and Africa's resources and approaches.

Concept Map

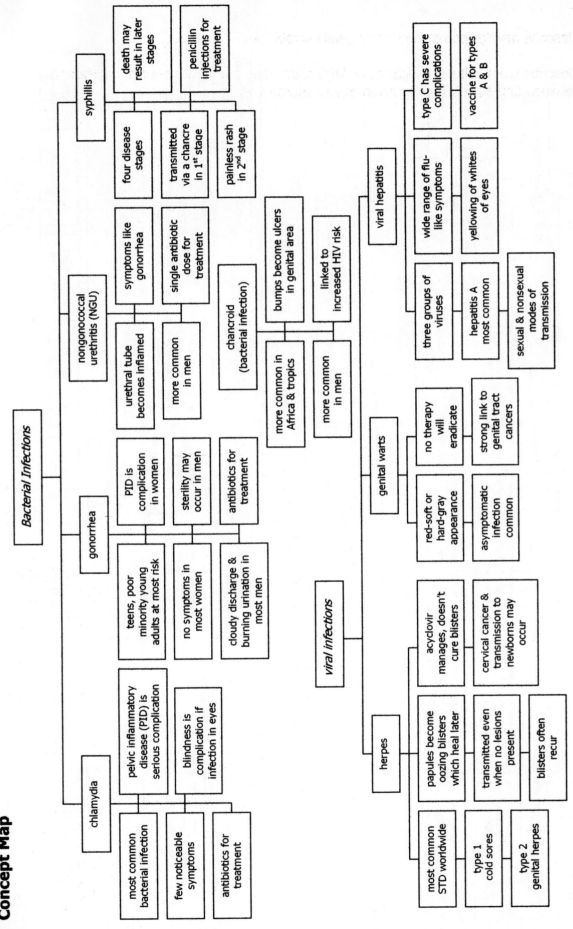

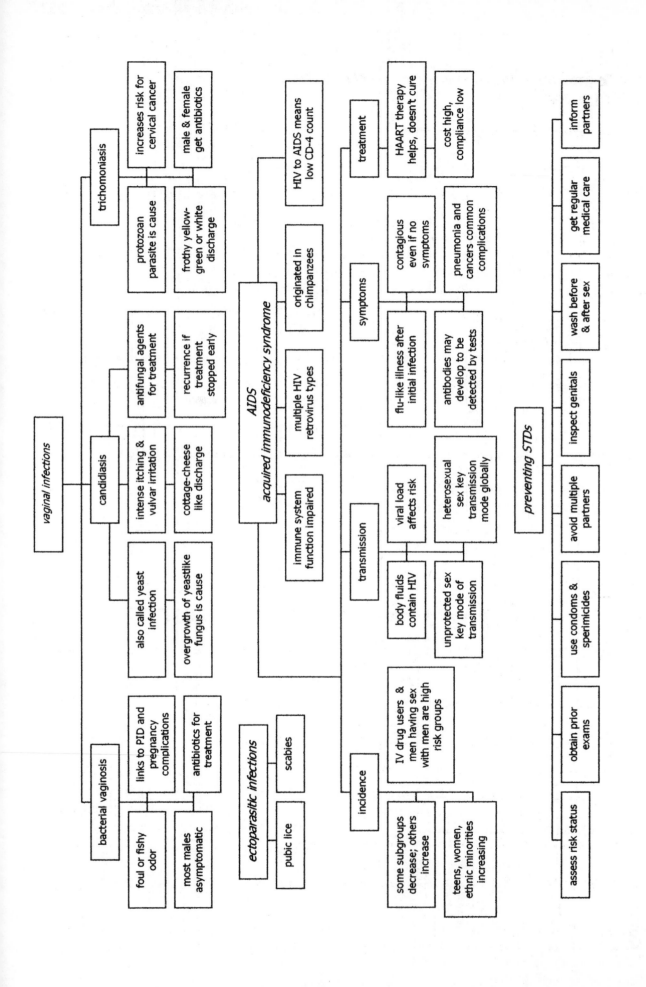

Key Terms. *Refer to the glossary or subject index in the back of your textbook for definitions and information.*

sexually transmitted diseases (STDs)
chlamydia
pelvic inflammatory disease (PID)
trachoma
conjunctivitis
gonorrhea
nongonococcal urethritis (NGU)
syphillis
chancre
chancroid
herpes
prodromal symptoms
genital warts (HPV)
viral hepatitis
vaginitis

leukorrhea
bacterial vaginosis
urethritis
cystitis
candidiasis
trichomoniasis
ectoparasites
pubic lice
scabies
acquired immunodeficiency syndrome
  (AIDS)
human immunodeficiency virus (HIV)
viral load
highly active antiretroviral therapies
  (HAART)

Concept-Checks. *Complete this section by filling in each blank after you have studied the corresponding pages from the text. Answers are provided at the back of this chapter.*

Chapter Opening, pp. 474-478
1. The majority of STD's in the United States occur among those aged _____ to
_____ .
2. Nearly 50% of the American population will contract an STD by the time they are
_____ years old.
3. The largest proportion of AIDS cases occurs among people in the 20's and 30's, who contracted the AIDS virus in their _____ and _____.
4. Factors that have helped fuel the rise of STDs include engaging in risky sex, having _____ partners, and having _____ sex.
5. Another important influence on the spread of STDs is that many of these diseases do not have _____ symptoms.

Bacterial Infections, pp. 478-486
Chlamydia
1. The most common infection reported to health departments nationwide is _____.
2. Sexually active teenagers, younger women who use _____ _____, and woman who _____ once a month or more are at greater risk for chlamydia infection.
3. Most women who contract chlamydia show no symptoms, but among those who do, _____ and cervicitis are common.
4. Chlamydia is also a major cause of _____ inflammatory disease.
5. Damage to the fallopian tubes caused by chlamydia is the most preventable cause of female _____ and ectopic pregnancy.
6. In men, chlamydia infection causes about 50% of cases of epidydimitis and nongonococcal _____.

7. Chlamydia can affect newborns, as chlamydia trachomatis is the most common cause of _____ infection in newborns.

8. Treatment of chlamydia consists of a seven-day regimen of doxycycline, an antibiotic, or a _____ dose of azithromycin.

Gonorrhea and Syphillis

9. Rates of gonorrhea are especially high among _____ and younger adults, and lower socioeconomic classes.

10. Symptoms of gonorrhea are more likely to be present in _____ than _____.

11. The two most common signs of gonorrhea infection in men are a _____, bad-smelling discharge from the penis, and a burning sensation after _____.

12. Symptoms in males will often disappear on their own, however the bacteria is still present so a _____ may be infected.

13. If gonorrhea symptoms are not treated in males, the infection will spread throughout the _____ tract.

14. Most women who contract gonorrhea do not show early _____ of the disease.

15. A major complication of untreated gonorrhea in females is _____ inflammatory disease, which may result in infertility.

16. Gonorrhea may also be present in the eyes, _____ and rectum.

17. Treating gonorrhea is difficult, as it is often confused with other _____.

18. Women who have contracted NGU (nongonococcal urethritis) typically have _____ symptoms, whereas men show symptoms similar to _____ infection.

19. In NGU the _____ tube is the initial site of this infection caused by bacteria other than gonococcus organisms.

20. The incidence of syphillis has been _____, yet unlike most STDs, syphllis can result in _____.

21. Syphillis is transmitted through open_____ to the mucous membranes of an uninfected partner through penile-vaginal, oral-_____, oral-anal, or genital-_____ contact.

22. Since syphilis can be spread from mother to fetus through the placenta blood, pregnant women should be tested for syphillis before the _____ month of pregnancy.

23. The key symptom of primary syphillis is a(n) _____, a painless sore that appears where the bacteria entered the body.

24. Secondary syphillis typically occurs two to _____ weeks afterward, and is characterized by a distinctive, painless _____ _____.

25. During the _____ stage, if syphillis remains untreated severe complications such as heart failure, paralysis, mental disturbance, or death may result.

26. Syphillis is treated by administering _____ injections.

Chancroid

27. Chancroid is more prevalent in _____, tropical, and semi-tropical areas.

28. Health officials are concerned because rates of chancroid have been _____ in recent years, and heretofore the disease was rather uncommon in the United States.

29. Chancroid is associated with increased prevalence of another STD, _____ infection.

30. Symptoms of chancroid are small bumps that eventually rupture and form _____ which provide an easy entry point for other infectious agents like HIV.

31. In response to the resurgence of STDs in mainland China, the government has launched campaign to control STDs which seems to have _____ impact.

Viral Infections, pp. 487-495
1. A virus is a cell that invades, reproduces and lives within another _____.

Herpes
2. Eight different herpes viruses infect humans, but only _____ of these are transmitted through sexual contact.
3. Herpes simplex virus (HSV) type _____ usually results in cold sores or fever blisters on the mouth or lips, whereas herpes simplex type _____ produces lesions in the genital area.
4. Genital herpes affects more people around the world than any other _____.
5. Oral herpes is primarily transmitted through _____, and secondarily through oral-genital contact.
6. Genital herpes is transmitted by penile-_____ , oral-genital, genital-_____ or oral-anal contact.
7. HSV may be transmitted when lesions and symptoms are absent through a process known as _____ _____.
8. Studies have demonstrated that HSV will not pass through _____ condoms.
9. HSV may be transmitted from a female to a male, even though he wears a condom, when vaginal secretions spread over the man's _____ area during intercourse.
10. People may spread HSV from one part of the body to another through _____ - _____, which is most likely after the infection has initially appeared.
11. Many individuals with herpes do not experience recognizable _____.
12. The key symptom of herpes is the presence of small, red bumps called _____ that typically appear on external genitals, vaginal opening and walls, or _____.
13. The bumps eventually form into blisters that rupture, making the person very _____ at this time.
14. Sores usually dry up and form a crust about _____ days after the first appearance of a red bump, then they heal in another ten days.
15. Oral herpes blisters form a crust and typically heal within 10 to _____ days.
16. After initial healing the herpes virus remains dormant in _____ cells in the neck or spinal cord, where the virus can cause periodic flare-ups throughout a person's life.
17. People who tend to have recurring flare-ups may show _____ symptoms which give advance notice that an eruption will occur.
18. Of the two sexes _____ are not likely to experience major complications from herpes.
19. Two serious, though uncommon, complications of herpes are cancer of the _____ and infection of a _____.
20. The key treatment for herpes is the antiviral drug _____, which may also be taken when symptoms are absent to prevent recurrence.
21. Reducing _____, keeping blisters clean and _____ , preventing urine from contacting lesions, and taking pain relieving medication can provide relief from herpes discomfort.

Genital Warts
22. Genital warts are caused by the _____ _____ virus (HPV).
23. Some researchers argue that HPV is the most _____ STD in North America.
24. Genital warts appear three weeks to _____ months after infection.

25. Transmission of HPV can occur when _____ are not present.
26. Warts may appear on the external genitalia and perineum of women and men, or on the inner walls and outer opening of the vagina, or on the _____.
27. HPV is usually transmitted though _____, anal, or oral-genital sexual activity.
28. If genital warts appear in a _____ skin area, they will be pink or red and soft.
29. If genital warts appear in a _____ skin area, they will be yellow-gray and hard.
30. Research has revealed a strong association between genital warts and _____ of the genitals and urethra.
31. Women with HPV have a much higher rate of developing _____ cancer.
32. No form of _____ has been shown that will completely eliminate HPV or prevent its recurrence.

Viral Hepatitis
33. Viral hepatitis affects functioning of the _____.
34. Of the three types of hepatitis, hepatitis _____ is most common, followed by type _____ and _____.
35. Type _____ and _____ hepatitis are transmitted sexually.
36. Hepatitis A is especially common among young homosexual _____, and types A and B are common among _____ drug users.
37. Hepatitis B is transmitted via blood, blood products, _____, vaginal secretions, _____, and from infected mothers to children during the perinatal period.
38. Stimulation of the _____ through various means is strongly associated with spreading Hepatitis B.
39. Nonsexual transmission of Hepatitis A occurs via the _____-_____ route, when food handlers do not follow proper handwashing procedures.
40. If symptoms of the various forms of hepatitis are present they may include _____ of the skin or whites of the eyes and flu-like symptoms that range from mild to severe.
41. Treatment of hepatitis A and B includes bed rest and adequate _____ intake, whereas treatment of hepatitis C is more difficult.

Common Vaginal Infections, pp. 495-498
1. Many organisms that cause vaginal infections live in the _____ and cause little trouble unless something happens that allows them to overgrow.
2. The pH of the vagina is normally _____ which prevents infection, yet certain conditions can change the pH, making an infection more likely.
3. Conditions such as antibiotic therapy, _____ _____ pills, menstruation, _____, wearing pantyhose or _____ underwear, douching, and lowered resistance from lack of sleep or stress can increase the likelihood of a vaginal infection.
4. Overgrowth of the bacteria *gardnerella vaginalis* is the most common cause of the vaginal infection _____ _____.
5. It is believed that bacterial vaginosis (BV) is primarily transmitted through _____, though the infection has been found in women who have not had sexual intercourse.
6. The key symptom of BV is a _____ smelling discharge that has the consistency of flour paste.
7. BV is associated with pelvic inflammatory disease and adverse _____ outcomes.
8. Most men who harbor BV are _____, although some may have urethritis or cystitis.
9. Current treatment for BV consists of taking _____, an antibiotic, by mouth, or intravaginally.

10. Current research has shown there is no benefit gained treating the _____ _____ of women who do not have recurrent BV.

11. Overgrowth of the fungus *Candida albicans* causes candidiasis, more commonly referred to as a _____ infection.

12. Factors which increase the likelihood of contracting candidiasis are pregnancy, diabetes, use of oral _____, and spermicidal creams and jellies.

13. Wiping from _____ to _____ after a bowel movement can spread the yeast organism to the vagina.

14. Symptoms of a yeast infection include intense _____ and soreness of the vaginal and vulval tissues and a white, _____ discharge that resembles cottage cheese.

15. Yeast infection treatment consists of vaginal _____ or creams, or less commonly, oral fluconazole.

16. In order for yeast infection treatment to be effective, treatment must be continued for the fully prescribed length of time, even though symptoms _____.

17. If frothy, white, or yellow-green discharge with an unpleasant odor is present, a woman might suspect that she has _____, a vaginal infection caused by a protozoan.

18. _____ are more likely than _____ to have no noticeable symptoms of trichomoniasis.

19. If a man does have symptoms, they may show as _____ and other genitourinary problems.

20. Prompt treatment for trichomoniasis may prevent the infection from spreading to the _____, or causing complications for pregnant women.

21. Unlike the other vaginal infections we have studied, both men and women must be treated with _____ or metronidazale, so long as the woman is not pregnant.

Ectoparasitic Infections, pp. 498-499

1. _____ and _____ _____ are two STD's caused by ectoparasites, organisms that live on the outer skin.

2. Pubic lice are spread during sexual contact when the _____ areas come into contact.

3. Female crabs may deposit _____ that can survive on underclothes or bedsheets for several days.

4. The key symptom of public lice is _____ that brings little relief, though a few people will experience no symptoms.

5. Lice treatment consists of a 1% permethrin cream rinse that is applied to all affected regions and washed off after _____ minutes.

6. Treatment should be _____ after seven days to kill eggs that may have hatched.

7. Scabies mites are too _____ to be seen by the naked _____.

8. Scabies is transmitted by close _____ contact that may be sexual or nonsexual.

9. Scabies symptoms are typically noticed when small _____ and/or a red rash appear that is accompanied by _____, especially at night.

10. Treatment for scabies consists of a topical scabicide that is applied from the neck to the _____ at bedtime and left on for 8-14 hours.

Acquired Immune Deficiency Syndrome (AIDS), pp. 499-514

1. In the United States AIDS is the _____ leading cause of death of persons 25-44 years of age.

2. AIDS works by destroying the ability of the _____ _____ to fight disease.

3. AIDS is caused by more than one _____.

4. It is now currently believed that AIDS originated in humans when it was transmitted from
_____ to humans living in Africa.
5. AIDS destroys the body's CD-4 _____ which coordinate the immune system's
response to disease.
6. This destruction of the immune system leaves the body vulnerable to _____ and
opportunistic infections.
7. In order to be diagnosed with AIDS, one must have HIV infection and have a CD4 count of
less than _____ cells per cubic millimeter of blood.
8. While the overall number of new HIV infections in the United States has stabilized, rates
among women, _____, and racial/ethnic minorities continue to rise
9. A majority of AIDS cases have been found among two groups, men who have sex with men
(MSM) and _____ drug users (IDUs).
10. Although AIDS cases among MSM are slowing, cases among _____ are rising.
11. _____ contact is the primary form of AIDS transmission worldwide.
12. During penis-vagina intercourse, the risk of becoming infected is greater for _____
than _____.
13. HIV is found in larger concentrations in _____ and _____, and in smaller
concentrations in vaginal secretions, saliva, urine, breast milk, cerebrospinal fluid, and amniotic
fluid.
14. Sexual contact is the mode of transmission of _____ percent of world-wide HIV
infections.
15. HIV may also be transmitted by sharing contaminated _____, from mother to child
before or during birth, during _____-_____ contact, vaginal or anal intercourse.
16. Viral load refers to the amount of HIV present in an infected person's _____.
17. Viral load is greatest during the period of _____ infection, or the time between
exposure to AIDS and the presence of AIDS antibodies in the blood -- a time when most people
do not know they infected.
18. HIV may be transmitted directly into the blood via small tears in _____ tissues or
_____ walls.
19. Newer studies have demonstrated that HIV may be transmitted to the _____
partner during oral sex when the virus comes into contact with mucous membranes, small tears
in the gums, or sores in the mouth.
20. It is believed that the risk of transmitting HIV through saliva, tears, and urine is very
_____.
21. There currently is no evidence which shows that HIV is transmitted through _____
contact such as hugging, shaking hands, or cooking together.
22. Behaviors that put one at high risk for contracting HIV include having multiple sex partners,
engaging in _____ sex, sexual contact with persons known to be at high risk, sharing
drug injection equipment, and using recreational drugs such as _____, marijuana, and
_____.
23. Sometimes people who are infected with HIV will show symptoms a few weeks after the
initial infection, these being: _____, muscle aches, skin rashes, loss of _____,
and swollen lymph glands.
24. These early symptoms of HIV _____ fairly rapidly.
25. Within a few _____ of being infected, most people develop antibodies to the virus
in a process called seroconversion.
26. Once infected with HIV a person should be considered _____, regardless of
whether or not signs of disease are present.

27. "Silent" HIV infections can be present in some persons for _____ years or more before standard blood tests can detect antibodies.

28. The incubation period, or time between infection and onset of symptoms linked to severe immune system impairment is typically _____ to 11 years or more.

29. The most common severe disease among HIV infected people is pneumocystic carnii _____, a disease that affects the lungs.

30. The most common cancer affecting people with AIDS is Kaposi's _____.

31. Death rates for people with AIDS have shown a significant _____ since 1996.

32. The preferred combination of drugs used to treat HIV , which was once called the "AIDS cocktail" is now referred to as highly active _____ therapy (HAART).

33. The high _____ of HAART remains a barrier for underinsured Americans and many people in developing nations.

34. The effectiveness of HAART rests on people being able to consistently follow a _____ schedule of taking medication over a long period of time.

35. Adherence rates for HAART are very _____, in part, because HAART produces toxic side effects that not all persons can tolerate.

36. Lack of adherence to the HAART regimen has resulted in less than optimal therapy, treatment failure, and the development of _____ - _____ strains of HIV.

37. HAART does not remove HIV that is hiding in the _____, lymph nodes, intestines, and other body tissues.

38. Recent studies have shown _____ sexual risk-taking since HAART became available.

39. The need for programs to provide zidovudine to mothers in developing nations remains _____, because most cases of mother-to-child transmission occur in these resource poor countries.

40. The only way to avoid getting HIV infection through sexual contact is to be involved in monogamous, _____ faithful relationship with an uninfected partner, or to abstain from all forms of sexual contact that put one at risk.

Preventing Sexually Transmitted Diseases, pp. 514-521

1. As you assess your partner's risk status, it is important to remember that a recent study of college students showed that _____ percent of men and _____ percent of women lied to their partners about pregnancy risk and prior sexual involvement in order to have sex.

2. This same study showed that people may not lie outright. Instead, people would report fewer partners than they actually had, as 47% of _____ and 42% of _____ did so.

3. A very recent study revealed that _____ percent of HIV infected persons did not tell all of their partners in the last six months their HIV status.

4. Even if your partner is open and honest with you, it is impossible to know if their prior sex partners were completely honest with them, so the authors recommend that couples obtain _____ examinations before beginning a sexual relationship.

5. The authors suggest that _____ condoms plus _____ be used to protect against STDs, even if contraception is not needed.

6. Spermicides containing _____ protect against transmission of bacteria, and *may* offer protection against HIV.

7. Condoms are less effective against the spread of herpes and _____ _____, offer no protection against pubic lice or scabies.

8. Condoms should be stored in a _____, dry place away from _____.

9. Condoms must be put on before _____ contact to prevent exposure to fluids that may contain infectious agents.

10. Lubricated condoms break less readily, so if adding lubricant only water-based products such as spermicides or _____ _____ should be used.

11. Condoms do not offer surefire protection against STDs, as one study showed that _____ percent of condom users reported one or more instances of breakage in the preceding year.

12. Rates of condom slippage and breakage are higher during _____ than _____ intercourse.

13. In order for condoms to offer STD protection, they must be used _____ time you have sex.

14. Avoiding sexual activity with _____ partners and inspecting your partner's _____ are other ways you can prevent STDs from affecting your life.

15. Using _____ focus pleasuring, as described in Chapter 16, may provide a way to explore your partner's genitals prior to sexual interaction.

16. Washing your own and your partner's _____ before and after sexual contact can also reduce your risk of contracting an STD.

17. Since most STDs do not have any noticeable symptoms, the authors suggest that people obtain regular _____ check-ups.

18. Many people do tell their current partner if they have an STD, yet studies have revealed subsequent sexual contacts are likely to remain _____.

Crossword

Across
2. the herpes virus remains dormant in these cells
5. HPV accounts for 85-90% of the risk for this cancer in women
8. a red rash appears in the secondary stage of this STD
9. cold sores and fever blisters represent one form of this virus
11. oral contraceptive use increases risk of this vaginal infection
12. HIV originated in this evolutionary relative

Down
1. _____ contact is the primary form of HIV transmission worldwide
3. erroneously considered a safe sex practice
4. don't cry, there's little HIV in here
6. the most commonly reported infectious disease in the United States
7. hepatitis impairs functioning of this organ
10. acronym describing a chlamydia complication that is a major cause of female infertility

Practice Test

This test will work best to guide your learning if you take it as part of a final review session before an exam.

1. Which of the following age groups is most likely to contract a sexually transmitted disease?
   a. adolescents
   b. young adults
   c. people 35 and over
   d. a and b
   e. b and c

2. Of the STDs listed below, which one is the <u>most</u> prevalent?
   a. syphillis
   b. chlamydia
   c. HIV
   d. gonorrhea

3. If chlamydia infection is left untreated in a female, what will result?
   a. pelvic inflammatory disease
   b. chancroid
   c. blindness
   d. liver damage

4. Most women and men with chlamydia
   a. will become infertile.
   b. will have a foul smelling discharge from the vagina or penis.
   c. display a rash on the scrotum or labia.
   d. show few or no symptoms.

5. All of the following complications may result from gonorrhea infection if a male is untreated <u>except</u>
   a. abcesses on the prostate.
   b. epidydimitis.
   c. adhesions in the spongy bodies of the penis.
   d. infertility.

6. Complications of untreated gonorrhea in women include
   a. vulvar vestibultitis.
   b. adenocarcinoma of the cervix.
   c. inflammed Skene's glands.
   d. infertility.

7. The symptoms of nongonococcal urethritis (NGU) in males are similar to those of
   a. syphillis.
   b. gonorrhea.
   c. AIDS.
   d. viral hepatitis.

8. About three weeks after syphillis infection, which symptom is typically manifested?
    a. a chancre
    b. a rash on the palms of hands or the soles of the feet
    c. a flu-like illness
    d. a watery vaginal discharge

9. During the tertiary stage of syphillis
    a. observable symptoms disappear.
    b. weight loss begins.
    c. complications may result in death.
    d. lymph glands reduce in size.

10. The herpes simplex virus may be spread
    a. when lesions are present.
    b. during the incubation period.
    c. if Zovirax treatment is stopped.
    d. even if no symptoms are present.

11. Which of the following is true regarding oral herpes?
    a. Oral herpes may spread to the genitals through oral sex.
    b. It is caused by HSV-2.
    c. It is caused by HSV-8.
    d. Unlike genital herpes, recurrence is not likely.

12. The discomfort of herpes blisters can be minimized by
    a. douching with plain yogurt.
    b. applying aloe lotion.
    c. keeping sores clean and dry.
    d. exposing the blisters to sunlight.

13. Studies indicate that _____ are more likely to experience major herpes complications than _____.
    a. younger women; older women
    b. heterosexuals; homosexuals
    c. older men; younger men;
    d. women; men

14. The preferred medication for managing herpes is
    a. acyclovir (Zovirax).
    b. metronidazole (Flagyl).
    c. zidovudine.
    d. doxycycline.

15. A serious complication of genital warts (HPV) is
    a. cervical erosion.
    b. prostatitis.
    c. cancer.
    d. nephritis.

16. Which of the following is <u>true</u> regarding genital warts (HPV)?
    a. In moist areas, warts have a hard, yellow-gray appearance.
    b. No known treatment exists that will completely eradicate HPV.
    c. If no warts are visible, the individual is considered cured.
    d. In dry areas, the warts have cauliflower-like appearance

17. The most common form of hepatitis in the United States is
    a. hepatitis A.
    b. hepatitis B.
    c. hepatitis C.
    d. non-A/non-B hepatitis.

18. Hepatitis A is transmitted by
    a. semen.
    b. vaginal fluid.
    c. oral-anal sexual activity.
    d. shared, contaminated needles.

19. A key symptom of viral hepatitis is
    a. swelling of the testicles.
    b. vulva irritation.
    c. intense itching of the lower abdomen.
    d. yellowinh of the whites of the eyes.

20. After she had intercourse, Sierra noticed a fishy odor and a foul-smelling vaginal discharge. Sierra's symptoms are characteristic of
    a. candidiasis.
    b. bacterial vaginosis.
    c. vulvodynia.
    d. trichomoniasis.

21. Griselda has intense itching and soreness in her vulva, and a white, clumpy discharge on her panties. Griselda's experiences are consistent with
    a. gardnerella vaginalis infection.
    b. gential herpes.
    c. a yeast infection.
    d. cystitis.

22. All of the following increase a woman's chance of contracting a vaginal infection <u>except</u>
    a. wearing nylon panties.
    b. taking antibiotics.
    c. using Norplant.
    d. pregnancy.

23. In order to prevent passing trichomoniasis back and forth between male and female sex partners, it is necessary to
    a. treat the male partner even if he has no symptoms.
    b. avoid sexual intercourse for six weeks.
    c. give the woman ampicillin in addition to Flagyl.
    d. apply gentian violet to the penis and scrotum.

24. Pubic lice may be transmitted through
    a. urine.
    b. blood.
    c. eggs deposited on clothing or bedsheets.
    d. poor genital hygiene.

25. Which of the following statements is <u>false</u> regarding AIDS in the United States?
    a. AIDS is the second leading cause of death for people aged 25-44.
    b. The proportion of AIDS cases among men having sex with men has declined.
    c. Higher rates of AIDS are found among ethnic/minority groups.
    d. HIV infection rates for women have been reduced.

26. HIV has been found in all of the following <u>except</u>
    a. blood.
    b. semen.
    c. skin.
    d. saliva.

27. The viral load for HIV is highest
    a. during the period of primary infection.
    b. when AIDS is in its late stages.
    c. when flu-like symptoms first appear.
    d. viral load remains relatively the same once a person is infected.

28. Which activity makes HIV transmission <u>least</u> likely?
    a. receptive oral sex
    b. penis-vagina intercourse
    c. open mouth kissing
    d. sharing injection drug equipment

29. All of the following factors play a role in spreading HIV infection in Africa <u>except</u>
    a. low status of women.
    b. "kept-boy" syndrome.
    c. lack of medical care.
    d. "dry" sex.

30. Which of the following is a symptom of HIV infection?
    a. jaundice
    b. oral candidiasis
    c. itchy skin
    d. weight gain

31. Complications associated with full-blown AIDS include
    a. pneumonia.
    b. Kaposi's sarcoma.
    c. cervical cancer.
    d. all of the above.

32. Although HAART is the preferred treatment for AIDS, the treatment is less than optimal because
    a. it is difficult to consistently and correctly follow this complicated treatment regimen.
    b. physicians are reluctant to prescribe HAART, due to FDA regulations.
    c. the Food and Drug Administrations (FDA) has restricted its use.
    d. HAART is more effective in women than men.

33. The best way to avoid contracting HIV sexually is to
    a. take the AIDS vaccine.
    b. use latex condoms and a spermicide with nonoxynol-9 during every act of sex.
    c. avoid getting too "run down" so that your immune system remains strong.
    d. avoid any form of sexual contact that places one at risk for infection.

34. Which statement is true regarding studies that have examined people's honesty about past sexual and drug use histories?
    a. Women were more likely than men to lie about past sexual involvements than men.
    b. Most HIV infected persons disclosed their status to their prior sex partners.
    c. Over 40% of college students would report fewer sex partners than they actually had.
    d. IV drug users were the least likely to disclose their HIV status.

35. All of the following describe proper condom use except
    a. wear a condom before any genital contact.
    b. withdraw the condom clad penis while it is still erect.
    c. store condoms in a warm, moist place.
    d. lubricate the condom with K-Y jelly if needed.

Answer Key – Chapter 17

<u>Concept Checks</u>

Chapter Opening, pp. 474-478
1. 15; 25
2. 35
3. teens; 20s
4. multiple; unprotected

Bacterial Infections, pp. 478-486

<u>Chlamydia</u>
1. chlamydia
2. oral contraceptives; douche
3. urethritis
4. pelvic
5. infertility
6. urethritis
7. eye
8. single

<u>Gonorrhea and Syphillis</u>
9. teenagers
10. men; women
11. cloudy; urination
12. partner
13. genitourinary
14. symptoms
15. pelvic
16. throat
17. diseases
18. no; chlamydia
19. urethral
20. decreasing; death
21. lesions; anal
22. fourth
23. chancre
24. eight; skin rash
25. tertiary
26. penicillin

<u>Chancroid</u>
27. Africa
28. increasing
29. HIV
30. ulcers
31. little

Viral Infections
1. cell

<u>Herpes</u>
2. two
3. 1; 2
4. STD
5. kissing
6. vaginal; anal
7. viral shedding
8. latex
9. scrotal
10. self-infection
11. symptoms
12. papules; cervix
13. contagious
14. ten
15. 16
16. nerve
17. prodromal
18. men
19. cervix; newborn
20. acyclovir
21. stress; dry

<u>Genital Warts</u>
22. human papilloma
23. prevalent
24. eight
25. warts
26. cervix
27. vaginal
28. moist
29. dry
30. cancer
31. cervical
32. therapy

<u>Viral Hepatitis</u>
33. liver
34. A; B; non-A/non-B
35. A; B
36. men; IV
37. semen; saliva
38. anus
39. oral-fecal
40. yellowing;
41. fluid

Common Vaginal Infections, pp. 495-498

1. vagina
2. acidic
3. birth control; pregnancy; nylon
4. bacterial vaginosis
5. coitus
6. foul
7. pregnancy
8. asymptomatic
9. metronidazole (or Flagyl)
10. male partners
11. yeast
12. contraceptives
13. back; front
14. itching; clumpy
15. suppositories
16. disappear
17. trichomoniasis
18. Women; men
19. urethritis
20. urethra
21. Flagyl

Ectoparasitic Infections, pp. 498-499

1. Scabies; pubic lice
2. pubic
3. eggs
4. itching
5. ten
6. repeated
7. small; eye
8. physical
9. bumps; itching
10. toes

Acquired Immune Deficiency Syndrome, pp. 499-514

1. second
2. immune system
3. virus
4. chimpanzees
5. lymphocytes
6. cancers
7. 200
8. teenagers
9. IV
10. IDUs

11. Heterosexual
12. women; men
13. blood; semen
14. 80
15. needles; oral-genital
16. blood
17. primary
18. rectal; vaginal
19. receptive
20. low
21. casual
22. unprotected; alcohol; cocaine
23. fevers; appetite
24. fade
25. weeks
26. contagious
27. three
28. eight
29. pneumonia
30. sarcoma
31. decline
32. anitretroviral
33. cost
34. complicated
35. poor
36. drug-resistant
37. brain
38. increased
39. enormous
40. mutually

Preventing Sexually Transmitted Diseases, pp. 514-521
1. 35; 10
2. men; women
3. 40
4. medical
5. latex; spermicide
6. nonoxynol-9
7. genital warts
8. cool; sunlight
9. genital
10. K-Y jelly
11. 23
12. anal; vaginal
13. every
14. multiple; genitals
15. sensate
16. genitals

17. medical
18. uninformed

Crossword Puzzle

Across
 2. nerve
 5. cervical
 8. syphillis
 9. herpes
11. yeast
12. chimpanzees

Down
 1. heterosexual
 3. oral
 4. tears
 6. chlamydia
 7. liver
10. PID

Practice Test

1. d 2. b 3. a 4. d 5. c 6. d 7. b 8. a 9. c 10. d 11. a 12. c 13. d
14. a 15. c 16. b 17. a 18. c 19. d 20. b 21. c 22. c 23. a 24. c 25. d
26. c 27. a 28. c 29. b 30. b 31. d 32. a 33. d 34. c 35. c

Chapter 18 – Atypical Sexual Behavior

Introduction

Less common forms of sexual expression are described in this chapter on atypical sexual behaviors, or paraphilias. The difference between "normal" and atypical sexual behaviors is often one of degree, since milder forms of some of these behaviors may exist within each of us. Exhibiting these behaviors in full form implies that this is someone's primary mode of sexual expression. Distinctions are drawn between coercive and noncoercive paraphilias. Methods of treating coercive paraphilias are discussed, and the controversial topic of sexual addiction is explored.

Learning Objectives. *In order to derive maximum benefit from these objectives, use these as soon as you begin reading the chapter. After you have completed reading and studying this chapter, you should be able to do the things listed below with ease, using only your memory.*

1. Define atypical sexual behavior and paraphilia and distinguish it from other labels such as deviant, perverted, abnormal, etc.

2. Explain each of the following considerations in discussing atypical sexual behavior:
    a. how these behaviors exist on a continuum
    b. what our knowledge base is regarding these various behaviors
    c. to what extent paraphilias may exist in clusters and the implications of that
    d. the impact of atypical sexual behavior both on the person exhibiting the behavior and on the recipient of the behavior

3. Distinguish between noncoercive and coercive paraphilias

4. Describe fetishism, making specific reference to the following:
    a. problems in defining it
    b. common fetish objects
    c. how it develops
    d. other offenses that may be associated with fetishism

5. Discuss each of the following in regard to transvestic fetishism:
    a. the range of behaviors that may comprise it
    b. who is most likely to engage in this behavior, citing relevant statistics
    c. what studies reveal regarding partner response to this behavior

6. Define sadomasochistic behavior, sexual sadism and sexual masochism and discuss each of the following in reference to these behaviors:
    a. the complexity involved in labeling these behaviors
    b. available statistics that indicate how common these behaviors may be
    c. the behavioral and psychological dynamics involved
    d. social views regarding these behaviors
    e. reasons why people may choose to engage in these behaviors

7. Describe each of the following noncoercive paraphilias:
    a. autoerotic asphyxiation

    b. klismaphilia
    c. coprophilia and urophilia

8. Define exhibitionism and discuss each of the following in regard to it:
    a. variations on this behavior
    b. what we know about the type of person who exhibits this behavior, and what some of the problems are with the available data
    c. theories regarding what influences the development of this behavior
    d. how likely exhibitionists are to engage in other illegal behaviors
    e. how to respond to exhibitionistic behavior

9. Explain what we know about the person who makes obscene phone calls, and the likelihood that this person will engage in other illegal sexual behaviors.

10. Outline several strategies for dealing with obscene phone calls.

11. Define voyeurism and discuss the problems in attempting to determine what qualifies as voyeuristic behavior.

12. Discuss common characteristics of voyeurs, the likelihood of voyeurs engaging in other serious offenses, and explain what factors may trigger voyeuristic behavior.

13. Briefly describe each of the following coercive paraphilias:
    a. frotteurism
    b. zoophilia
    c. necrophilia

14. Describe each of the following treatment alternatives for coercive paraphilias:
    a. psychotherapy
    b. behavior therapy
    c. aversive conditioning
    d. systematic desensitizing
    e. orgasmic reconditioning
    f. satiation therapy
    g. drug treatment
    h. social skills training

15. Discuss the controversy surrounding sexual addiction—what it is, how to categorize it and how to treat it.

Concept Map

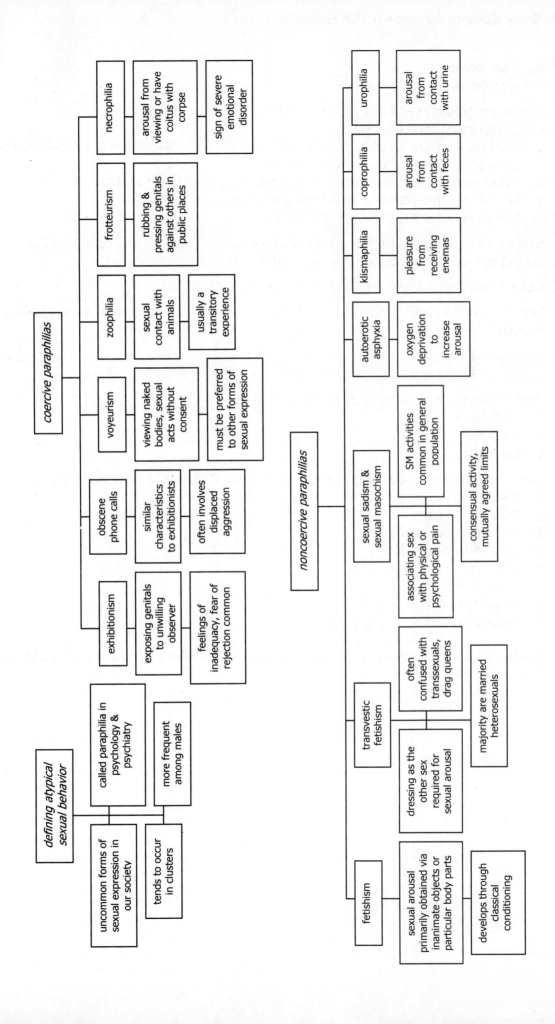

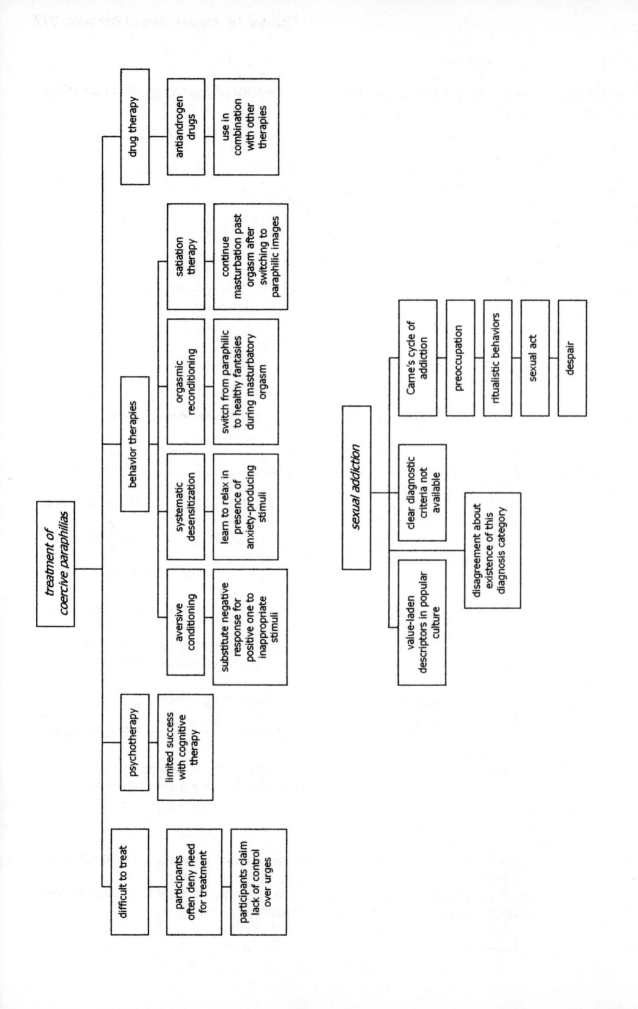

Key Terms. *Refer to the glossary or subject index in the back of your textbook for definitions and information.*

paraphilia
atypical sexual behaviors
fetishism
transvestic fetishism
sadomasochistic behavior
sexual sadism
sexual masochism
bondage
autoerotic asphyxia
klismaphilia
coprophilia
urophilia

exhibitionism
voyeurism
zoophilia
necrophilia
psychotherapy
cognitive therapies
aversive conditioning
systematic desensitization
orgasmic reconditioning
satiation therapy
antiandrogen drugs
social skills training

Concept-Checks. *Complete this section by filling in each blank after you have studied the corresponding pages from the text. Answers are provided at the back of this chapter.*

What Constitutes Atypical Sexual Behavior?, pp. 526-527
1. The term paraphilia literally means "beyond usual or typical _____", and is used to describe uncommon types of _____ _____.
2. The authors prefer to use the term _____ sexual behaviors because these behaviors, when fully developed, are not typically shown by most people in our society.
3. Although the atypical behaviors described in this chapter exist in various degrees, many of us recognize some aspect of these behaviors or feelings within _____.
4. Most people who report practicing atypical forms of sexual expression tend to be

_____.
5. Sexologist John Money believes that _____ erotosexual differentiation is more complex than _____, therefore more errors may result.
6. Since atypical sexual behaviors tend to occur in _____, engaging in one form of atypical sexual expression lessens _____ so that engaging in another atypical sexual behavior becomes more likely.
7. Many persons who exhibit atypical sexual behavior find it difficult to have _____ or intimate relationships with _____.
8. Since noncoercive atypical sexual behaviors do not involve violating someone's basic rights, some people believe that these behaviors are _____.
9. Some people question whether coercive sexual behaviors should be labeled "_____" offenses, since some research indicates that people progress from these offenses to more serious ones.

Noncoercive Paraphilias, pp. 527-534
1. When an individual's preferred way to become sexually aroused involves focusing upon an inanimate object or part of the human body, _____ occurs.
2. In some cases, sexual response in the absence of the fetish object is not possible, whereas in other cases sexual response has a _____ intensity.

3. For other people fetish objects act as _____ for human contact and are not used if a human partner is available.
4. Some researchers argue that fetishism results from the process of classical _____, where objects become associated with sexual arousal.
5. Another explanation for fetishism is that a fetish object becomes endowed with the power of an _____ significant person, and so the fetishist responds to the object as though it were that person.
6. Only rarely does fetishism evolve into something that may harm someone, and this key exception is the crime of _____.
7. The term transvestite is now applied only to persons who dress as the other sex in order to experience _____ _____.
8. Transsexuals cross-dress in order to attain some sense of physical and emotional _____, rather than for sexual gratification.
9. A key distinction between fetishism and transvestic fetishism is that in transvestic fetishism the object is actually _____, instead of being just viewed or touched.
10. Many members of the _____ community believe that transvestic fetishism is legitimate way to become sexually aroused and do not agree with the notion that it is an abnormal form of sexual expression.
11. Current guidelines specify that only _____ males can receive the diagnosis of transvestic fetishism.
12. Research studies have demonstrated that _____ men with a _____ orientation comprise the majority of transvestic fetishists.
13. One explanation for transvestic fetishism states that it develops through a process of _____ similar to other fetishes.
14. Transvestic fetishism seems to be more common among societies where males have a greater _____ burden than females.
15. One group of transvestic fetishists are heterosexual males who want to express the _____ side of personality in a society that forces males to adopt rigid gender roles.
16. Sadomasochistic behavior involves associating sex with _____, and this may be physical or _____.
17. Sexual sadism involves achieving arousal by _____ pain whereas sexual masochism involves achieving arousal through _____ pain.
18. Engaging in sexual sadism does not necessarily imply that one also engages in sexual masochism, so the American Psychiatric Association has _____ categories for each of these paraphilias.
19. Labeling sexual expression as sadism or masochism is problematic, as one recent study of 975 people found that _____ percent reported occasionally engaging in an SM activity with a partner.
20. Most people who engage in SM activities stay within _____ agreed-on limits.
21. In mild forms of sexual sadism the pain that is inflicted is often more _____ than _____.
22. _____ involves receiving sexual pleasure from being bound up, tied, or restricted.
23. Persons with sadistic tendencies are _____ common than those with masochistic tendencies.
24. Studies with better research methodology have revealed that SM is a form of sexual enhancement involving elements of dominance, submission, role-playing and _____.
25. Many people who participate in SM activities do so out of a desire to experience _____ or _____ rather than pain.

26. One theory proposed by Baumeister asserts that SM provides an opportunity to escape from high levels of _____-_____.
27. Clinical cases studies also suggest that SM practitioners often have _____ experiences that established a connection between sex and pain.
28. The authors suggest that many people, perhaps the majority, do not depend on SM activities to experience sexual _____ and _____.
29. When sexual arousal is enhanced by using pressure to deprive oneself of oxygen, the paraphilia is called _____ _____.
30. Persons engage in oxygen deprivation alone or with a _____.
31. Autoerotic asphyxia is extremely _____ and life threatening.
32. Some sexologists have suggested that autoerotic asphyxia is a variation of _____ _____ with bondage themes.
33. _____ refers to obtaining sexual arousal from receiving enemas.
34. Coprophilia describes obtaining sexual gratification from contact with _____, whereas _____ describes obtaining sexual arousal from contact with urine.
35. "Water sport" and "golden showers" are other names for the paraphilia called _____.

Coercive Paraphilias, pp. 535-541
1. Exhibitionism has also been referred to as _____ _____.
2. Exhibitionism involves exposing one's _____ to a(n) _____ observer.
3. The victims of exhibitionism are usually _____ and _____.
4. What we know about people who engage in exhibitionism comes from samples of arrested offenders, an _____ sample. This requires that we interpret such data with caution.
5. The limited data tells us that most people who exhibit themselves are _____ in their 20s or 30s, and over half are or have been _____.
6. Those who engage in exhibitionism are frequently very _____ and nonassertive, and they often feel _____ and have problems with intimacy.
7. People who engage in exhibitionism often function _____ in their daily lives.
8. Most men who participate in exhibitionism _____ this activity to exposing themselves to others, and do not escalate the behavior any further or physically harm the victim.
9. Victims of exhibitionists may be emotionally _____ by the experience.
10. If you are the victim of an exhibitionist, the authors suggest calmly _____ the offender, as most exhibitionists want to elicit reactions of disgust or fear from victims.
11. People who make obscene phone calls are similar to those who engage in _____.
12. Those who engage in obscene phone calls show greater anxiety and _____ than exhibitionists.
13. Obscene phone callers often _____ during or following a call, and _____ follow up with a physical confrontation with the victim.
14. If you are the victim of an obscene phone call, the authors suggest simply setting down the _____ and going about your business, and if the phone rings again do not _____ it.
15. Some degree of _____ is socially acceptable, as when we view movies, so it is sometimes difficult to determine when this behavior becomes a problem.
16. In order to be considered an atypical sexual behavior, voyeurism must be preferred to sexual relations with _____ or engaged in with some _____.
17. Voyeurs are most often aroused when the threat of discovery is _____.
18. People who engage in voyeurism have characteristics similar to _____.

19. Voyeurs typically have poor social skills, and strong feelings of _____ and inferiority, and are males in their early _____.
20. Those who engage in voyeurism prefer to "peep" at _____ rather than someone known to them.
21. Pressing or rubbing one's body against another's in a public place is referred to as

_____.
22. During the activity described above, orgasm may be experienced, yet it is more common to integrate mental images of the act during fantasies used while _____ later.
23. Zoophilia is sometimes referred to as _____.
24. Zoophilia is considered a coercive paraphilia because the participant(s) are _____.
25. Sexual contact with animals is typically a _____ event, when a partner is unavailable.
26. True zoophilia exists only when sexual contact with animals is _____ regardless of what other forms of sexual expression are possible.
27. When someone experiences sexual arousal when viewing or being sexually intimate with a corpse, _____ is said to occur.
28. Persons who engage in the behavior described above tend to be males who display severe _____ disorders.
29. Some necrophiles have acted out desires by having contact with _____ corpses, such as prostitutes who dress and act like dead persons.

Treatment of Coercive Paraphilias, pp. 541-544
1. People who engage in coercive paraphilias typically do not _____ that they are in need of _____.
2. Those who engage in coercive paraphilias also claim that they are unable to _____ their compulsions.
3. A pivotal step in treatment is dispelling the paraphiliac's belief that he is _____ to change his behavior.
4. Talking with a psychologist, social worker, or psychiatrist during individual _____ has not been demonstrated as an effective way to treat coercive paraphilias.
5. _____ therapy rests on the notion that distortions in thinking produce psychological disorders.
6. Maladaptive behaviors have been learned, so they can be unlearned, according to _____ therapy.
7. Steve receives painful, but not damaging, electric shocks while he masturbates and fantasizes about past incidents where he exposed himself to unwilling victims. Steve seems to be experiencing _____ conditioning therapy.
8. Most men who receive aversive conditioning are required by the _____ _____ to undergo this course of treatment.
9. Exposing persons to anxiety-provoking situations while training them to relax constitutes _____ _____ therapy.
10. The goal of the therapy described above is to help people overcome feelings of anxiety due to feelings of _____ and poor social skills.
11. During orgasmic reconditioning the client masturbates to his usual fantasies, then as _____ approaches, he switches to more socially appropriate imagery.
12. As orgasmic reconditioning progresses, the client is instructed to move the appropriate images to _____ phases of his masturbation-induced sexual response cycle.

13. _____ therapy is in some ways the opposite of orgasmic reconditioning therapy, as the client masturbates to appropriate images, then switches to inappropriate ones right after orgasm, while continuing to masturbate.

14. Drugs such as Depo-Provera are termed _____ and may block inappropriate sexual arousal by reducing testosterone levels in the body.

15. Drug treatment tends to work best when it is _____ with other therapies.

16. Developing the skills needed to establish and maintain the healthy interpersonal relationships that allow access to appropriate forms of sexual expression is called _____ _____ training.

Sexual Addiction: Fact, Fiction, or Misnomer? pp. 544-545

1. Terms such as _____ for women and _____ for men are pejorative ways of describing the concept of sexual addiction.

2. The authors believe that guidelines used to establish alleged conditions of hypersexuality are subjective and value-laden, because there are no clear criteria as to what are _____ levels of sexual involvement.

3. Carnes' controversial book established four phases of sexual addiction, these being preoccupation, _____ behaviors, the sexual act, and _____.

4. Sexologist Eli Coleman proposed the concept of sexual _____ rather than addiction.

5. According to Coleman, such persons suffer from feelings of shame, unworthiness, _____ and _____, which cause pain, and lead to the search for a "fix" to numb the pain.

Crossword

Across
3. in klismaphilia this is needed to produce sexual arousal
4. Carne's last phase of the sexual addiction cycle
7. transvestic fetishism has this goal, cross dressing does not
9. "partner" of someone with necrophilic tendencies
10. systematic desensitization seeks to substitute this for arousal
11. frotteurism venue
12. reading pornographic magazines is a mild form of this behavior

Down
1. conditioning that substitutes a negative response for a positive one to inappropriate stimuli
2. people engaging in coercive paraphilias believe they cannot _____ their behavior
5. common feeling among persons engaging in coercive paraphilias
6. atypical sexual behaviors often occur in this fashion
8. 25% of Rubin's respondents engaged in the SM activity

Practice Test

This test will work best to guide your learning if you take it as part of a final review session before an exam.

1. Paraphilias are _____ sexual behaviors.
   a. deviant
   b. perverted
   c. atypical
   d. illegal

2. Most persons who disclose that they have engaged in a paraphilia are
   a. psychologically disordered.
   b. male.
   c. adults with histories of childhood maltreatment.
   d. erotosexually undifferentiated.

3. A person who dresses in the clothes of the other sex in order to obtain sexual arousal is referred to as a(n)
   a. homosexual.
   b. transsexual.
   c. transgendered person.
   d. transvestite.

4. Obtaining sexual pleasure by receiving physical or psychological pain is called
   a. sexual masochism.
   b. sexual sadism.
   c. bondage.
   d. domination.

5. Rubbing or pressing one's genitals against an unwilling or unaware person while in a public place is best described as
   a. klismaphilia.
   b. coprophilia.
   c. exhibitionism.
   d. frotteurism.

6. Urophilia describes the act of experiencing sexual arousal due to contact with _____ .
   a. diapers
   b. rubber
   c. urine
   d. feces

7. Someone who engages in fetishism becomes sexually aroused by
   a. inanimate objects or particular parts of the body.
   b. violent or degrading pornographic films.
   c. engaging in ritualized stroking of housecats.
   d. viewing childhood pornography.

8. Which paraphilia listed below may result in death for the person engaging in it?
   a. necrophilia
   b. autoerotic asphyxiation
   c. frotteurism
   d. telephone scatalogia

9. Seeking sexual gratification by exposing one's genitals to an unwilling observer is termed
   a. exhibitionism.
   b. sadism.
   c. voyeurism.
   d. nudism.

10. Fetishism is thought to develop through
    a. abusive childhood discipline.
    b. aversion conditioning.
    c. classical conditioning.
    d. instrumental conditioning.

11. The majority of persons who engage in transvestic fetishism are
    a. heterosexual.
    b. bisexual.
    c. homosexual.
    d. celibate.

12. Anthropologists have noted that transvestic fetishism is more common in societies where
    a. gender roles are fluid.
    b. participation in organized religion is low.
    c. males have more economic responsibility than women.
    d. homosexuality is sanctioned.

13. A study of SM participants in a nonclinical environment found that SM activities involve
    a. consensuality.
    b. the expression of both sadism and masochism within the same encounter.
    c. coercion.
    d. severe physical pain.

14. A large study of 975 persons found that _____ of the respondents reported at least occasionally engaging in some form of SM.
    a. 5%
    b. 10%
    c. 15%
    d. 25%

15. Some theorists have suggested that SM allows participants to
    a. increase self-awareness.
    b. relinquish ego control.
    c. escape from restrictive roles they occupy in everyday life.
    d. express thanatological urges.

16. All of the following are characteristics of persons who engage in exhibitionism <u>except</u>
    a. They often feel inadequate.
    b. Most go on to physically assault the victim.
    c. Most exhibitionists are married men.
    d. They have difficulty with intimacy.

17. All of the following are strategies suggested to deal with obscene phone calls <u>except</u>
    a. slamming down the phone.
    b. pretending to be hard-of-hearing.
    c. calmly hanging up the phone.
    d. ignoring the phone if it rings again.

18. People who engage in voyeurism are similar to
    a. rapists.
    b. sexual sadists.
    c. exhibitionists.
    d. pedophiles.

19. Which statement regarding zoophilia is <u>true</u>?
    a. It is commonly a transitory experience.
    b. The National Health and Social Life Survey found a decrease in this behavior since Kinsey's time.
    c. Zoophilia is considered a noncoercive paraphilia.
    c. Females typically have contact with farm animals.

20. Treating coercive paraphilias is difficult because
    a. few treatment modalities are available.
    b. malpractice suits are more likely to be brought against a therapist by this client type.
    c. people with coercive paraphilias often do not believe they need treatment.
    d. rates of depression and suicide are high.

21. All of the following are methods of treating coercive paraphilias <u>except</u>
    a. psychoanalysis.
    b. cognitive therapy.
    c. orgasmic reconditioning.
    d. aversive conditioning.

22. Antiandrogen drugs work to reduce compulsive, paraphiliac urges by
    a. stimulating estrogen production.
    b. reducing testosterone levels.
    c. prompting the prostate gland to release prostate-specific-antigen.
    d. temporarily stopping sperm production.

23. Sexologists disagree about the existence of sexual addiction because
    a. there are no clear criteria about what normal levels of sexual activity are.
    b. the disorder is not distinguishable from other compulsive disorders.
    c. the disorder negates individual responsibility.
    d. all of the above are true.

Answer Key – Chapter 18

Concept Checks

What Constitutes Atypical Sexual Behavior?
1. love; sexual behavior
2. atypical
3. ourselves
4. male
5. male; female
6. clusters; inhibitions
7. sexual; others
8. harmless
9. nuisance

Noncoercive Paraphilias
1. fetishism
2. diminshed
3. substitute
4. conditioning
5. emotionally
6. burglary
7. sexual arousal
8. completeness
9. worn
10. transgendered
11. heterosexual
12. married; heterosexual
13. conditioning
14. economic
15. feminine
16. pain; psychological
17. giving; receiving
18. separate
19. 25
20. mutually
21. symbolic; real
22. Bondage
23. less
24. consensuality
25. dominance; submission
26. self-awareness
27. early
28. arousal; orgasm
29. autoerotic asphyxia
30. partner
31. dangerous
32. sexual masochism

33. Klismaphilia
34. feces; urophilia
35. urophilia

Coercive Paraphilias
 1. indecent exposure
 2. genitals; unwilling
 3. women; children
 4. unrepresentative
 5. males; married
 6. shy; inadequate
 7. effectively
 8. limit
 9. traumatized
10. ignoring
11. exhibitionism
12. hostility
13. masturbate; rarely
14. phone; answer
15. voyeurism
16. others; risk
17. high
18. exhibitionists
19. inadequacy; 20s
20. strangers
21. frotteurism
22. masturbating
23. bestiality
24. unwilling
25. transitory
26. preferred
27. necrophilia
28. emotional
29. simulated

Treatment of Coercive Paraphilias
 1. acknowledge; treatment
 2. control
 3. powerless
 4. psychotherapy
 5. Cognitive
 6. behavior
 7. aversive
 8. legal system
 9. systematic desensitization
10. inadequacy
11. orgasm
12. earlier

13. Satiation
14. antiandrogens
15. combined
16. social skills

Sexual Addiction: Fact, Fiction, or Misnomer?
 1. nymphomania; satyriasis
 2. normal
 3. ritualistic; despair
 4. compulsion
 5. inadequacy; loneliness

Crossword Puzzle

Across
 3. enema
 4. despair
 7. arousal
 9. corpse
10. relaxation
11. bus
12. voyeurism

Down
 1. aversive
 2. control
 5. inadequacy
 6. clusters
 8. bondage

Practice Test

1. c 2. b 3. d 4. a 5. d 6. c 7. a 8. b 9. a 10. c 11. a 12. c
13. a 14. d 15. c 16. b 17. a 18. c 19. a 20. c 21. a 22. b 23. a

Chapter 19 – Sexual Victimization

Introduction

Our nation is becoming increasingly aware of the staggering frequency of sexual victimization within its borders. This chapter focuses attention on sociocultural phenomena that create a society in which rape, sexual abuse of children, and sexual harassment are commonplace events. Both clinical experience and current research are utilized to discuss characteristics of perpetrators and experiences of victims. Strategies for preventing and coping with rape, reducing child sexual abuse, and dealing with sexual harassment are also described.

Learning Objectives. In order to derive maximum benefit from these objectives, use these as soon as you begin reading the chapter. After you have completed reading and studying this chapter, you should be able to do the things listed below with ease, using only your memory.

1. Define all of the key terms and concepts for this chapter listed in the margin of the text and be able to integrate them with all relevant material outlined below.

2. Discuss the difficulties in obtaining accurate statistics on the number of rapes and rape survivors in the U.S. and cite some of the variations in currently available statistics.

3. Identify and elaborate upon five false beliefs regarding rape.

4. Citing relevant research, describe some of the psychosocial bases of rape.

5. Discuss what research has revealed regarding the impact of sexually violent and degrading media on the attitudes and behaviors of rapists and nonrapists.

6. Describe the characteristics of men who rape.

7. Discuss the arguments for and against a sociobiological explanation of rape.

8. Discuss recent research regarding acquaintance rape and sexual coercion, making specific reference to the following:
   a. how prevalent it is
   b. factors that might contribute to people engaging in unwanted sexual activity
   c. the use of the drugs such as Rohypnol to facilitate sexual conquest or to incapacitate victims who are then raped or molested

9. Cite examples of how and for what purposes wartime rape has been used.

10. Explain the short-term and long-term effects of rape on female survivors, making specific reference to the following:
    a. rape trauma syndrome
    b. suggestions regarding how to respond to a partner who has been raped

11. Discuss how frequently the rape and sexual assault of males occurs, who the perpetrators are, and what some of the problems are with the data in this area.

13. Describe some of the physical, psychological and sexual effects are on men who have been raped.

14. List and briefly describe nine suggestions for reducing the risk of stranger rape.

15. List and briefly describe five suggestions for how to deal with threatening situations involving strangers.

16. List and briefly describe six suggestions for reducing the risk of acquaintance rape.

17. List and briefly describe five ways in which a woman may take action if she has been raped.

18. Distinguish between pedophilia and incest, and discuss some of the differences in defining child molestation.

19. Discuss the problem of pedophiles in cyberspace and what might be done to combat this problem.

20. Discuss the sexual abuse of children, citing specific information and current research as it relates to the following:
    a. in what situations and under what conditions it most commonly occurs
    b. how prevalent it is and the problems with these statistics
    c. how incidence of abuse in girls compares to that of boys

21. Discuss the results of a controversial meta-analysis concerning the effects of sexual abuse on children.

22. Describe the factors that contribute to how severely abuse affects the victim and what these effects might be.

23. Identify treatment programs available for child sexual abuse survivors.

24. Describe the characteristics of the person who sexually abuses children.

25. Discuss the controversy surrounding the issue of recovered memories of child sexual abuse.

26. List and describe ten suggestions for preventing childhood sexual abuse.

27. Explain what kinds of responses might be helpful in the event you discovered that your own child had been molested by an adult.

28. Define sexual harassment and describe two types of sexual harassment as provided by the EEOC guidelines.

29. Discuss the various forms that sexual harassment can take.

30. Citing relevant statistics, discuss how common sexual harassment is among men and women.

31. Discuss some of the problems unique to same-sex sexual harassment.

32. Discuss the effects of on-the-job harassment on victims.

33. Outline and describe six guidelines for dealing with sexual harassment in the workplace.

34. Discuss sexual harassment that may occur in an academic setting, making specific reference to the following:
    a. who the perpetrators are
    b. differences between harassment that occurs in an academic setting vs. the workplace
    c. how common sexual harassment is in this setting
    d. how to deal with sexual harassment in an academic environment

35. Discuss how different cultures may punish women who have been raped.

Concept Map

Rape

coitus without consent under actual or threatened force

types & prevalence

- women are victims more than men
- majority of first rapes under 25 years of age
- most rapes not reported to police
- *statutory* – under age of consent
- *acquaintance* – more common than stranger rape
- stranger rape

rape myths abound

- help justify male aggression & deny extent of rape

factors promoting rape

rapist characteristics
- no single profile
- unrepresentative samples hinder research
- anger, power and sexual gratification play some role

rape-prone society
- unequal power between sexes
- glorification of male violence
- peer group support of sexual aggression
- mass media

acquaintance rape issues

- 20-35% of women are victims
- sexual scripts promote poor communication

aftermath

- guilt & shame common
- physical symptoms common
- avoidance of or reduced sexual activity

sexual harassment

unwelcome advances, requests, creation of hostile environment

types

- quid pro quo
  - compliance is condition of employment or advancement
- hostile or offensive environment
  - no power imbalance present

prevalence

- women: 40-82% across variety of jobs
- men: 15-22% on more limited data

impact on victim

- adverse effects common on finances & career
- most victims experience psychological distress

academic settings

- effects 20-50% of high school & college students

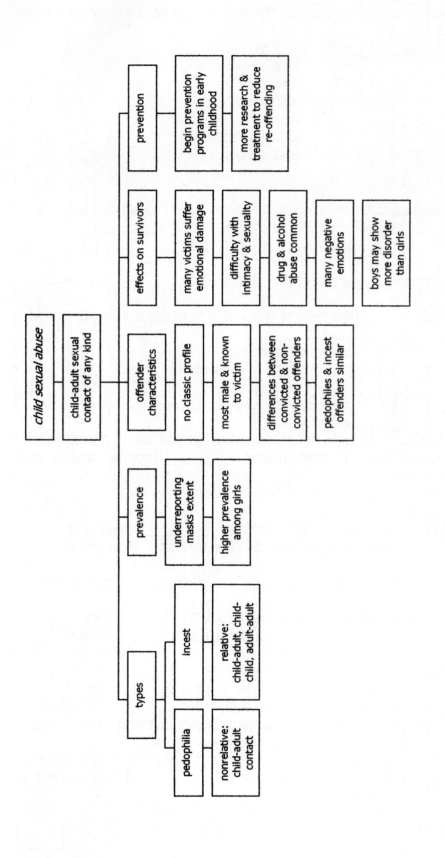

child sexual abuse

child-adult sexual contact of any kind

types

pedophilia

nonrelative: child-adult contact

incest

relative: child-adult, child-child, adult-adult

prevalence

underreporting masks extent

higher prevalence among girls

offender characteristics

no classic profile

most male & known to victim

differences between convicted & non-convicted offenders

pedophiles & incest offenders similar

effects on survivors

many victims suffer emotional damage

difficulty with intimacy & sexuality

drug & alcohol abuse common

many negative emotions

boys may show more disorder than girls

prevention

begin prevention programs in early childhood

more research & treatment to reduce re-offending

Key Terms. *Refer to the glossary or subject index in the back of your textbook for definitions and information.*

rape

acquaintance rape

date rape

statutory rape

sexual scripts

posttraumatic stress disorder

child sexual abuse

pedophilia

child molestation

incest

sexual harassment

quid pro quo

Concept-Checks. *Complete this section by filling in each blank after you have studied the corresponding pages from the text. Answers are provided at the back of this chapter.*

Rape, pp. 548-560

1. Most state laws define rape as sexual intercourse that occurs without _____ as a result of actual or _____ force.

2. _____ rape and _____ rape refer to types of rape where the perpetrator is known to the victim.

3. _____ rape describes rape by an unknown assailant.

4. When intercourse occurs with someone below the age of consent, it is called _____ rape.

5. Estimates of the percentage of rapes that are actually reported to law enforcement agencies range from 11.9 percent to _____ percent.

6. Many rape victims do not report the crime to the police because of self-blame, fear of being _____ by others, mistrust of the legal system, fear of _____ by the victim or his family, and a desire to avoid unwanted publicity.

7. Many acquaintance rapes are not reported because they do not fit a woman's _____ notion of what a "real" rape may be.

8. A new study with acceptable methodological rigor found that _____ percent of women and _____ percent of men reported they had been the victim of a real or attempted rape.

9. Rape myths promote the justification of male _____ and place _____ on the victim.

10. The notion that "women can't be raped if they don't want to be" is false because a) men are physically larger and _____ than women; b) gender role conditioning teaches women to be _____ and _____ and c) the _____ chooses the time and place for the attack to occur, creating a rather large advantage.

11. The false belief that "women say no when they mean yes" implies that women want to be _____ into sexual activity, and that the act was not rape, but "_____" sex play.

12. The notion that "women cry rape" is false because research shows that women are actually _____ likely to experience rape and not report the crime to any authority.

13. The notion that "all women want to be raped" should be questioned because in a fantasy, the person retains _____, and fantasy carries no risk of _____ or death, whereas a rape does.

14. The notion that "rapists are 'obviously' mentally ill" is mistaken because it breeds the feeling that we are safe with someone we know, yet most rapes are committed by someone _____ to the victim.

15. The belief that "male sex drive is so high that men cannot control their urges" is questionable because it shifts responsibility from the _____ to the _____.

16. Most researchers and therapists believe that rape results primarily from _____ processes within society as a whole, rather than disorder within individual rapists.

17. Anthropologist Peggy Reeves Sanday distinguishes between rape-prone societies that tolerate and glorify masculine _____ , allow men to remain distanced and uninvolved with "women's work", and have great power imbalances between the sexes, and rape-free societies where women and men share _____ and _____, and children of both sexes are raised to value nurturance and avoid aggression.

18. The United States has the _____ incidence of rape among Western nations.

19. Several studies have demonstrated that males who have _____ that act sexually aggressive or condone the use of aggression to gain access to women are more likely to engage in sexually aggressive behavior.

20. The notion that rape is a sexualization of violence is supported by _____ evidence, calling for more research to make sense of these findings.

21. Studies examining the characteristics of rapists are flawed because they are based upon men who are _____ of rape, making the samples highly unrepresentative.

22. Men who uphold _____ gender roles, who have _____-_____ personalities, and have _____ toward women are more likely to sexually assault women.

23. Gene Abel's careful research supports the notion that some rapists may engage in progressively more _____ sexual offenses.

24. Over 50% of women who were raped indicated that their first rape occurred before age _____, and 22% of women stated that their first rape occurred before age _____.

25. Prison inmates, _____ _____ and prisoners of war are men who have a higher risk of being raped.

26. Men are especially likely to avoid reporting rape, because men who report being the victim of sex crimes are judged especially harshly by other _____.

27. Another reason that sexual assault of males is infrequently reported is that such assaults are rarely reported in the _____ and in the medical and psychological literature.

28. Sexual assaults on _____ males are more violent than assaults on _____ males.

29. The risk of stranger rape may be reduced by changing behavior in accordance with the results of one study which showed that rapists were more likely to select victims who exhibited _____ and _____.

30. Several studies have also shown that women who offer verbal or physical _____ are more likely to avoid being raped than women who cry or plead.

31. To minimize the risk of acquaintance rape, using _____ communication can reduce a man's tendency to force unwanted sexual activity, or to feel he was "led on".

32. If a woman who has been raped begins to blame herself, the authors suggest that she remember that being raped is not a _____.

33. The sociobiological explanation of rape states that there is an evolutionary advantage for men to have sex with many women and produce as many _____ as possible.

34. The sociobiological explanation for rape is not supported by a careful analysis of data, as the odds are less than _____ in 100 that a rape would offer an evolutionary advantage.

35. The ways a culture teaches us to behave in sexual situations are referred to as
_____ _____.

36. If a woman cuddles with a man after she has clearly expressed her desire not to have sex, sexual scripts may lead her male date to interpret her behavior as "_____
_____", inferring that she does not want to appear too "easy".

37. A study of female college students revealed that _____ percent had engaged in token resistance at least once.

38. The issues surrounding "token resistance" underscore the notion that many sexual interactions are plagued by _____ communication.

39. One study on sexual communication revealed that women and men most frequently indicated sexual consent by _____ _____.

40. Several studies have demonstrated that many men believe rape is _____ if a man feels he was lead on, if a woman dresses suggestively, or if she goes to his home.

41. The so-called "date rape" drug Rohypnol is an odorless, colorless, tasteless drug that produces muscle relaxation, sedation, and _____, making discovery and prosecution of rape very difficult.

42. Studies of wartime rape indicate that it is used to _____, humiliate, and control women, and to terrorize a whole _____.

43. Initially after a rape, feelings of _____, anger, _____, guilt and a sense of powerlessness are common.

44. Physical symptoms such as nausea, _____, gastrointestinal disturbances, genital injuries, and _____ disorders may also occur after rape.

45. One long term study of rape survivors found that 40% abstained from sexual activity for six months to a year after the rape, and another 75% experienced reduced sexual activity for up to _____ years.

46. Some survivors of rape or attempted rape may experience reactions severe enough to be diagnosed with _____ _____ disorder.

47. Key symptoms of the disorder described above include flashbacks of the traumatic experience, disturbing _____, anxiety, _____ and feelings of extreme vulnerability.

48. Studies reveal that people who received _____ soon after an assault suffer fewer emotional repercussions than those who delay treatment.

49. The first and most important thing a partner or friend can do for someone who is raped is to _____ to her/him.

Sexual Abuse of Children, pp. 560-570

1. Child sexual abuse is defined as inappropriate _____, oral-genital contact,
_____ and the like, even if no overt violence or threats occur.

2. Child sexual abuse is considered illegal because children are not deemed mature enough to provide _____ _____ to sexual activity.

3. Nonrelative child abuse is called _____ or child molestation.

4. Sexual contact between related persons is termed _____, and includes sexual contact between _____, between children and parents, children and step-parents, grandparents, uncles, aunts, and cousins.

5. The age of consent in the United States varies from state to state, but is typically between _____ and 18 years of age.

6. Incest occurs across all _____ levels and is illegal regardless of the _____ of those involved.

7. _____-_____ and first-cousin contacts are the most common forms of incest.

8. _____-_____ sexual abuse is most likely to be reported to the authorities.

9. Daughters may be extremely reluctant to report father-daughter incest because of fear of family _____ or fear of being blamed.

10. There is no classic profile of child sex offenders that would allow for easy identification, except that offenders are _____ and _____ to the victim.

11. One study suggested that non-incestuous child sex offenders tend to engage in _____ atypical sexual behaviors than did incestuous sex offenders.

12. Pedophile offenders who are prosecuted are more likely to be shy, lonely, _____ informed about sexuality, very moralistic, have poor interpersonal relationships with adults, and feel socially _____ and inferior.

13. Child sex offenders found outside the legal system may be well educated, successful, socially _____, and civic-minded.

14. Incest offenders share several of the characteristics of _____.

15. Many incest offenders have _____ ideas about adult-child sex.

16. Estimating the prevalence of childhood sexual abuse is _____, so researchers tend to rely upon reports provided by adults regarding their childhood experiences.

17. A recent meta-analysis which combined the results from several studies on child abuse found that _____ percent of adult women and _____ percent of adult men living in Canada and the USA reported being sexually abused during childhood.

18. _____ and Ireland have the lowest rates of childhood sexual abuse.

19. Regarding the controversy surrounding recovered memories of childhood abuse, both the American Psychological Association and American Psychiatric Association have issued statements _____ the notion that forgotten memories can be recovered later in life.

20. These same organizations also acknowledge that a memory may be _____ and then remembered as true.

21. Cyberspace pedophiles, like other pedophiles, first gain a child's _____ by expressing genuine interest and concern in their problems.

22. Some cyberspace pedophiles send pornographic material to suggest that adult-child sex is _____ and _____.

23. The limited data available thus far suggest that no stereotype of cyberspace pedophiles exists, and that many are upper-middle-class males from a variety of _____.

24. The 1996 Communications Decency Act (CDA) prohibited distributing indecent materials by computer, yet in 1997 the Supreme Court _____ the CDA saying it infringed upon free speech.

25. Much research indicates that survivors of childhood sexual abuse have difficulty forming _____ relationships.

26. In addition, abuse survivors often show low _____-_____, guilt, shame, depression, alienation, and lack of _____ in others, revulsion at being _____, drug and alcohol abuse, obesity, elevated suicide rates, and some long term medical problems.

27. People who seek treatment for _____ difficulties frequently have histories of sexual abuse.

28. Responses to childhood sexual abuse are influenced by the duration of the molestation, the intrusiveness of the abuse, whether _____ occurred, and the _____ of the relationship of the offender to the victim.

29. A recent study has indicated that sexually abused _____ showed considerably more emotional and behavioral problems than sexually abused _____ .

30. Suicidality was _____ times more common in girls who were sexually abused than girls with no history of such abuse.

31. Suggestions to prevent child sexual abuse include presenting prevention material to very a) _____ children ; keeping presentations and discussions b) _____; refraining from frightening discussions; explaining differences between okay and not-okay touches; encouraging children to believe they have c) _____ ; encouraging children to tell someone right away if they have been touched in a way that produces discomfort; discussing strategies that adults may use to get children to d) _____ in sexual activities; and discussing strategies to get away from uncomfortable situations; encouraging children to tell adults who touch them inappropriately that they will tell a responsible e) _____; and discussing the positive aspects about sexuality between loving adults.

32. The authors stress that adults should remain _____ in the face of a child disclosing sexual abuse, because if parents act with extreme agitation, children are likely to experience even more negativity and distress than they probably already feel.

Sexual Harassment, pp. 570-575

1. Sexual harassment is said to occur when _____ sexual advances, requests for sexual favors, or when the actions of others create a _____ or offensive work or academic environment.

2. The guidelines of the Equal Employment and Opportunity Commission (EEOC) specify that in the *quid pro quo* type of sexual harassment, compliance with unwanted advances is a condition for securing a _____ or education benefits, or for _____ treatment at school or in the workplace.

3. *Quid pro quo* harassment is often associated with _____ for refusal to comply.

4. The second type of sexual harassment, "hostile or offensive environment" is described less clearly in the EEOC guidelines, but is more _____ than the *quid pro quo* type.

5. Unlike quid pro quo harassment, "hostile or offensive" environment does not necessarily involve _____ or _____ differences.

6. A large-scale study of federal employees revealed that _____ percent of women and _____ percent of men reported experiencing sexual harassment, as reported in a 1996 update.

7. A survey of active-duty military personnel found that _____ or more of women in each branch of military service believed they had been sexually harassed.

8. Another study of medical students reported that _____ percent of female doctors and _____ percent of male doctors reported experiencing sexual harassment during their residency.

9. People who are victims of same-sex sexual harassment have found little recourse in the courts due to the _____ of federal laws specifically prohibiting same-sex harassment.

10. Various surveys have indicated that between _____ percent and _____ percent of harassed workers report psychological distress.

11. Studies of victims of sexual harassment show a sense of helpless and degradation that is similar to that experienced by _____ victims.

12. Other studies show that being the victim of sexual harassment can cause harm to the victim's _____ status, job performance, career opportunities, and _____ relationships.

13. Many women keep silent after being sexually harassed, in part, because of a desire to protect one's _____, fear that formal reporting will not be helpful, and that they will be _____ evaluated by others.

14. Both sexes experience sexual harassment in academic settings, and it is most common for _____ faculty members to harass _____ students.

15. The discussion regarding faculty-student romances is centered on the notion that such relationships may seem _____ on the surface, yet in actuality they may not be, as professors have a great deal of influence over a student's academic and professional future.

16. If a student believes they have been harassed, the authors advise students to _____ the harassment, perhaps to the department chairperson or Dean.

17. One reason to report sexual harassment to college officials is to _____ the likelihood that others may be victimized by the same faculty member.

Crossword

Across

6. sexual _____ comprise "the rules" for sexual interaction
7. memory altering effect of Rohypnol
8. common reaction of rape survivors that deters reporting
9. many child sexual abuse victims have difficulty forming this type of relationship
10. sexual activity stimulates this, not arousal, in many rape survivors
12. more negative effects occur when victim and perpetrator have this type of relationship

Down

1. fear of disrupting this unit silences many child sex abuse victims
2. sexual harassment may create this type of work environment
3. rape myths shift responsibility for the crime onto this person
4. children are not mature enough to provide this, though many pedophiles disagree
5. most likely perpetrator of rape
11. first rape most common in this age group

Practice Test

This test will work best to guide your learning if you take it as part of a final review session before an exam.

1. A woman may be reluctant to report having been raped for which of the following reasons?
   a. She blames herself for what happened.
   b. She fears reprisal from the rapist or his family and friends.
   c. She wishes to avoid recalling a traumatic event.
   d. Her experience of acquaintance rape does not match her idea of rape as a violent attack by a stranger.
   e. All of the above are true.

2. The belief that "rapists are 'obviously' mentally ill" is false because
   a. mental illness is not common.
   b. sex offenses are not classified as mental disorders.
   c. it describes rapists as crazed strangers and runs contrary to research which shows that most rapes are committed by someone the victim knows.
   d. mental illnesses are uncontrollable, therefore a rapist cannot be held responsible for acts committed while ill.

3. The notion that "women say 'no' when they mean 'yes'" is false because
   a. women are socialized to be better communicators than men.
   b. women are trained to lead men on.
   c. it helps rapists justify their behavior as normal sex play, not rape.
   d. the role of seducer demands that women act coy.

4. Which characteristic was found in the rape-prone societies studied by anthropologist Peggy Reeves Sanday?
   a. shared power between the sexes
   b. glorification of masculine violence
   c. expectations that both sexes contribute to the welfare of the community
   d. higher rates of psychological disorder among men

5. The highest incidence of rape among Western nations is found in
   a. the United States.
   b. Mexico.
   c. Macedonia.
   d. Colombia.

6. All of the following are characteristic of men who are more likely to rape except
   a. having male friends who are sexually aggressive
   b. having low self-esteem.
   c. feeling anger towards women.
   d. holding traditional gender roles.

7. The majority of first rapes occurred before the victim was _____ years old.
   a. 12
   b. 18
   c. 35
   d. 50

8. A sociobiological explanation for rape cannot be supported at this time because
   a. cross cultural studies have not been carried out.
   b. studies have not been conducted on nonhuman primates.
   c. the odds that rape offers an evolutionary advantage are very low.
   d. scientists lack the appropriate techniques to study biological adaptations like rape.

9. Ahmet believes that he should be aggressive and make the first sexual advance, whereas his girlfriend Frankie believes she should act passively so she does not appear "too easy". Ahmet and Frankie's behavior best illustrates the influence of
   a. poor childhood socialization.
   b. sexual scripts.
   c. sexual personae.
   d. poor communication skills.

10. In a study of college women all of the following were reasons given for offering token resistance <u>except</u>
    a. not wanting to appear promiscuous.
    b. undesirable surroundings.
    c. uncertainty about a partner's feelings.
    d. desire to avoid game-playing.

11. One study of rape survivors showed that nearly 75% had reduced levels of sexual activity for as long as
    a. six months.
    b. one year.
    c. three years.
    d. six years.

12. Which of the following best describes initial emotional reactions to being raped?
    a. hypersexuality and depression
    b. drug or alcohol use and sleep disturbances
    c. shame, anger, guilt, fear, feelings of powerlessness
    d. anger, aggression, and recklessness

13. _____ refers to sexual contact between relatives whereas _____ refers to sexual contact between an adult and child who are not related.
    a. Pedophilia; incest
    b. Incest; pedophilia
    c. Incest; statutory rape
    d. Pedophilia; paraphilia

14. Which type of sexual abuse is the most common?
    a. father-daughter
    b. stranger-child
    c. brother-sister
    d. uncle-niece

15. Pedophiles who are prosecuted have which of the following characteristics?
    a. religious
    b. lonely
    c. poorly informed about sexuality
    d. two of the above
    e. all of the above

16. A summarization of several studies indicated that _____ percent of women and _____ percent of men reported being abused as children.
    a.   8; 3
    b. 11; 5
    c. 17; 6
    d. 22; 9

17. Which of the following statements best reflects the position of the American Psychological and American Psychiatric Associations regarding recovered memories of sexual abuse?
    a. Both associations agree that the majority of recovered memories were implanted by unqualified therapists.
    b. The American Psychiatric Association disputes the notion that memories can be recovered, whereas the American Psychological Association disagrees.
    c. Both associations agree that forgotten memories can be recovered later in life.
    d. Both associations agree that memories recovered under hypnosis are more trustworthy than memories recovered using other methods.

18. Which of the following is not a frequently encountered effect of childhood sexual abuse?
    a. abstaining from drug and alcohol use
    b. difficulty forming intimate relationships
    c. depression
    d. revulsion at being touched

19. In order to prevent childhood sexual abuse it is recommended that prevention programs reach children younger than age _____, as 25% of abuse occurs before that age.
    a. thirteen
    b. ten
    c. eight
    d. seven

20. Which of the following is the <u>best</u> example of *quid pro quo* sexual harassment?
    a. Janelle finds pictures of nude women taped to her locker at work.
    b. Sarah's supervisor says she can keep her job if she performs fellatio.
    c. Maria's co-worker repeatedly asks her out for dates, even after she refuses.
    d. Teesha's patrol partner regularly makes comments about her breasts, even though she has told him to stop.

21. All of the following are effects of sexual harassment on victims <u>except</u>
    a. financial gain.
    b. feeling ashamed.
    c. feeling irritable.
    d. lack of motivation.

22. A survey of high school students revealed that _____ percent experienced sexual harassment.
    a. 12%
    b. 18%
    c. 34%
    d. 50%

23. The authors suggest that if you experience sexual harassment on campus you should
    a. avoid the harasser by dropping the class.
    b. circulate a petition among students to send to the professor's dean.
    c. report it so that the inappropriate behavior will stop.
    d. find a way to endure the term and then tell other students about the professor's unprofessional behavior, so they won't take his or her classes.

Answer Key – Chapter 19

Concept Checks

Rape
1. consent; threatened
2. Acquaintance; date
3. Stranger
4. statutory
5. 16
6. blamed; reprisal
7. preconceived
8. 17.6; 3
9. aggression; blame
10. a) stronger b) compliant, submissive c) rapist
11. coerced; normal
12. more
13. control; harm
14. known
15. rapist; victim
16. socialization
17. violence; power; authority
18. highest
19. friends
20. equivocal
21. convicted
22. traditional; self-centered; anger
23. violent
24. 18; 12
25. gay men
26. men
27. media
28. gay; heterosexual
29. passivity; submissiveness
30. resistance
31. direct
32. crime
33. offspring
34. one
35. sexual scripts
36. token resistance
37. 39
38. poor
39. not resisting
40. justified
41. amnesia
42. dominate; community
43. shame; fear

44. headaches; sleep
45. six
46. post traumatic
47. dreams; depression
48. counseling
49. listen

Sexual Abuse of Children
1. touching; coitus
2. informed consent
3. pedophilia
4. incest; adults
5. 16
6. socioeconomic; ages
7. Brother-sister
8. Father-daughter
9. disruption
10. male; known
11. more
12. religious; inadequate
13. adept
14. pedophiles
15. distorted
16. difficult
17. 22; 9
18. Finland
19. supporting
20. suggested
21. trust
22. normal; appropriate
23. profession
24. overturned
25. intimate
26. self-esteem; trust; touched
27. sexual
28. violence; closeness
29. boys; girls
30. five
31. a) young b)simple c) rights d) participate e) adult
32. calm

Sexual Harassment
1. unwelcome; hostile
2. employment; preferential
3. reprisals
4. common
5. power; authority
6. 44; 19

 7. half
 8. 73; 22
 9. absence
10. 75; 90
11. rape
12. financial; personal
13. career; negatively
14. male; female
15. consensual
16. report
17. reduce

Crossword Puzzle

Across
 6. scripts
 7. amnesia
 8. self-blame
 9. intimate
10. anxiety
12. close

Down
 1. family
 2. hostile
 3. victim
 4. consent
 5. acquaintance
11. young

Practice Test

1. e 2. c 3. c 4. b 5. a 6. b 7. b 8. c 9. b 10. d 11. a 12. c 13. b
14. c 15. e 16. d 17. c 18. a 19. d 20. b 21. a 22. d 23. c

Introduction

The topic of sex as a business is explored in this chapter that focuses on two ways that sex generates profits: pornography and prostitution. The historical development of these money-making enterprises are traced, as well as the personal, social, and legal ramifications of sex for sale.

Learning Objectives. *In order to derive maximum benefit from these objectives, use these as soon as you begin reading the chapter. After you have completed reading and studying this chapter, you should be able to do the things listed below with ease, using only your memory.*

1. Define pornography and explain some of the problems in establishing a contemporary definition of it.

2. Discuss the legal controversies surrounding pornography as they relate to the following:
    a. evaluating what is obscene from a legal standpoint
    b. freedom of speech
    c. regulating the dissemination of pornography
    d. addressing the dissemination of pornographic materials on the Internet

3. Describe the effects of sexually explicit materials, making specific reference to the following:
    a. the outcome of President Johnson's Commission on Obscenity and Pornography
    b. the limitations of research results in this area
    c. three types of sexually explicit materials
    d. the extent to which pornography affects intimate relationships between men and women
    e. the process and outcome of the 1986 U.S. Attorney General's Commission on Pornography (the Meese Commission)
    f. China's laws regarding sexually explicit materials

4. Define prostitution and discuss the ways in which it has manifested itself throughout history.

5. Identify the characteristics of the female prostitute's typical customer.

6. Describe some characteristics of the typical prostitute and explain some of the motivations for being a prostitute.

7. Explain the controversy that exists in this country regarding the legal status of prostitution, and in doing so, distinguish between legalization and decriminalization.

8. Explain how AIDS is a concern for prostitution, and citing relevant statistics, discuss the extent to which AIDS is a problem in the U.S. as opposed to parts of Africa.

9. Discuss teenage prostitution, making reference to the following:
    a. what prompts some teenagers to become prostitutes
    b. common characteristics in the lives and backgrounds of teenage prostitutes
    c. according to one study, who the children are that are used in child pornography

    d. how federal laws have affected child pornography

    e. what many consumers of child pornography have in common

    f. how children who are involved in child prostitution are affected socially, emotionally, and psychologically

10. List and briefly describe three types of female prostitutes and the services they may provide.

11. Define the role that a brothel has played in prostitution.

12. List and briefly describe five types of male prostitutes.

13. Discuss the various people, agencies, businesses and institutions that benefit economically from prostitution.

14. Describe how women and children worldwide have come to be exploited through prostitution.

15. Describe the influence of the Internet on prostitution services.

Concept Map

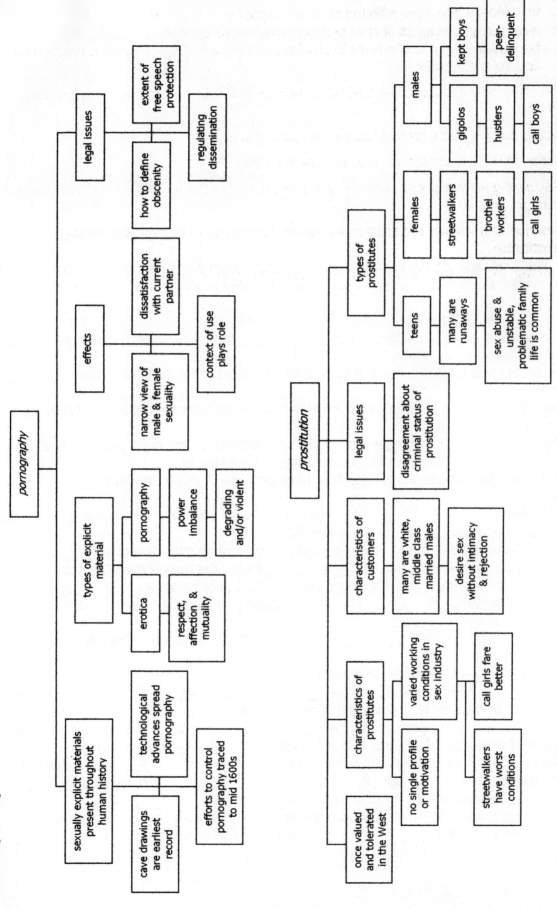

pornography

legal issues
- extent of free speech protection
- how to define obscenity
  - regulating dissemination

effects
- dissatisfaction with current partner
- narrow view of male & female sexuality
  - context of use plays role

types of explicit material
- erotica
  - respect, affection & mutuality
- pornography
  - power imbalance
  - degrading and/or violent

sexually explicit materials present throughout human history
- technological advances spread pornography
- cave drawings are earliest record
- efforts to control pornography traced to mid 1600s

prostitution

types of prostitutes
- teens
  - many are runaways
  - sex abuse & unstable, problematic family life is common
- females
  - streetwalkers
  - brothel workers
  - call girls
- males
  - gigolos
  - kept boys
  - hustlers
  - peer-delinquent
  - call boys

legal issues
- disagreement about criminal status of prostitution

characteristics of customers
- many are white, middle class married males
- desire sex without intimacy & rejection

characteristics of prostitutes
- no single profile or motivation
- varied working conditions in sex industry
  - call girls fare better
  - streetwalkers have worst conditions

once valued and tolerated in the West

Key Terms. *Refer to the glossary or subject index in the back of your textbook for definitions and information.*

pornogrpahy	call girl
erotica	gigolo
degrading pornography	hustler
violent pornography	call boy
obscene	kept boy
prostitution	peer-delinquent prostitute
brothel	pimp
streetwalker	

Concept-Checks. *Complete this section by filling in each blank after you have studied the corresponding pages from the text. Answers are provided at the back of this chapter.*

Pornography, pp. 579-587

1. Pornography refers to written, visual, or _____ material of a sexual nature that is used for the purpose of sexual arousal.

2. Pictorial representations of sexual activity can be found as far back as ancient _____ drawings.

3. Depictions of coitus in Schunga paintings and woodcuts from the 1600s and 1700s were made by the _____ people.

4. The invention of the printing press in 1450 help allowed for the mass production of _____ stories, which helped the populace become literate.

5. In the mid sixteenth century, Pope Paul IV created the Church's first list of _____ books.

6. The invention of _____ in the mid 1800s created another technology that furthered the spread of pornographic and erotic materials.

7. Control over the distribution of pornography became more difficult, as the _____, automobile, private shipping, and the _____ loosed the hold of the US Postal Service.

8. Pornography emerged as big business with the 1953 publication of _____ magazine.

9. The 1973 movie _____ _____ moved pornography from an underground market to public movie houses.

10. The 1973 Supreme Court _____ versus California decisions created federal antiobscenity laws.

11. Other technological advances that made pornography more difficult to control included _____ television, the VCR, and the _____, allowing people to view pornography in the privacy of their homes, rather than a public venue.

12. Many people consider pornography to be _____-core when the genitals are explicitly featured and when genitals are not shown the label _____-core applies.

13. Erotica differs from pornography as sexuality is shown with _____ and affection.

14. The root of the word *pornography* means female _____, thereby implying domination of women and an unequal balance of power.

15. In a study of reactions to films depicting explicit sex, both college men and women rated the video that was highly _____ and highly explicit as being most _____.

16. _____ pornography objectifies and deprecates the participants, often by using racial stereotypes whereas _____ pornography involves aggression and brutality.

17. Pornography often emphasizes male _____ and _____ rather than pleasure and the expression of affection.

18. Male sexuality is often represented in a restricted fashion with an overemphasis on _____ size and performance.

19. Sex therapist Bernie Zilbergeld believes that pornography perpetuates myths about male sexuality, namely that a "real" man should always be ready for _____, and that he should get it without regard for the other person or his own complex _____ as a man.

20. Women in pornographic media are often shown as being wildly _____ to any stimulation from a male, and this may result in men feeling _____ or cheated, with women doubting the normality of their sexuality.

21. After repeated exposure to pornography, men and women become _____ satisfied with the appearance and performance of their sexual partners.

22. Media critic Laura Kipnis believes that pornography has some value as social criticism, because pornography has historically challenged the _____ sexuality of women.

23. If a person or social group judges something to be offensive, the material may be labeled _____.

24. The U.S. Supreme Court uses three guidelines for establishing obscenity, and these focus upon a) a _____ interest in sex b) community standards for offensiveness and c) the _____ the work has for literature, art, politics, or science.

25. Critics believe that current criteria for establishing obscenity are highly _____.

26. The debate surrounding obscene materials struggles with the notion of whether sexually explicit materials are protected by freedom of _____.

27. In China most pornographic materials have been _____ since 1989.

28. A 1970 presidential commission reviewed the scientific research literature to date and recommended _____ laws prohibiting access to pornography, yet President Nixon and the Senate rejected those recommendations.

29. The Meese Commission concluded that _____, nondegrading erotica was destructive to society.

30. The Meese Commission's report generated much controversy, as the commission's conclusions about violent pornography _____ with scientific research which showed that it is "violence, whether or not it is accompanied by sex" that promotes violence against women.

31. The Supreme Court recently extended free speech protection to sexually explicit materials found on the _____.

32. Public debate is also focused on how the _____ of pornography should be regulated.

33. _____ pornography is not included under First Amendment free speech protection, and this applies to computer-generated materials.

Prostitution, pp. 587-593

1. Prostitution is defined as the exchange of _____ _____ for money.

2. The exchange of money for sexual services can occur between a woman and a man, two _____, or two women.

3. Elements of prostitution are present in everyday life, as when a woman marries a good financial _____ instead of her true love.

4.   Prostitution has been revered and tolerated throughout human history as exemplified during the _____ era, when prostitution was considered a "scandalous, but necessary sexual and social outlet for men".

5. The typical customer of a prostitute is white, middle-aged, _____ class and married.

6. Motivations for using the services of a prostitute include providing sexual contact without any expectation of _____ or commitment, reducing the risk of _____, and offering the opportunity to engage in sexual practices that the customer would not do with a current partner.

7. There is no singular reason why people enter prostitution, yet _____ incentive seems to be common.

8. One observer summarizes characteristics of prostitutes, noting that "prostitutes have _____ histories, aspirations, and current life conditions".

9. The conditions of sex work vary, as strippers, nude dancers and prostitutes have _____ personal health and safety, whereas phone sex, Internet workers, and video conference models have safer and less oppressive working conditions.

10. The typical pay of high-tech sex workers is _____ than entry level service jobs, such as working as a cashier.

11. Some reasons cited in favor of making prostitution illegal include that more women would become prostitutes if it were not punishable, and that it would be more difficult to enforce _____ on prostitution activities.

12. Some say that prostitution should not have criminal status because illegal prostitution encourages ties to organized _____, and that penalties are applied in a discriminatory manner as it is the _____ who is more likely to suffer arrest, prosecution, and imprisonment.

13. Other reasons to decriminalize or legalize prostitution center on the notion that prostitution is a "_____" crime, and that ties to organized crime would be weakened and victimization of _____ by pimps, customers, the judicial system, and others would be reduced as a result.

14. One study showed that _____ percent of New York City streetwalker prostitutes tested positive HIV.

15. Prostitutes in county-licensed facilities in the state of _____ are required to be tested monthly for HIV and must use condoms during their work.

16. Many teenage prostitutes enter the business because they have run away from home, _____ percent have been victims of sexual abuse, and most have been abandoned by their _____.

17. _____ are at the bottom of the hierarchy in prostitution, are the group of prostitutes most likely to have traumatic family backgrounds and experience abuse at the hands of customers and pimps.

18. A house in which a group of prostitutes work is called a(n) _____.

19. One study indicated that most massage parlor customers where white-collar businessmen over the age of _____.

20. Call girls generally earn _____ than other types of prostitutes.

21. Call girls and brothel workers are _____ likely to be arrested than other types of prostitutes.

22. In modern times there is no _____ male prostitute.

23. Unlike female prostitutes, male prostitutes appear to work _____, without a pimp or madam.

24. Males who provide sexual services to women in exchange for money or goods are called _____.
25. The male counterpart to a call girl is a(n) _____.
26. Male prostitutes that service other men are called _____, call _____, and _____ boys.
27. _____-_____ prostitutes work in groups and use sex work as a way to assault and rob customers.

Crossword

Across
1. group of prostitutes most likely to be victimized
3. pornography type without First Amendment protection
7. prostitution penalties miss this target
9. non-puritantical obscenity criterion
10. primary incentive for entering prostitution

Down
1. pornography myths stress that men are always ready for this
2. the Greek god Eros would have liked this form of sexually explicit material
3. moniker of the prostitute's union
4. racial stereotypes embody just one form of this pornography quality
5. Larry Flynt magazine-male prostitute
6. working conditions in these Nevada houses are difficult at best
8. Sanger nemesis and anti-obscenity crusader

Practice Test

This test will work best to guide your learning if you take it as part of a final review session before an exam.

1. All of the following expanded pornography and extended access of sexually explicit materials <u>except</u>
   a. The Miller v. California decision.
   b. photography.
   c. the railroad.
   d. VCR's.

2. Erotica can be distinguished from pornography because
   a. pornography depicts genitalia; erotica does not.
   b. erotica is made primarily by females; pornography is made primarily by males.
   c. pornography connotes domination of women; erotica portrays sexuality respectfully.
   d. erotica is soft-core; pornography is hard-core.

3. Which of the following is <u>true</u> regarding the impact of pornography on sexuality?
   a. Pornography emphasizes female pleasure and autonomy.
   b. Pornography shows the complex nature of male sexuality.
   c. Pornography depicts men as always being ready for sex.
   d. Pornography shows women acting coy and shy in response to stimulation from males.

4. In the study of college students who were shown four video segments, which video was rated as most arousing?
   a. the hard-core video with no romance, by men only
   b. the hard-core video with romance, by women and men
   c. the soft-core video with no romance, by women and men
   d. the soft-core video with romance, by women only

5. Zillman & Bryant's study demonstrated that when women and men were repeatedly exposed to pornography
   a. both women and men became less satisfied with their partners physical appearance and sexual performance.
   b. women became more active and responsive during sexual interaction with their partners.
   c. men broadened their repertoire of sexual behaviors to include activities other than sexual intercourse.
   d. women and men reported an increase in the frequency of sexual activity.

6. What do violent and degrading pornography have in common?
   a. use of hard-core, explicit images
   b. aggression and brutality
   c. use of nontraditional gender roles
   d. imbalance of power

7. Legal issues surrounding pornography have focused on defining what is
   a. degrading.
   b. depraving and corrupting to the user.
   d. obscene.
   d. violent.

8. Our nation and legal system are still debating whether or not sexually explicit materials should be protected by
   a. the Geneva Declaration.
   b. freedom of speech.
   c. universal human rights principles.
   d. United Nations Resolutions.

9. Which of the following statements is false regarding the history of prostitution?
   a. Prostitutes were valued for the intellectual companionship in ancient Greece.
   b. Sexual relations between men and prostitutes occurred in religious temples.
   c. Prostitution was banned in medieval Europe.
   d. Prostitution was considered scandalous but necessary during the Victorian era.

10. Which statement is true concerning the background of female prostitutes?
    a. Prostitutes are a diverse group and no single theory or profile describes them.
    b. Most have a history of sexual abuse.
    c. The majority are poorly educated.
    d. They exhibited higher rates of problem behavior during adolescence.

11. All of the following comprise arguments against the criminal status of prostitution except
    a. Prostitution thrives despite criminal penalties.
    b. Prostitution encourages connections with organized crime.
    c. The government has a responsibility to regulate morals.
    d. Penalties against prostitution target prostitutes more than customers.

12. Which statement is true regarding teenage prostitution?
    a. Many are runaways from stable middle class families
    b. Most show remarkable resiliency against the troubles of sex work.
    c. Most work in phone sex or lingerie modeling.
    d. The overwhelming majority have been sexual abuse victims.

13. Which type of prostitute is lowest in the hierarchy of prostitution and faces the worst work conditions?
    a. a brothel worker
    b. a massage parlor worker
    c. a streetwalker
    d. a call girl

14. Which term is out of place here among these descriptors of male prostitutes?
    a. pimp
    b. gigolo
    c. kept boy
    d. hustler

15. _____ often use prostitution as a way to commit robbery and assault.
    a. Streetwalkers
    b. Madams
    c. Call boys
    d. Peer-delinquent prostitutes

Answer Key

<u>Concept Checks</u>

Pornography
1. spoken
2. cave
3. Japanese
4. pornographic
5. prohibited
6. photography
7. railroad; airplane
8. Playboy
9. Deep Throat
10. Miller
11. cable; Internet
12. hard; soft
13. respect
14. captive
15. romantic; arousing
16. Degrading; violent
17. performance; conquest
18. penile
19. sex; sexuality
20. responsive; inadequate
21. less
22. restricted
23. obscene
24. a) prurient c) value
25. subjective
26. speech
27. banned
28. repealing
29. nonviolent
30. disagreed
31. Internet
32. dissemination
33. Child

Prostitution
1. sexual services
2. men
3. prospect
4. Victorian
5. middle
6. Intimacy; rejection
7. economic
8. diverse

9. diminished
10. more
11. restrictions
12. crime; prostitute
13. victimless; prostitutes
14. 35
15. Nevada
16. 95; families
17. Streetwalkers
18. brothel
19. 35
20. more
21. less
22. typical
23. independently
24. gigolos
25. gigolo
26. hustlers; boys; kept
27. Peer-delinquent

Crossword Puzzle

Across
1. streetwalker
3. child
7. customer
9. prurience
10. economic

Down
1. sex
2. erotica
3. COYOTE
4. degredation
5. hustler
6. brothel
8. Comstock

Practice Test

1. a 2. c 3. c 4. b 5. a 6. d 7. c 8. b 9. c 10. a 11. c
12. d 13. c 14. a 15. d